ASPECTS OF DEVELOPMENT IN COLONIAL PERIOD 1800-1947

ANANTAPUR DISTRICT, ANDHRA PRADESH

ASPECTS OF DEVELOPMENT IN COLONIAL PERIOD 1800-1947

ANANTAPUR DISTRICT, ANDHRA PRADESH

Penukonda Jyothi

KALPAZ

Published by

Kalpaz Publications
C-30, Satyawati Nagar,
Delhi – 110052
Ph.: 011-47034999, 9811692060
www.kalpazpublications.com
E-mail: kalpaz@hotmail.com

Distribution Network
gyanbooks.com
India, USA, Canada, UK, Australia, France

ISBN: 978-93-5722-275-4 (HB)

First Published, 2023

Printed at: Gyan Press, Delhi.

ASPECTS OF DEVELOPMENT IN COLONIAL PERIOD 1800-1947
Author: PENUKONDA JYOTHI

Foreword

The impact of the British rule and the struggle for independence in India is a fascinating and absorbing. Some of the burṇing socio-economic and political problems of contemporary India can be traced back to the colonial rule. It ever since was attracted by the developments in the country. As such my attention was very much drawn towards Indian affairs including conditions inherited form the British dominance and to the understanding of the past with a view to suggesting ways and means to shape the present and future. Naturally, I always cherished the hope of writing a book presenting the colonial exploitation or the tragic story of the Indian people and their glorious struggles against the British and their aspects of development in colonial period in Andhra Pradesh.

The situation which enabled a Company of merchant to conquer India, its impact on India and the Indian response, in the form of regional and national struggles, especially some parts of Andhra Pradesh, have been deals with in this book. British attitudes were colonial in that information and perspectives were sought so as to possess, categorise and at time subvert India. British strategies were imperial because they were designed both to protect and extend the empire and also, out of a sense of responsibility, to meet what were thought to be positive goals.

The crucial importence of the period of 18th century in the economic history of Andhradesa in general and that of its trade and commerce in particular is too well-known. This period witnessed many fluctuations in the trading and commercial life of the region due to rapid contemporary political changes and also the emergence of certain external forces.The seventeenth and the eighteenth centuries mark a transitional period in the history of India. During these centuries, India, because of the cumulative influence and total effect of a number of political, social and economic factors, commenced on its course of moving from the medieval age towards the modern age and from the feudal age towards the colonial age. From the limited perspective of trade and commerce these two centuries may also be called as the age of European East India Companies.

In Andhradesa, as elsewhere in some other regions of India, so far as the aspect of trade and commerce is concerned, the seventeenth and the eighteenth centuries have acquired a special significance. This significance lies in the fact that a foreign and extraneous element in the form of European East India Companies, the Portuguese, the Dutch, the English and the French entered the economic scene through channels of trade and commerce; the 'factors' of these Companies founded 'Factories' at several port-towns, along the eastern and the western coasts of the southern peninsula and also at a few places in the interior of the country. Though the Portuguese presence was there in the early part of the seventeenth century on the eastern coast, its effect on the trade and Commerce in Andhradesa, if not next to nothing, was minimal and marginal. It was largely confined to San Thome and Madras and to places and ports south of Madras; to the north of Madras it never extended beyond Pulicat; the trade relations and activities of the Portuguese were mainly with the Vijayanagar empire, which was on the wane of its power.

Anantapur district is the place where dry and hot climate prevails most of the time in a year. Evasion of monsoons is the main cause for precarious agricultural conditions in the district. As the district is far away from the seam, the north-east monsoons do not visit this region. The Western Gluts prevent the south-western monsoons from entering into this district. The rainy season is mainly experienced during the months of May-November. The average rainfall in the district is 440.4mm. Agriculture is the main stay of the people of the district The main crops that are produced in the district are paddy, jowar, bajra and maize. The important commercial crops in the distinct are grams and peanuts Though the district relies much on rains for agriculture, cultivation in certain area, is under major and minor irrigation projects.

Anantapur region was under the rule of various divisions dynasties during the ancient period. Different systems of land revenue policies came into vogue in this region. After the third Mysore war in 1799 A.D. the Nizam of Hyderabad entered into an alliance with British East India Company which is known as Subsidiary Alliance in A.D. 1800. According to which the districts of Ballary (inclusive of Anantapur district) Cuddapah. and Kurnool passed into the hands of British East India Company. Anantapur was made head quarters in 1807 A.D. and the region was called ceded districts. This region was divided into two Collectorates of Bellary and Cuddapah and so remained until 1858 when Kurnool was constituted into separate district.

Dr. Talari Rangaiah
Member of Parliament
Andhra Pradesh

Preface

The study of British imperialism was more pragmatic than that of other colonial powers. Its motivation primarily based on its economic interests. At first the main purpose was to achieve a monopolistic trading position. Later, it was felt that a regime of free trade would make India a major market for British goods and a source of raw materials, but British capitalists who invested in India, or who sold banking or shipping services there, continued effectively to enjoy monopolistic privileges. The Britishers relied on market forces to deal with problems like famine. They did nothing to stimulate agriculture or protect industry. In the light of that, its deals with the economic development of the region under colonial regime. India was ruled by different dynasties in different periods of history. As a consequence, several factors such as political, social, economic, religious and cultural etc. had come to influence the growth and pattern of urbanization of the country in varying degrees in different periods of time. Of them, religious and cultural factors were the basis of the urban growth in the early and medieval era. Among the economic factors, trade was the major one to affect the early urbanization. However, clear definitions of trade and urbanization came to India only during colonial period. Trade and urbanization went hand in hand during this period. The coastal Andhra region too experienced urban growth from seventeenth century due to maritime trade and establishment of European settlements. Along the Andhra coastline, several port cities emerged which sustained on extensive overseas trading relations. The numerous trading centres were not only specialised in different branches of trade but also varied in the composition of trading communities. The diversity and the tradition in overseas commerce, led to the coexistence of different indigenous and foreign merchant communities.

The colonial homogenised assumptions about Orientalism and the imposing of absolute distinction between the self and the other, made the emergent Indian Nationalism to feel equally imperative to stake out claims to sole representational authority over the self. In the colonial economy with its new agrarian and industrial relations accompanied by a vast and expanding administrative structure, existing dominant groups began to be forged into a middle class or bourgeoisie. This class tried to reform itself initiating campaigns against idolatry, caste system, polytheism, child marriage etc. seeing them as elements of a pre modern. In all these practices, women were figured as the victims. Rationalism endowed with scientific temperament had induced the Intelligentsia to produce the literature and lead the social reform movements. During the 19th century, all over the world, transforming indigenous cultures had been an agenda central to colonial domination. The colonial state and its agencies, both through direct intervention and indirect influence, communicated and reproduced a cultural ideal, attractive and powerful enough for the local intelligentsia to internalise and disseminate. The new cultural scenario brought by British was a result of interventions by the ideological apparatuses of state, as of participation and collaboration by the local intelligentsia in the process of colonial hegemonisation.

The colonial government made institutional changes in agriculture by transforming traditionally circumscribed property rights into something more closely resembling the unencumbered private property characteristic of Western capitalism. The beneficiaries of these new rights varied in different parts of India. The jagirdari system was abolished and the bulk of the old warlord aristocracy was dispossessed. Their previous income from land revenue, and that of the Moghul state, was now appropriated by the British as land tax. In the Madras Presidency, of which Andhra Pradesh in particular Anantapur is a part, the British dispossessed many of the old Moghul and Maharatta nobility and big zamindars, and vested property rights and tax obligations in individual 'peasants'. Thus there was no change in social structure at the village level, except that the new ownership rights gave greater opportunities for sale and mortgage, and the security of the tenant was less than it had been under the previous system. The administration was rather remote from individual villages (with a district officer responsible for over a thousand villages), and many British administrators had a personal bias in favour of customary tenant rights because by maintaining them they could avoid political trouble. The British were more concerned with arrangements which would guarantee their revenue and not provoke too much political disturbance rather than in increasing productivity or introducing capitalist institutions. The class of landless agricultural labourers grew in size under British rule. Little was done to promote agricultural technology. There was some improvement in seeds, but new no extension service, no improvement in livestock and no official encouragement to use fertilizer.

With the object of helping the farmer with latest ideas on agriculture an Agricultural Society was started at Penukonda by the government in 1901. The society is still active and members are on its rolls belonging to the district and 200 members are from outside of the district. The district Collector is its President. The society publishes a periodical, which is mainly devoted to agricultural matters, and organizes lectures on these subjects. It also conducts crop exhibitions motivating some of its members to experiment with ground-nut and potatoes in a piece of wet land under the Penukonda tank which serves as a trial ground and model farm. Anantapur was not particularly well known for any industries although some places seem to have specialized in manufacturing of certain types of products which have now almost disappeared. There is no proper record of evidence to show that the district was rich like some of its neighbouring districts in iron ore smelting or the manufacture of earth salt, salt-petre and or even indigo dye etc. However, casual references were made in the old' records about some of these industries, which, in course of time, failed to survive. Of these to mention some, (the making of bangles at Gutturu (Penukonda), and of handmade paper at Nyamaddala (Dharmavaram), the hand printing of cloth at Pamidi (Gooty), the manufacture of candles at

Gooty and the preparation of indigo dye at a few places in Tadipatri taluk deserve mention. The production of the synthetic dye rendered the manufacture of indigo un-remunerative while the local candles could not withstand competition from those of the foreign variety.

In those times, English educated intelligentsia became the receivers and carriers of new cultural taste and sensibility. The cultural ideal in literature, theatre, painting, music dress, food, conversation, etiquette and so on was now drawn from the coloniser's world. The cultural impact of the new literacy was not confined to English literates. There was a spill over effect on vernacular readers. With the printing press, the written word as a cultural factor became increasingly important and influential during the course of the 19th century. The availability of print literature contributed to a change in attitude towards leisure itself. New literary genres like the novel were a product of this process; they emerged simultaneously with the educated middle class being drawn in to the colonial cultural world. A true literature is the artistic expression of life and it was fully immersed in Telugu life. The advent of the British brought the Telugu's culture into contact with the vitalising influences of western literatures and arts. Literary tastes have changed and literary ideals underwent radical transformations. New ideals challenged attention and evoked enthusiasm. New watch words sprang up. When love for the vernaculars was intensified, there was also a growing a petulant, impatience with old forms and ideals.

Rayalaseema region as backward region in education There was no college in any part of the region or districts, and there are only two high or upper secondary institutions established. One of these is the municipal school at Anantapur headquarters. This began in 1882 as a Government middle school was transferred to the council in 1884 and was raised to high school standard in 1885-86. It is at present in a flourishing condition, financially and otherwise. Four lower secondary schools exist in the district. Three of these are at Penukonda taluk board and the Railway schools at Guntakal and Gooty, all the schools are English schools and the fourth, the London Mission boarding school for Native Christians at Gooty, is a vernacular institution. The other upper secondary school is the London Mission's Anglovernacular school at Gooty, which was raised from a lower secondary institution to an upper secondary institution in 1897-98.7 The training schools include the Government institution at Anantapur maintained by the London Mission at Gooty opened in 1900-01. There are no schools for girls above the primary level and no Industrial or commercial institutions in this region of the state.

Although prose was not unknown in Indian literatures, it's potentiality and possibilities as an effective instrument of communication, both literary and non-literary, was realised only during the course of the nineteenth century. Hence the first novel in Telugu, Rajasekhara Charitra by Kandukuri Veeresalingam pantulu appeared in 1880. This new genre was not generated exclusively by external stimulus. Infact it was rooted in the intellectual needs and aesthetic sensibility of the middle class. The contradictions, ambiguities and uncertainties of the middle class in their social and cultural life, which arose out of the mix of a hegemonising colonial culture and contending traditional cultures, formed the contexts in which a literary sensibility found expression in 19th century. Apart from the movement, the social reform campaigns began to develop in South India in the last of the nineteenth century. they remained rela weak until the turn of the century. In 1871, a remarriage association was started in Madra was short-lived; it was revived in 1880s by D Bahadur Raghunatha Rao. In 1878, Veeresali started the Rajamundry social reform Assoc which focussed on widow remarriage.

The government which was keen on collecting land revenue from the peasants did not bother to improve the irrigation facilities in the country. The invasion of Nawab of Arcot to collect tributes and the resultant revolts of Palayakkarars had destroyed the irrigation channels in Tamil Country. The British on assumption of power did not do anything to repair the irrigation channels. Nor did they initiate measures to build new irrigation embankments to facilitate development of agriculture in the first half of nineteenth century. Madurai Collector R. Peter, seeing the wretched condition of tanks in his district wrote to the Board of Revenue in 1816: ...most of them could not have been repaired for many, many years and the consequence has been that large tracts of land have remained uncultivated for want of a regular supply of water. The inhabitants of every village I passed begged that I would look at their tanks and asked how it was possible for them to increase the cultivation, or indeed to cultivate at all, in the condition in which they then were'51 With the erosion in the political authority of zamindars, their interest in maintaining the tanks also declined. But they had no compunction in raising the rent of the tenants and exploiting them mercilessly.

The Company government, after entrenching itself comfortably in power, in pursuance of its two pronged commercial policy of carrying raw material from India and dumping the finished English factory made goods on Indian markets, allowed unrestricted flow of imports of British goods into India that competed with the domestic product on equal terms. At the same time Indian manufactures were prohibited from entering into England in view of high protective duties levied by the English government there. This proved ruinous to the Indian traders and weavers. The government built roads connecting the cotton cultivating districts to the ports, and developed harbor facilities there for export of raw cotton. Exempting cotton soil from land taxes, and enactment of laws for the prevention of adulteration of raw cotton were the other two supportive measures initiated by the Company administrationtoprovide stimulus to cotton cultivation and trade in Madras Presidency. With a view to targeting the investible surplus capital in England/they adopted the doctrine of free trade and private enterprise from 1833.

The impact of such a commercial policy on Indian weaving sector was disastrous. A nineteenth century record portrays the melancholic condition of weaving industry in Madras thus: Time was when the principal part of the Madras investment of piece goods was provided in Ganjam, but now there were few vestiges of industry. South Arcot formerly carried on a very profitable export trade in piece goods with the Malay Archipelago, but British manufactures had ousted the Indian trade.... In every district, it was the same tale of decay and distress.The effects of the blow to the weaving industry in the aftermath of import of British mill made textiles was most acutely felt, because of the ubiquitous presence of handlooms, providing employment to a very a large number of people, including "millions of women".

Repairing a damaged tank embankment would lead to hiking of tax rate and this prevented repair from being undertaken. E.B. Thomas, collector of Tirunelveli, during the 1840s, pointed out that exorbitant tax rates discouraged farmers from digging wells. Ludden quotes the proclamation made by an English man in 1843 that 'as long as one drop of water is allowed to run waste into the sea, we must take blame unto ourselves for not exerting our best efforts to obviate the evils of poverty or the dreadful effects of famine.Under British rule, small and scattered drainage irrigation works never received government funding in proportion to their importance in agriculture. Until 1868 almost all government funding supported what were called "repairs". There were bureaucrats who believed irrigation 'to infinitely more important for the wants of the country than railways. Sir Arthur Cotton, famous builder of Godavari and Kaveri canals told a Parliament Committee: My great point is this. That what India wants is water carriage; that the railways have completely failed they cannot carry the quantities and they cost the country three million a year.But the colonial state, as a military power, weighed the benefits of railways with the building of an irrigation network and preferred the former, as it had to keep its garrisons moving constantly from one end of the other to crush any possible rebellions or insurrections of indigenous rulers and chieftains.

In Andhra Pradesh state of Anantapur district, less than three-quarters of the population, depend directly upon agricultural and pastoral pursuits for their daily life. Anantapur along with other territories of Madras Presidency, the British dispossessed many of the old Moghul and Maharatta nobility and big zamindars, and vested property rights and tax obligations on individual peasants. This settlement was known as the ryotwari system (peasant tenure). However, the term peasant is misleading, because most of those who acquired land titles belonged to the traditionally dominant castes in rural villages. The peasants belonging to lower-caste cultivators in villages became their tenants. Thus there was no change in social structure at the village level, except that the new ownership rights gave greater opportunities for sale and mortgage, and the security of the tenant was less than it had been under the previous system.

Cattle are bred for sale in considerable numbers at Pamudurti, the retail trade being chiefly in the hands of the Lambadis. Goats and sheep are valued as manuring agents and for their skins; sheep provide in addition mutton and wool. The wool is sold to the people of Kuruba community to make the blankets. Sheep are collected in large quantities at Hindupur and driven for sale every week to Bangalore to be converted into mutton.

Out of the total non-agricultural population, (the percentage who subsists by handicrafts other than those of the ordinary village artisans is smaller than in almost any district) Such of these callings as exist, moreover, with the single exception of the textile occupations, not only economically unimportant but artistically and industrially insignificant. Weavers are more numerous in proportion to the total population than in any other district except Bellary. They may be divided into weavers of gunny, cotton, silk and wool.) Gunny is made from locally grown sunn hemp (crotolaria juncea) in a few villages in Anantapur, among which may be mentioned, Byadigera in Madakasira taluk, Chilumutturu and Hindupur.

The cotton-weaving industry consists mainly in the making of the coarse white sheeting which the average ryot wears and the coloured cloths used by the women. There is in addition some little manufacture of tapes for cots (chiefly by Dudekulas) and of cloths for turbans and bodices, and in Uravakonda five or six families occasionally make striped cotton rugs similar to those woven at Adoni.

During 1800-1825, there were only four famines but between 1875 and 1900 there were 22 famines. The new facilities of transport and communication changed famine from a regional to a class problem and left the laboring class and small plot holders exposed to starvation. The lives of five millions of human being were lost during the famine of 1876-78s William Digby wrote the situation in Madras in November, 1876:

Especially in Andhra Pradesh state of Anantapur region is economically very backward and frequent drought conditions keep the people in distress. Soil and climatic conditions of the district are adverse and the ryot, the farmer, is ignorant of modern technology and industries other than rural are almost non-existent during the British regime. In 1871 Anantapur district had a density of population of only 152 to the square mile, as against 226 of the Madras Presidency. The distress in 1877-78 was probably severest in Anantapur and Bellary districts; hence the pressure of population on an area was not the cause of famine, but the pressure upon the existing means and methods of getting a livelihood and raising crops. Capital will not descend from the sky (though it can arise out of the earth) and it seems that there is no way of making the district regularly maintain itself other than by acting on the ryot in the matter of education in rural economy.

The rise in grain prices and the development of cash cropping helped large. landholders to take advantage of the new market situation and reap the profits from many of their neighbours cultivation. During 1871-1901 the inhabitants of the district only increased at the rate of 6 per cent. The people of the district suffered very severely in the great famine of 1876-78 and at the census of 1881 their numbers were one-fifth fewer than they had been in 1871. In the next decade the usual rebound after the famine took place and the population increased at the rate of 17 per cent., but in the ten years between 1891 and 1901 it grew at little more than the average pace in the Presidency as a whole. Emigration and immigration have affected the figures but slightly. The population continued to grow up to 1941 with minor variations. Eighty per cent of the people speak Telugu, 11 per cent Kannada, and six per cent Hindustani. Kannada is the vernacular along the western border and in Madakasira two-fifths of the population talks it. In case of education Anantapur is the most backward in the whole Madras Presidency. The occupations of the people reveal that the percentage of the people who depend for their livelihood upon agricultural and pastoral pursuits is even higher than usual. White garments seem to be generally preferred to coloured. Women generally wear handloom sarees of varying colours and patterns. Rice constitutes the staple food of the people both in towns and villages. Korra, cholam, ragi and sajja are also consumed in places where they are grown. Young and old, people of all castes and communities play a variety of indigenous games.

At the beginning of the 19th century, India was pre-eminent in arts and crafts.' Even as late as 1813, Sir Thomas Munro stated that India produced its essential articles much cheaper and better than in Europe. The manufactures Munro mentioned, amongst other things, were cotton and silk products, leather, paper, domestic utensils of brass and iron and agricultural implements. The East India Company as a trading firm first exported Indian textiles to England. It encouraged the cotton manufacturers in India with the support of required expertise and machinery. When the Company became a territorial power it provided them with relief from transit duties and local taxes. It even abolished the tax on looms (Moturpha). There were commercial residents, agents and Board of Trade to monitor and regulate the supply of goods. The industrial revolution in textile production that took place in England reversed this trend. The cheap machine made British goods began to flood Indian markets while Indian cotton piece goods began to lose export markets gradually. From 1818 on English factories came to be closed down one by one and finally the Board of Trade itself was abolished in 1824. Cotton cloth exports by sea from Madras fell from 53% of all exports, by value in 1820 to 29 per cent in 1840 and then steeply to 11 per cent in 1850,

In view of the flooding of mill-made cotton manufactures from England, Tirunelveli, which was exporting textile goods to countries abroad earlier, had to rest content with exporting raw cotton after 1838. Cotton exports which were valued at 30 percent of Madras government revenue in the 1830s rose to 150 per cent in the 1870s and peaked at 400 percent during the American Civil War (1861-'65)." As D.H. Buchannan wrote, 'the Europeans were able to outbid the Indian craftsman on two important scores. They could pay more for Indian food grains and cotton than he could afford and they could sell manufactures cheaper than he could make them. Thus the farmers sold their produce abroad and brought power manufactures from Manchester and Birmingham, while the craftsmen who had formerly been paid in goods were left with neither occupation nor income'.

The traditional traders notably Chettiyars became money lenders, merchants and businessmen. The prominent place occupied by European agency firms had inspired some wealthy Hindu merchants to invest their surplus capital in these firms. Those with greater enterprise and capital resources decided to float agency firms of their own. In 1851, the Madras Almanac listed three Hindu agency houses operating in the city. These were essentially family partnerships, started by wealthy Chettis, Komatis and Naidus, 'to compete with their European rivals for a share in the export-import business, speculate in indigo, cotton and textile fabrics, and participate in the retail trade. This class of merchants was not like the old dubashis, who were dependent on government patronage and tied to an European clientele for its existence'.

The proponents of ryotwari system proposed to create a large body of independent peasant proprietors, who would be protected from the 'corrupt and faithless zamindar'. The destruction of the previous social order strengthened the position of dominant caste in each village. A shift in power relations within the ruling bloc that took place in the colonial era strengthened Brahmans in relation to erstwhile Kshatriya ruling class. "As the British bureaucracy extended its hold, writes Pamela Price, 'it was its "servants" or employees who extended their power, and it was largely the literate castes, primarily Brahmans, who managed to gain new monopolies of these bureaucratic positions via the British educational system'.

As the incidence of litigation increased, in view of the confusion the British rule created over land, "the sons and grandsons of agraharam villages" took to legal education in a decisive way."By the last quarter of nineteenth century Tamil and Telugu lawyers could attain status, respectability and wealth and begin to acquire power as a professional group. In the words of Pamila Price, the great fortunes of the "lions" and "luminaries" of the Madras Bar were the products of litigation involving the great landholding families of Madras Presidency.

As we have seen in the foregoing pages, the onslaught of British colonialism has been so devastating on the lower and "depressed" classes and this has left a legacy of their increasing assertion in demanding social justice. If the much trumpeted concept of reorganization of states on linguistic basis is contested today, it is mainly because of the colonial past, which proved to be a boon to the well entrenched higher classes and a bane to those pushed to the periphery of the social order during nineteenth century colonial Madras.

Penukonda Jyothi

Contents

List of Tables, Figures and Maps

Tables

Figures

Maps

1

Introduction

Local history is the study of history in a geographically local context and it often concentrates on the local community incorporating cultural and social aspects of the past. Historic plaques are one form of documentation of significant occurrences in the past and oral histories are another. It is often documented by local historical societies or groups that form to preserve a local historic building or other historic site. Many works of local history are compiled by amateur historians working independently or archivists employed by various organisations. An important aspect of local history is the publication and cataloguing of documents preserved in local or national records which relate to particular areas.

Definition of Local History:

The term "local history" is not as simple as it might first appear. Conventionally, local histories have been thought of as writings about a town, region or state written by an amateur writer for a local audience. Since the late nineteenth century professionalisation of history, many accredited historians have held amateur local historians and their writings in disdain and have not considered them to be part of the profession. In contrast, in the last decades of the twentieth century, some academics appropriated the term local history to refer to community studies-highly academic monographs that explore questions about a particular community. More recently, historians like Terry Barnhart broadened the parameters of local history to include the work of historical geographers and anthropologists as well as case studies of national, regional or community history. He writes, "Local history is a big tent-the demographic province of both amateurs and professionals-and local historians are as diverse as their audiences."[1]

Barnhart criticised the amateur historians for their "inordinate preoccupation with pioneers and first families," though he does acknowledge some of these early scholars were skilled. Some of the principal scholars of local history hold a similarly conflicted view of conventional local histories. While wanting to support and acknowledge the value of amateur historians, they also upbraid them for not adhering to basic standards of historical inquiry. Carol Kammen in her definition of local history, which is simple at first- "the study of past events, or of people or groups, in a given geographic area," — but then she continues with how she thinks local history ought to be done:

"[local history is] a study based on a wide variety of documentary evidence and placed in a comparative context that should be both regional and national. Such study ought to be accomplished by a historian using methods appropriate to the topic under consideration while following general rules of historical inquiry: open-mindedness, honesty, accountability, and accuracy."[2]

Kammen's "Encyclopedia of Local History, are useful resources for amateur historians seeking help in writing their narratives. However, implicit in this desire to help amateur, local historians write more contextually as professional historians do, is the assumption that the way many amateurs have been writing is inferior. The hope is that if more local historians write better local history, the entire reputation of the profession will improve as well. It will begin to edge the local historian away from the negative stereotype of the "old lady in tennis shoes."[3]

On the other hand, British historian William D. Rubenstein believes such a view tends to exclude from academic history a variety of amateur writings that are valued by much of the population and that, viewed critically, can enhance an understanding of a community. Furthermore, he asserts amateur and professional historians share basic methodologies: both weigh evidence and follow methods to do their research. Acknowledging that the perspective of the local historian is often less complex and more sanguine than that of the academic historian, Rubenstein argues the writings of the nonacademic historian offer the academic historian both important information and insight into the past. Suggesting professional historians can learn from their amateur counterparts, Rubenstein writes, "it would do the academic historian no harm at all to become better acquainted with this vast world of which, too often, he or she knows too little."[4]

In keeping with the above definitions one can view that for a formal definition of an academic field of local history that expands the boundaries of local history to include a variety of academic and non-academic local history narratives. Like public history or political history, local history is a concept. It can be thought of as a narrative or genre trope that assumes a referent to a place nearby. This geographical place varies with each book and each author. It can be a multi-state region, a street, a neighbourhood, a town, a body of water, or a piece of the landscape. The focus of the local history can be the place itself, the people who lived there or events that took place in a particular location. The study of local history narrative brings together writings about the past, amateur and academic, that share a relationship to a place. There is no other academic category that puts these writings in one place together. The collected writings about the past of a place constitute the local history narrative tradition. Practicing local history allows historians to reach a wider audience beyond their students and colleagues. As some professional historians have long understood, local history narrative is extremely popular with ordinary people, far more popular than most monographs. Further, the historiography of local history can provide historians with valuable insight into a community that they may not find elsewhere and it provides an important historiographical base for academic study of a community. William D. Rubenstein rightly pointed out that, "local historiography does provide in most cases a firm and valuable basis for more sophisticated histories which should, perhaps, be better known to today's graduate students and researchers whose iconoclasm and search for conflict based in socio-economic factors may have gone too far in the other direction."[5]

Studying local history provides the reader with increased interest in the larger subject of history. It advances from memorising names; dates and places, to the desire of knowing what was being said about people, places or events. It gives a better sense of realism. It's a body of information that can be relevant to the readers' own surroundings. The subject matter of today's learning institutions should not be isolated from the matter of life. The community and its institutions can be a laboratory for learning and the while community provides a sense of immediacy and reality about both the past and the present. It is a fact that there is local history everywhere, but we know little about what it is, how it was practiced, and who the practitioners are. Keeping in view of this the present study makes an attempt to study the local history of Anantapur district under colonial rule. It is the crucial period of transition from traditionalists to modernity in the history of this region of the country.

Anantapur:

The history of Anantapur [now called as Ananthapuramu] presented by two great British historians Col. Mackenzie, Sir C.P. Brown. The Telugu scholar printed a version of these for the use of students of the language and added a translation of them under the C.P. Brown presented legendry history of Anantapur in his book "The Wars of the Rajas."[6]

A big tank was constructed by Chikkappa Udaiyer, Diwan to king Bukka I of Vijayanagar, who ruled from 1343 to 1379. At each end of the embankment he built a waste weir and near each weir a village. The village at the eastern end was named as Bukkaraya Samudram in memory of his master Bukka and that at the western end Anantasagaram in memory of Chikkappa

Udaiyer's wife. Bukkarayasamudram is still in existence and still known by its original name. The Anantapur was called after the tank Anantasagaram.

With regard to Anantasagaram one local fable is famous even today. As per this fable, the tank Anantasagaram used to breach frequently due to heavy rains. The breach of tank often resulted loss of life as well as loss of crops to the dwellers of Bukkarayasamudram, as it is located in the down streams of Anantasagaram. To come out of this calamity the people of Bukkarayasamudram devoted '*Gangammatalli*' (goddess of waters). In response to their devotion '*Gangammatalli*' entered the body of a woman and explained out of her mouth that if someone was thrown into the breach she (the goddess) would stay within her proper limits and damage the bund no further. Accordingly Musalamma, daughter-in-law of Basi Reddi of Bukkaraya Samudram, was thrown into the breach and built up within it.[7] Three margosa trees, under which are a *virukal* and some other stones, still mark the spot and sheep, fowls and so on are still occasionally offered to the shade of the girl. For a long time, says local tradition, she used to answer when called upon after such sacrifices, but one day an impertinent woman called out to her " O Musalamma! Has not thy voice yet drowned? " and since then she has kept silence.[8]

During the time of Rama Raja, the usurper of the Vijayanagar throne, Anantapur and the country around it were granted to Hanumappa Nayudu of Hande family, who had helped that ruler to put down an insurrection. Hence the place was known thereafter as Hande Anantapur, a name which indeed survived even for several years after the English came into possession of it. Hanumappa was succeeded by his son Immadi Hampa Nayudu, who was in turn followed by his son Malakappa. The latter was present at the battle of Tallikota. Munro says that he was Diwan of Vijayanagar and that he afterwards submitted to the king of Bijapur and was granted a jaghir paying a peshkash of 45,772 Kanthiraya pagodas, or about Rs 1,30,000. He was thus at that time a gentleman of substance.[9]

Hanumappa was followed by his son Hampa Nayudu (1619-31) and then by Siddappa Nayudu (1631-59). Pavadappa Nayudu

(1659- 71) was the next chief, and during his time the country was invaded by the poligar of Rayadurg in Bellary district, who made his way as far as Dharmavaram and left a garrison there. On Pavadappa's death his wife Ramakka managed the estate for some years during the minority of her son Siddappa. During her rule, the Delhi Emperor Aurangzeb came into possession of the suzerainty of the country and he reduced the *peshkash* to 11,200 pagodas but required the *poligar* to keep up 1200 foot and 150 horses for service if called upon.

Siddappa died in 1696 and was succeeded by his eldest son Prasanappa Nayudu (1696-1720). He helped the Nawab of Cuddapah, to whom he was now subject, to attack the forces of the Rayadurgpoligar, and the Nawab eventually released him from the obligation of keeping up any military force. He was murdered in 1720 by his concubine Vasantamma, with whom he was living because his wife was childless and by whom he had had four children.[10]

The next chief, Pavadappa Nayudu (1720-37), brother of Prasanappa Nayudu declined to pay the usual tribute to the Nawab of Cuddapah and beat off a force sent against him. He was followed by his son Siddappa (1737-40), a dissolute youth squandered the resources of the estate. His men chief rebelled against him and set up his cousin Ramappa, the son of Prasanappa, as a claimant to his place. Siddappa obtained help from the poligar of Tadimarri but Ramappa's faction called in Mordri Rao of Gooty, captured Anantapur and imprisoned Siddappa.

Ramappa (1740-52) thus became chief. During this time the peshkash of the estate was reduced by the Marathas to Rs 18,000, but in addition a tribute of Rs.5,000 was paid to Mordri Rao. Ramappa was of a fighting turn and began by attacking Kanumukkala, a village eight miles south of Dharmavaram, which had been captured from his predecessors by the poligar of Rayadurg.[11] The attack failed and in the next year (1741) Rayadurg besieged Bukkapatnam. Just as the place was about to capitulate, Ramappa Nayudu entered it by a path over the hills which stand to the east of it and made such a vigorous sortie against the Rayadurg forces that they retired to Dharmavaram. Another attack of theirs on the same place in the next year was also repulsed. Meanwhile trouble was brewing. The widow of Siddappa, the cousin whom Ramappa had ousted, had fled to the protection of the poligar of Bellary, who was a kinsman of the Hande family. At her suggestion this poligar proposed to Ramappa that he (the Bellary poligar) should adopt Ramappa's eldest son Siddappa. Ramappa agreed and the boy was sent to Bellary. Some time afterwards Ramappa went there to see him. After he had gone back to Anantapur the Bellary poligar with a considerable force paid him a return visit. The fort at Anantapur was too small to hold the followers of both parties, so with unwise politeness Ramappa invited the Bellary people to occupy it and withdrew his own garrison,- stopping in the fort himself without attendants to look after his guest. Next morning the Bellary poligar murdered him and made himself master of the place. He next seized most of the country round about, except the forts at Bukkapatnam, Kottacheruvu and Raptadu. Thereafter, he returned to Bellary and there he threw into prison Siddappa, the son of Ramappa whom he had adopted. The boy however bribed his jailors, escaped, and fled with his brother-in-law Basappa to Hirehelu, a fort some twelve miles south of Bellary which belonged to Morari Rao. By Morari Rao's orders Basappa was supplied with some troops by the amin of the fort and with these he marched to Raptadu. Here he was joined by many adherents of the Hande family and eventually was strong enough to attack Bukkardyasamudram,[12] the place was however relieved by troops from Bellary after a fierce fight. Basappa then obtained help from the Nawab of Cuddapah and the garrisons of both Bukkardyasamudram and Anantapur thereupon fled. Basappa thus secured possession of the estate and having established order he sent for Siddappa and installed him as poligar in 1753 AD.

In 1757 AD, Anantapur was attacked by Morari Rao. It resisted stoutly for some time but at length bought off the enemy for Rs 50,000. The estate had been so much impoverished by the struggles it had recently gone through that there was the greatest difficulty in raising the amount. Partly for this reason and partly to revenge himself upon those who had refused to help him in his hour of need, Basappa sent out plundering expeditions, and these ravaged a number of important places such as Tadipatri, Yollutla, Roddam, and others.

Basappa died in 1772 AD from over-fatigue incurred in trying to stop a breach in the Bukkapatnam tank. In 1775, Haidar Ali took Bellary and Gooty and became suzerain of Anantapur. The peshkash was raised to 23,625 Kanthiraya pagodas, or about Rs 69,000. This was more than the estate could pay and it speedily fell into arrears. One of Haidar's officers therefore came down and arrested the poligar and attached his property. Thenceforward the decline of the family was rapid. The old poligar's two eldest sons were drafted into Haidar's army and were killed in action and the third son, Siddappa Nayudu, was sent to *Seringapatam*. Crushed by all his troubles, the old poligar died in 1788.[13]

In order to prevent any chance of risings, Tipu Sulthan hanged all the males of the family who were at Anantapur. Siddappa however escaped from Seringapatam and after Tipu's death in 1799 he succeeded in taking Anantapur. He afterwards submitted to the Nizam, to whom the country had been transferred by the treaty of 1799, and was given the village of Siddarampuram as a Jaghir. He was granted a pension by Munro and some of his descendants were drawn stipends up to 1860.

Setting of Anantapur:

Anantapur is one among the four districts of Rayalaseema situated in the South-Western most tip of Andhra Pradesh between latitude 13°41'-15°14'N longitude 76°76'-78°86'E with its vast expanse of 19,130 Sq.kms. It is one of the largest districts not only in Rayalaseema but also in the state of Andhra Pradesh. Anantapur at present is bounded on the North by Kurnool district, on the east by Cuddapah district, on the south by Kolar district of Karnataka and Chittoor district and West by Bellary district of Karnataka state. The entire district is divided into three natural divisions as the Northern taluks of Gooty, Guntakal, Uravakonda and Tadipatri with large expanse of Black Cotton soil. The central taluks of Anantapur, Rayadurg, Kalyandurg, Kanekal, Kambadur, Dharmavaram and Penukonda with arid tree less expanse of poor soil, the southern taluks consisting of Madakasira, Hindupur and Kadiri with comparatively less in hospitable soils.

The hills that pass through the district are mostly plain rocks with no vegetation and do not stand comparison in size height or thickness with those in the neighbouring districts or Kurnool and Cuddapah. Even these few ranges run from North to South without bearing any specific name. However, there are the Muchukota hills in Gooty, Tadipatri and Anantapur Taluks, Nagasamudram hills in Gooty, Anantapur, Dharmavaram Taluks, Nallappa hills in Penukonda Taluk, Akkamma hills in Hindupur Taluk and Laguvamma hills in Kadiri Taluk are famous in the region.

The major river system of the district is Pennar, Chitravathi, Papagni Tadakaleru which are not perennial and only during the rainy season that they become active. Naturally, the people of the district depend purely on Monsoons for the purpose of irrigation. Due to the geographical position, this is a drought-prone area famines are being a common feature in the district because of the impediment of the high ghats.

Anantapur in 1882

The district is made up of the eight taluks of Anantapur, Dharmavaram, Gooty, Hindupur, Kalyandurg, Madakasira, Penukonda and Tadipatri. The Kalyandurg taluk was constituted in December 1893 out of the portions of Dharmavaram and of the Rayadurg taluk of Bellary, the old Dharmavaram taluk being found to be unwieldy. Their headquarters are at the towns from which each is named. Besides these eight places, the other towns of any importance are Pamidi and Uravakonda in Gooty Taluk and Yadiki in Tadipatri Taluk.

The taluks of the district may be said to roughly arrange themselves into three natural divisions, namely Gooty and Tadipatri in the north, which contain large areas of black cotton-soil; Anantapur, Kalyandurg , Dharmavaram and Penukonda in the centre, which are mainly made up of arid, treeless expanses of poor red soils ; and Madakasira and Hindupur in the south, which connect with the Mysore plateau and stand at a higher elevation than the rest of the district and in which the soil, though still red, is a loam of a kind superior to that found in the central taluks.[14]

The cotton-soil areas are fertile and in parts of Hindupur and Madakasira (the latter of which is sometimes somewhat grandiloquently called the garden of the district) there is plenty of cultivation and vegetation. But most of the rest of Anantapur is made up of barren undulating wastes clothed with a miserably thin grass and dotted with scattered stunted trees. Much of the soil is so poor that it will not stand continuous cropping and is consequently more often fallow than under cultivation, which gives the country a poverty-stricken appearance. The wide plains are broken up by ridges, lines and clusters of rocky hills which, like the ground around them, are covered with poor grass and a few small trees. In the moister valleys are occasional topes, but on the uplands and the hills—even those which are forest reserves-the tree-growth is never large or dense. An artist, however, might find compensation for the inhospitable appearance of this central portion of the district in the wonderful colouring of its hills, which changes from hour to hour in sympathy with every alteration in the atmospheric conditions of the day.

Review of Literature:

Literary evidences are the next important source material for the present study while the direct contribution to the regional history from this sources are thus seen to be little importance the indirect value of the literature to a historian can hardly be overrated. Just they enable us to picture of the social and religious milieu in which the characters of the region lived and more also acted.

There are very few literary works which help us in the course of present study. They are indeed district Gazetteers, village manuals or kaifiyats or local records, Sthalapuranas or Sthanika Itihasas, temple chronicles and other works. Andhra Pradesh District Gazetteers[15] is the nearest approach to study the geographical and historical background of the district.

C.P. Brown in his work entitled "In the Wars of Rajas"[16] made an attempt to study several myths and legends, which are popular in Anantapur region.

Krishna Murthy M.S. in his work entitled "The Nolambas"[17] stated the glory of a local dynasty called as Nolamba Pallavas and he also refers their political alliances with neighbouring rulers of the region. It is useful to know the genealogical information of this rulers and socio-economic conditions of the period.

Krishna Sastri V. V., in his book entitled "The Proto and early Historical Culture of Andhra Pradesh"[18] discussed the history of Andhra Pradesh on the basis of archaeological sources. It is considered as an authentic evidence for the regional archaeology of Anantapur district. It describes the lifestyle of the people of Paleolithic and Neolithic periods in the region.

Rama Mohan Rao K., in his work entitled "Directory of Monuments Antiquarian"[19] provides information on the archaeological aspects like pre-proto and historical sites, monuments, and sculptures of the region. It serves as the important source material for the study of the district.

Chandrasekar, A., in his scholarly work entitled "Fairs and Festivals of Anantapur District"[20] made an attempt to make a complete and comprehensive collection of information on every fair and festival celebrated in the villages and towns of Anantapur district. It is more useful to describe the religious and cultural practices of the people in the district.

Sampat Kumar, M.D., in his work entitled "Chittoor through the Ages"[21] made an attempt on the history of Chittoor district, which is the adjoining region of Anantapur district. It provides useful information about the relationship between the local rulers and neighbouring dynasties.

Ranganatham, G.B., in his dissertation entitled "History and Monuments of Penukonda"[22] made a monumental survey of the district in general and that of the history of Penukonda in particular. It helps to picturize the prehistoric sites of the district.

Gopala Krishnamurthy, P., in his manuscript entitled "Khadri Sthalapuranamu"[23] described the origin of the name of the place. It also states the socio-cultural activities of the local people and refers to the historical background of the Lakshmi Narasimha Temple at Kadiri.

Narayana Charyulu, P., in his manuscript entitled "Penukonda-Lakshmi"[24] portrays the historical importance of Penukonda in Anantapur district. It is also considered as the "Sthanika Itihasa" of the Penukonda region and contains fruitful information on the socio-economic conditions of the people in the region. It also makes a special reference to the administration of the region.

Ranganatham, G. B., in his paper entitled "Rock Paintings of Budagavi and Kothasivaram"[25] provided good information about the socio-economic conditions of the Neolithic and Mesolithic periods in the region. It also mention about a number of stone artifacts and a few iron implements of the early man in this region.

Jawaharlal, G., in his paper entitled "Antiquities of Budagavi"[26] made an attempt to provide some glimpses of the pre-historic background of this region and also presented sufficiently a broad spectrum of the socio-religious and cultural aspects of the region.

Venkata Ramana, K., in his work entitled "Early rulers of Anantapur District"[27] illustrates the history of early rulers in the district describing the socio-economic conditions of the period in the region.

Nilakanta Sastri, K. A., in his work entitled "Early History of the Andhra Country"[28] cites that the power of Ikshvakus extended as far north as Kanheri and as far east as Anantapur. According to author the Ipur seal resembles a symbol much like that found on the coins of the Cutus in the Anantapur District.

The Journal of Geological Society of India in its Correspondence entitled "Glory of Diamonds in India"[29] established that Anantapur was one of the main diamond producing areas of the country. The author recorded that to protect the interests of South African diamond mining companies (owned by Britishers), the giant Indian diamond industry of that time was forced to close down by British rulers.

Dhanaraju Vulli, in his scholarly article entitled "History of 'Colonial Education' in Andhra: Response from Various Castes"[30] critically analyzes that the growth of education among the various castes during colonial period in Andhra as well as Anantapur district. The intervention of colonial rule witnessed greater progress in the growth of education among the lower castes. In the second half of the nineteenth century government revised educational code and adopted a new scheme of payments which influenced the growth of education among the non-Brahman castes. The series of Acts were as catalysts for a wider change in the middle classes as well as the depressed castes in the society. The new forces created by the British rule and western education weakened the traditional social order and broke down the intellectuals monopoly of the Brahmins. Not only did it break the traditional order of the society and Brahmin's domination, in the post-formation of Andhra Pradesh the non-Brahmin castes also got the political power in the state and continued the same kind of domination as the Brahmins played during colonial period. But the lower caste situation was the same. By analysing colonial education and its importance in the wider socio-historical context this paper would address responses of the various castes towards colonial education in Andhra. The author analyzes the literacy rates in Anantapur district during 1891-1911.

Reddeppa, S., in his research article entitled "The Role of Christian Missionaries in Madras Presidency – A Historical Study"[31] explains the role of Christian missionaries in the development of education in Madras Presidency in general and Anantapur district in particular. As per the study, the modern education was introduced by the Christian Missionaries under the British rule. It presents that the Christian Missionaries in Madras Presidency was to introduce English education as well as English culture and tradition. The Missionary schools have done wonderful job. They inculcated moral values and spiritual values in students.

The colonial historians and administrators have studied the history of the backward region from the administrative point of view. But all these studies have their own limitations and they could not provide complete information. Hence, it is felt essential to analyze and to study the impact of colonial rule on this region. Keeping this in view, it is proposed to study the Anantapur district of Andhra Pradesh of the colonial rule 1800-1947. The study period assumes importance in the history of Andhra Pradesh as it is one of the territories handed over to Britishers under Subsidiary Alliance System of Lordwellesley. It is the period, which brought several changes in socio-economic and cultural life of the people in this region particularly Anantapur district. The period assumes significance in the history of the district as it is faced several famines, which received little attention by foreign rulers.

Objectives of the Study:

The present study is an attempt to focus on the Aspects of Development in colonial period 1800-1947 Anantapur District, Andhra Pradesh.

The specific objectives of the study are as follows:

1. To portray the historical background of Anantapur district with special reference to political developments.
2. To evaluate the role of British Indian Government in mitigating the miseries of the people of the district during famines and epidemics, Andhra Pradesh.

3. To study the demographic features and socio-religious life of people under colonial rule in Anantapur district.
4. To analyze the contribution of British Indian Government for industrial and banking development in the study area, and
5. To evaluate the developments taken place in rural and urban local self-governments during British rule in Anantapur district of Andhra Pradesh.

Methodology:

The present study look into different parameters and paradigms of Anantapur district, Andhra Pradesh under Colonial region from 1800-1947. The study is both analytical and descriptive and is based on primary and secondary data. The methodology employed in this research is a combination of historical and descriptive. The source available for the present study includes both literary and archaeological material. The study is chiefly based on the information contained in the numerous lithic and other inscriptions found in various parts of Anantapur district, Andhra Pradesh to trace the history of this region. The secondary source material includes the Andhra Pradesh district gazetteers, reports of various commissions and committees, administrative reports etc.

Area of the Study:

The area chosen for the present study is Anantapur district located in Rayalaseema region of Andhra Pradesh State. The district directly came under the British rule in 1800, when it was ceded by the Nizam of Hyderabad. It was made as the district in 1882.

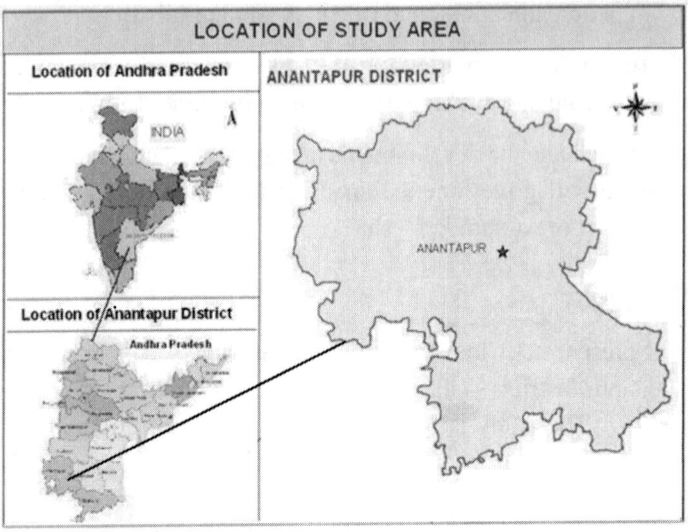

Organisation of the Study:

The present thesis is divided into Eight chapters including introduction and conclusion.

The first chapter- Introduction- defines and traces the importance of studying local history. It covers the setting of Anantapur district and significance of Anantapur in the history of Andhra Pradesh. It also contains review of literature, objectives of study, methodology, data collection and plan of the study.

The second chapter- 'Historical Sketch of Anantapur District': is devoted to study the pre-history and history of Anantapur district before it came under the colonial rule. The chapter also throws light on the history of Anantapur during the ancient, the medieval and the modern periods.

The third chapter presents- Social Development: Myths and Realities- traces the growth and development of people with special emphasis on linguistic, religious, educational, social and occupational aspects. The chapter also covers the conditions of women and various religious castes in the district under colonial rule.

The fourth chapter deals with the- Economic Development of the People under British rule- It discusses the extent of agricultural, industrial, banking and communication development of the region and the way how the colonial administration initiated steps to develop Industrial and Banking sector.

Chapter five deals with the- Development of Local Self Government institutions in Anantapur under colonial administration. Further, it presents the functioning of local bodies and developmental activities during colonial rule.

The sixth chapter presents- Public Grievances and the Response of Government- illustrates the condition of people during famines and other epidemics in Anantapur district, and it evaluates the measures taken by the government to ameliorate the conditions of people during public grievances.

The seventh chapter deals with the Historical perspectives of developments in Andhra under the colonial period an intensive work into these Aspects i.e., trade and commerce and Andhra Desa eighteenth centuries, will definitely help the proper reconstruction of the history of this region and also proper understanding of the causes for the decline of internal Trade and commerce and the unfavourable balance of foreign trade that characterised the British colonial rule in India as well as in Andhra in the succeeding period. It covered many interesting aspects of the theme such as sea port, commodity structure of external and Internal Trade. The rule of European Trading Companies, Merchant Communities, means of Transport and communications, Trade and State etc.

The eighth chapter presents- Summary and Conclusion of the study.

REFERENCES

1. Terry Barnhart, "Of Whole and Parts: Local History and the American Experience," *Research and Review Series*, 7 (2000), p. 10.

2. Carol Kammen and Norma Prendergast, *Encyclopedia of Local History*, (Lanman, Maryland: Rowman, Alta Mira, 2000), p. 74.
3. *Ibid.*, p. 79.
4. William D. Rubenstein, "History and 'amateur' history" in Peter Lambert and Phillipp Schofield ed., Making History: *An Introduction to the History and Practices of a Discipline* (London: Routledge, 2004), pp. 272-273.
5. *Ibid.*, 273.
6. Soma Reddy, R. 1980, *History of Religious Institutions in Andhra Desa from A.D. 1300-1600.* Hyderabad, p. 260.
7. Rubies, J.P., *Travel and Ethnology in the Renaissance: South India Through European Eyes, 1250-1625*, Cambridge University Press, Cambridge, 2000, p. 41.
8. Settar, S., Hampi, *A Medieval Metropolis*, Kala Yatra, Bangalore [1990]. An introduction to the site emphasising contemporary literary sources, p. 58.
9. Sewell, Robert, *A Forgotten Empire (Vijayanagar): A Contribution to the History of India*, [reprint] Asian Educational Services, New Delhi, 2000, p. 12.
10. Wagoner, Phillip B., *Tidings of the King: A Translation and Ethnohistorical Analysis of the Rayavacakamu*, University of Hawaii Press, Honolulu, 1993, p. 30.
11. Sinopoli, Carla M. 2003, *The Political Economy of Craft Production: Crafting Empire in South India, c. 1350-1650.* Cambridge University Press, p. 131.
12. W. Francis, Madras District gazetteers, A*nantapur District gazetteer 1905,* Addison & Company, Madras, 1905, p. 124.
13. *Ibid.*, p. 147.
14. *Ibid.*, p. 148.
15. Shiva Shankar Narayana (E.D), *Andhra Pradesh District GazettersAnantapur District*, Govt. of Andhra Pradesh, 1970, p. 57.
16. Brown C.P. : *The wars of Rajas*. Asian educational service. New Delhi, 1988, p. 11.
17. Krishna Murthy M. S., *The Nolambas*. University of Mysore 1980, p. 13.
18. Krishna sastri V. V., *The Proto and early Historical Culture of Andhra Pradesh*, Govt. of Andhra Pradesh, Hyderabad, 1983.

19. Rama Mohan Rao, K., Directory of Monuments Antiquarian, Subramanyam B. *Remains of Andhra Pradesh*. Dept, of Archaeology and Museum A.P., Hyderabad. 1993.

20. Chandrasekar. A., *Fairs and Festivals of Anantapur Dis*trict, Census Publications, Andhra Pradesh, 1961, p. 127.

21. Sampat Kumar, M.D, *Chittoor through the Ages*. B.R. Publishing Corporation, Delhi 1980, p. 129.

22. Ranganatham. G.B. *History and Monuments of Penukonda* (un Published Ph.D. dissertation,) SK University, Anantapur, 1990, p. 17.

23. Gopala Krishnamurthy, P., *Khadri Sthalapuranamu* (unpublished Manuscript), Khadri, 1983, p. 46.

24. Narayana Charyulu, P., *Penukonda Lakshmi*, (unpublished Manuscript), Proddutur, 1980, p. 103.

25. Ranganatham, G.B., *Rock Paintings of Budagavi and Kotha Sivaram*, Andhra Pradesh History Congress Proceedings XIII Session, Sri Sailam, 1989, p. 41.

26. Jawaharlal, G., *Antiquities of Budagavi and Kotha Sivaram*, Andhra Pradesh History Congress Proceedings XIII Session, Sri Sailam, 1989, p. 65.

27. Venkata Ramana, K., *Early Rulers of Anantapur District, Budagavi and Kotha Sivaram*, Andhra Pradesh History Congress Proceedings XIV Session, Warangal, 1990, pp. 39-42.

28. Nilakanta Sastri, K. A., *Early History of the Andhra Country*, Madras University Historical Series, No. 16, G. S. Press, Madras, 1941.

29. ______ Correspondence, "Glory of Diamonds in India", *Journal of Geological Society of India*, Vol. 67, June 2006, pp. 818-819.

30. Dhanaraju Vulli, "History of 'Colonial Education' in Andhra: Response from Various Castes", *Research Journal of Educational Sciences*, Vol. 1, No. 6, September 2013, pp. 8-17.

31. Reddeppa, S., "The Role of Christian Missionaries in Madras Presidency– A Historical Study", *Indian Journal of Applied Research*, Vol. 4, No. 2, February 2014, pp. 4-6.

2

Historical Sketch of Anantapur District

Anantapur region offers vivid glimpses of the prehistoric past. Bruce Foote surveyed the northern part of this district towards the end of the nineteenth century. According to Forte, it is an open country with a number of granite hills which are castellated and which once offered strongly defensible sites. The plain at their base must have been securely cultivated by the people, who kept a watch from the top of the strong rocky fastnesses to get timely warning of the approach of enemies.[1] The Paleolithic age, in which man fashioned his tools and weapons by chipping hard stones of convenient size and shape, is represented by the only Paleolithic's recovered from the Vidapanakallu west hill in this district. It is made of quartzite and is of squarish oval shape.

Foote collected several Neolithic artifacts. Nearly twenty-three localities in the district yielded very interesting objects. Eight of them are highly important; nine are of moderate importance and the rest comparatively insignificant. The important sites include the Lattavaram hill, Budihal or Budikonda, Vidupanakallu Fort or East hill and West hill, Velpumadugu or Yellapadugu (all in Gooty), the riverside site east of Tadipatri, the Havaligi hill (Gooty) and Kalamedevur hill (Dharmavaram). To the moderately important category belong Vajrakarur, Uravakonda, Karakumukkala, the Guntakal Railway junction (all in Gooty), Bhogasamudram

(Penukonda), the hill north of Havaligi hill (Gooty), Mutchukota (Tadipatri), the Jambuladinne hill (Anantapur) and the Yerragudi hill (Gooty).[2]

The neolith artifacts gathered by Foote covered a large number of used and broken implements, about a dozen corn-crushers of pistacite rock from the Lattavaram hill. Budihal or Budikonda is also a fine, castellated hill with many capital rock shelters, yielding a small pestle made of diorite, a rare large oval mealing stone made of grey crystalline limestone, a broken mealing stone of chrome-mica and a fragment of a grey earthenware vase. He found a long shallow stone trough between two good rock seats and a very remarkable oblong terrace with a flat bare rocky floor where people carried on their mealing work. On the east and west hills of Vidupanakallu there are a large number of celts, chisels, flakes, strike-a-lights, scrapers and cores made mostly of chert, agate, chalcedony and quartzite. The agates must have been obtained from a considerable distance, probably from the valley of the Tungabhadra. Foote collected quite a number of celts, scrapers, flakes, flake knives and cores from the velupumadugu hill at the east of Tadipatri he picked up many potsherds of highly decorated and good quality, presumably belonging to the well-to-do classes. The most interesting finds on the Havaligi hill belong to the fine series of artifacts of chert and agate. The site at the Kalamedevur hill revealed the existence of a flake factory, which include numerous broken celts, corn-crushers, pounders and potsherds of excellent quality.[3]

An outcrop of black trap rock runs near Demaketapalle (Hindupur) along the crest of a hill. The boulders of the rock show signs of having been struck with stone hammers for producing flakes required for working into finished celts. Hundreds of flakes and unfinished stone implements lie scattered at the base of these boulders. This site must have once been used as a factory for manufacturing celts. At the moderately important sites celts, flakes, chisels, hammers, corn-crushers, mealing stones, cores, potsherds and linchets were commonly met with. The only wooden prehistoric object of the Neolithic age which survived till today was a small comb which was discovered at the Guntakal Railway Junction by

Cornelius Cardew, a friend of Foote. Many of Cardew's findings are now preserved in the Madras Museum.[4]

A few dolmens were discovered at Kalyandurg and Kambaduru. Hundreds of kistvaens were found to occur at Mudigallu, Devadulabetta, Malyavantam, Kondapuram and Puleru. The existence of cairns at places like Mudigallu, Devadulabetta, Kalyandurg and Thodagutta was also brought to light. The dolmens were usually found intermingled with cairns and kistvaens and appeared to have been erected as tombs in memory of the departed and also as receptacles for votive offerings to propitiate the spirits of the dead. Dolmens were sometimes converted into hero-shrines dedicated to some local chief or warrior or into shrines of Siva with stone lingams installed in them. Such shrines can still be seen at Kalyandurg and Kambaduru.

The remnants of the post Neolithic period included the fortification on an isolated granite hill at Velpumadugu in Gooty. Foote's exploration revealed that there are many signs of continued settlements in the middle and eastern parts of the Havaligi hill. Traces of an Iron Age settlement which succeeded the Neolithic ones evidenced by the shape of iron slags strewn all over the surface were brought to light at Kalamedevur (Dharmavaram). Cornelius Cardew made some excavations and found an iron and Bronze Age site near the Guntakal Railway station from which valuable series of earthenware and iron articles were obtained.[5] As civilisation advanced, other metals like gold, copper and bronze came into existence, and it was referred as the 'later Iron' Age, by the archaeologists, passed down into the proto-historic age which formed the link between the prehistoric and historic ages.

Mauryan Period:

The historical period of Anantapur commences with the rule of Mauryan Empire. There are no evidences that Ashoka conquered Anantapur region of the south India, although his edicts are found in this region. Bindusara was a peaceful ruler and his father Chandragupta Maurya established his State at Pataliputra and defeated Selucus Nicator, who was an armed General of Alexander of Macedonia. No other conquests are attributed to him and there is no direct evidence, it may even to surmise that the Nandas could have annexed these territories to their empire. There is a clear indication in the form of the edicts of Ashoka which were found at Erragudi in the district [near Gooty] and Rajulamandagiri in Kurnool district. The Erragudi site is more important because it has all the fourteen rock edicts and also two minor rock edicts of Ashoka. All these edicts are engraved on the rocks adjacent to Erragudi village. Unfortunately, there are no remains of a town discovered here. No excavations also have been conducted here. But, it is quite possible that this was a frontier town with a route leading to south India. Except for this stray reference there is no other evidence to give us details of the polity, the economy or the social structure of the period in the region. Buddhism obviously had its stronghold in the region. The Buddhist missionaries of Ashoka might have passed through this area to the south.

The edicts of Ashoka at Erragudi in Gooty mandal of Anantapur district are engraved on a boulder in the nearby hill rock, which is generally called "Nallaenugulakonda.[6] Most of these records are in the form of instructions given to the Rajjukas by the Mahamatras to follow the path of Dhamma and these contain commentaries on Dhamma. In the minor edicts of Ashoka declared that although he accepted Buddhism two and a half years before the edict was issued, it was only after one year that he commenced his efforts to follow the principles of Buddhism and also to propagate its principles. This record came into existence in 256 days after he started his tour. Whether the number given here is with reference to days or to the year in which he was ruling is not clear. In this edict he clearly states that spiritual merit is not only for the rich, even the poor can, if they follow Dharma with a pure heart, can attain salvation. The second edict is addressed not only to Rajjukas but also to the Rashtrikas. It contains simple but prominent principles like obeying the parents, respecting the elders, sympathetic towards other beings speaking truth and following Dhamma. He desires that these principles are propagated by the Teachers, Brahmanas, Gajarohakas and Ratharudhas.

These edicts of Ashoka show that this area was reasonably populated and thus formed part of Mauryan administration. The Brahmagiri edict refers to the instruction of the (prince) Aryaputra and the Mahamatra (officers) at Suvarnagiri to the Mahamatras at Isila. Suvarnagiri is identified with Jonnagiri near Erragudi. If this identification is accepted, then the region around Erragudi had an important city or town at Suvarnagiri presently known as Jonnagiri. Therefore, it could be inferred that it was populous region and Ashoka felt that he should have propagated his Dharma here. This may be one of the reasons for the existence of all the edicts of Ashoka here. However, there is no further evidence to know more about the society of the region and nevertheless it is possible that due to Ashoka's influence many people got converted into Buddhism. But there are no traces of any survival of Buddhism in this region. This area comprises the south-east part of the present Andhra Pradesh, with certain parts of Rayalaseema. There are other monuments right up to Guntur district at Amaravati which testify to the fact that in those northern regions Buddhism had a very stronghold. Whether the Rayalaseema region came deeply under the influence of Buddhism cannot be vouchsafed, but Ashokan edicts are the only available epigraphical evidences.

Sathavahana period:

The Satavahanas were successors of Mauryas in Andhra country. The dynastic history of Andhra Country is traced only from the history of Satavahanas. But, the early part of the history of this region is full of controversies. Srimuka is generally taken to be the Satavahana king responsible for killing the last Mauryan ruler in Pataliputra. However, there is also a view that the last king of Mauryan dynasty was killed by Simuka.[7] Surprisingly, Simuka was not interested in establishing a kingdom for himself in Magadha and he came over to Deccan. The earliest epigraph of Satavahana is found in Maharashtra and it is held that the Satavahanas, there upon migrated from Maharashtra to Andhra Pradesh, more so after Gautamiputra Satakarni. But the Puranas like the Vayu, Mastya, Vishnu and Bhagavata called Sathavanas as Andhras. This is taken to mean that they referred to the clan (jati) of Andhras, while the rulers belonged to the family (kula) of Satavahanas. There is an ample evidence to indicate that this region came under the rule of Sathavahanas. At Myakadoni, [8] near Bellary found there an inscription belonging to Pulamavi, the later Satavahana ruler of the third century A.D. It speaks that the region is referred to as Satavahanahara i.e., the ahara is an administrative unit or division of the Satavahana kingdom. Ananatapur district naturally must have been a part of this division called Satavahanahara. This region is also called as Satavahaniratta, i.e., Satavahanarashtra or the territory of the Satavahanas in the Hirehadagalli plates[9] of Pallava Sivaskandavarms.

The discovery of few coins bearing legend Harathi belonging to 'vinhukada chutukulananda' and a large number of un-inscribed lead coins with horse on the obverse and the characteristic ten arched chaitya hill with a very line, below, assignable to the Maharathis, who were feudatories of the Satavahanas,[10] Further the discovery of a hitherto unknown early historic site at Sasanakota in Hindupur taluk, which yielded traces of Satavahana culture viz., coins, terracotta figurines, typical red polished and red slipped wares, brick built structures, supports the assumption that Anantapur district was indeed in the hands of a branch of Satavahanas and their feudatories i.e.. Maharathis who held sway over the region with Banavasi in Chitradurga district. However, it is interesting to note that this part of the Deccan never felt the presence of the imperial Satavahanas.

Western Gangas:

The Pallavas were the political successors of the Satavahanas in the area under study. But it is not known that how far and how long this area was remained under the suzerainty of Pallavas. Very soon, in the south Karnataka region, the Western Gangas rose to a political power to reckon with. Gangas with Talakadu in Mysore district as their capital had good relations with the Pallavas in the beginning. Anantapur district became a part of the Ganga kingdom, perhaps, because the Pallavas had a soft corner towards the Gangas whom they allowed to rule over this distant region. There are two copper-plate grants of the Gangas found in Anantapur district. The first one is in Sasanakota in Hindupur taluk.[11] It refers to the rule of Madhavarma I, son of Koganivarman, the Ganga King dated the regional year first· Phalguna su.10. This is in characters of fourth and fifth century AD. The record grants the village Velputuru in Paruvi-vishaya to a Brahmana named Dharasarma by the king for his own merit. The other copper-plate is from Penukonda.[12] This is a record of Madhava-II alias Simhavarmas son of Aryavarma and grandson of Madhava-I. The record states that Aryavarma was anointed by Pallava Simhavarma, while his son Madhava was anointed by Pallava Skandhavarma. Aryavarma is also referred to as Harivarma or Krishnavarma. It is argued that these names belonged to three different sons of Madhava-I they are–Harivarma, Aryavarma, Krishnavarma originated three different branches of the Ganga family Viz., Paruvi, Kaivara and Talakad. But the record of Avinita of Talakad shows that paruvivishaya (paruvi region) was a part of his kingdom. Therefore, it is difficult to agree with a view that there were different branches. The Penukonda plates register a gift of 72 Khandugas of land of Karmatura field under the tank of paruvi-vishaya,[13] according to Bramhadeva system to Kumarasarma of Vatsa–Gotra and Taittiriya-Charana. The fact that Aryavarma was anointed by Pallava Simhavarma and his son Madhava anointed by Pallava Skandhavarma indicate that the affinity and cordial relationship between the Pallavas and Gangas in the early centuries. Madhava-I is assigned a period of 25 years of rule from 350 to 375 A.D., while Madhava-II seems to have ruled from 400 to 420 A.D.

All the above accounts would show that after the Pallavas, the Western Gangas of Talakad had their hegemony over Ananatapur district in the last quarter of the fourth century A.D. and first quarter of the fifth century A.D. As stated above, Avinita, grandson of Vishnugopa, the younger brother of Madhava-II seems to have continued his rule over this region in the last quarter of the fifth century. Paruvi–vishya was one of the Administrative units of the Ganga kindom, Paruvi being identified with Parigi in Hindupur Taluk. The genealogy of this dynasty may then be represented as follows:

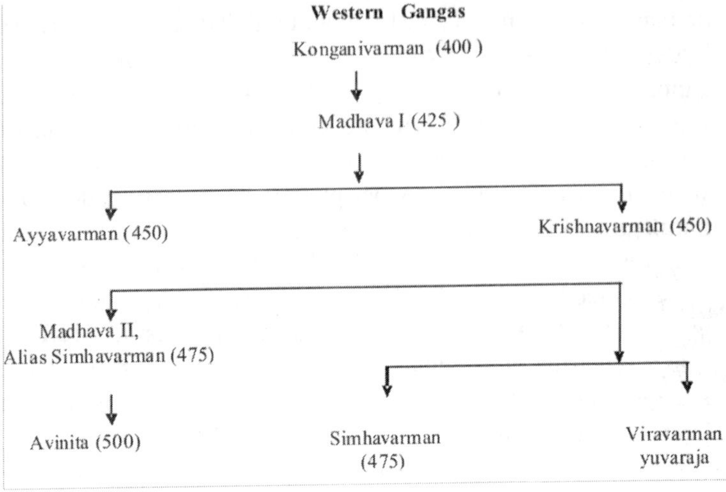

Banas

An important feudatory dynasty intimately connected with the territory now falling within the confines of Anantapur region was that of the Banas whose history can be traced almost from the middle of the fourth century A.D. The epigraphs in which they figure are, with the exception of a few, found in the northern taluks of Gooty and Tadipatri. The Banas were at first tributary to Mayurasarman and were later conquered by the Western Gangas. They then shifted their loyalty to the victorious Chalukyas of Badami and later to the Pallavas for a period of about twelve years. Some of the important members of the dynasty were Ranavikrama, Balikulatilaka Narasimha Banadhiraja, his son Vikramaditya Bali Indra Banaraja and Prithvi Banaraja. The tracts over which the Bana chieftains ruled were Vanganurunadu, Turamaravishaya and Gangarenadu comprising portions of this district. Sometime between A.D. 375 and A.D. 425 they left Kurnool and occupied a portion of Anantapur, then known as Paruvivishaya and ruled from Parigi in Hindupur taluk. They came into conflict with the Nolambas and the Western Gangas and fought battles in alliance with the Vaidumbas at Mandavi, Mudumaduvu and Soremati in Penukonda taluk which resulted in their victory. Some of the epigraphs of the ninth, tenth and twelfth centuries A.D. found at Senagalaguduru, Chinnapappuru (both in Tadipatri), Miduturu (Gooty) and Paideti (Hindupur) also refer to certain other Bana chiefs like Chandiyanna, Agappa, Mahasamanta Chilaparasa, Mahamandalesvara Chittarasa and Prabhumeru Anniga Dhananjaya, who were directly connected with the district.[14]

Chalukyas of Badami :

After the Western Gangas, Anantapur region appears to have passed into the hands of the Chalukyas of Badami. Avinita ruled between 469-529 A.D. and was succeeded by his son Avinita who also ruled for about 50 years from 529 to 579 A.D. In the Chalukya reign his contemporaries were Pulakesin-I and Kirtivarma-I. Pulakesin-I is said to have performed the Asvamedha sacrifice and is quite possible that he extended his small kingdom, but, his son Kirtivarma I might have waged several wars in course of his conquests. The Nalas of Nalavadi and the Gangas of Talakad were defeated by him. The Nalas of Nalavadi were ruling over the areas between Bellary and Kurnool districts. It is quite possible that in course of this campaign that the parts of Anantapur region fell into the hands of the Chalukyas. The Peddavaduguru epigraph[15] is an undated record of Kannada referring to the rule of Ereyitiyadigal after his subjugation of Ranavikrama. Originally, it was thought that this Ranavikrama was a Bana king. But, it is now shown that Ranavikrama of the record was Mangalesa-I, the uncle of Pulakesin-II. And it is a fact that Ranavikrama was a favourite epithet of Mangalesa.[16] The inscription has direct bearing on the battle for the throne waged by Pulakesin-II against his uncle. In this region, the Banas were ruling probably as subordinates of the Chalukyas and when Mangalesa became antagonistic to Pulakesi, the latter sought shelter in the Bana dominion. Mangalesa, provoked by this rebellious attitude of this nephew, invaded the Bana territory and gave battle to Ereya at Elpattu Simbhige in Nandanur.

The inscription at Peddavaduguru records the grant of a village, Elpattu Simbhige, to the mahajanas who were asked to choose a piece of land for their maintenance and livelihood. The Mahajanas requested king Pulakesin-II, to grant them a village called Nandanur. They also requested the king to free them from all encumbrances.

The king not only made such a grant but also donated to the Mahajan the income from ponnatere levied and collected in the agrahara situated in the vishaya (district) of the Bana ruler. This is one among the several evidences to show that the Anantapur district was under the hegemony of the Chalukyas and the Banas were ruling there as subordinate rulers of the Chalukyas of Badami.

There are some more inscriptions of the Chalukyas in the district. One of them is the Dimmagudi stone inscription[17] in Gooty taluk, dated the twenty seventh regnal year of Vikramaditya. This is an incomplete and damaged record available in Telugu, and refers to a gift by the king. King Vikramaditya ruled from c. 655-681 A.D., and was succeeded by his son Vinayaditya (681-96 A.D.), whose record also found in Virareddipalli[18] in Tadipatri taluk. This is a Telugu record in archaic Telugu characters dated the tenth regnal year of the king. It registers a gift of land at Nitturu. (The name of the donor is lost), when Vanaraja belonging to the Bana family was governing over Vanganuru-nadu. There is another inscription of the same king at guduru (Anantapur taluk) dated the fourteenth regnal year of the king. The Inscription records a gift of land by the Bana feudatory ruling over Ganga-Renadu.[19]

There are almost ten records of Vijayaditya available in the district. In Tadipatri mandal the Chandana stone inscription[20] recorded in Telugu language is dated during second regnal year of the king corresponding to 697 to 698 A.D. This inscription records a gift of land at Chenjona as pannavisa to Sandayaru, who is a Brahmana, by Chola Mutturaju, when Banaraju was ruling over Ganga-Renadu. The Nitturu inscription[21] dated 697 to 698 A.D. refers to a Bana feudatory who is stated to have been ruling over Vanganuru-vishaya. It is the same feudatory that is referred in the Kottapalli inscription dated the third regnal year (698-699) of Vijayaditya during 698-699 A.D.[22] It mentions another Bana feudatory of the king as ruling over Vanganuru-vishaya. In Tadipatri at Kotturu village there is another Telugu inscription[23] available of the same king dated the fourth regnal year, corresponding to 700 A.D. In this inscription, the king is found to be associated with the usual titles Prithvivallabha, Maharajadiraja and Paramesvara. It is stated that Vanaraja was governing the Vanganuru-vishaya, when a gift of eight units of cultivable land as pannasa in the village

Penukaparuthi was made by Pullamukki Balakanamayaru, after announcement of the royal order to the effect and in the presence of Chappiliraja and the residents of the two villages. The donee was Kumarasarma of Bharadvaja-gotra. Vanaganuru-nadu is identified with the region with the present day village of Vanganuru in Tadipatri mandal. Penukaparthi seems to have situated near Kotturu and is probably the same as Penukalapadu in Tadipatri.

At Kondapalli in Gooty taluk, a Kannada Inscription[24] which registers a gift of land to a donee whose name was not mentioned during Vikramaditya-Balli-Indra Banaraja of the Balli family was governing Turumara-Vishaya. This inscription is dated during twenty third year of the ruler, which corresponding to 718-719 A.D. The Betapalli inscription[25] of the period of Vijayaditya, (the date of the issue of the record not available), registers a grant of 20 mattars of black soil, 50 mattars of red soil, one mattar of wet land and two mattars of garden land to one Telereyar by Vikramaditya, the uncle of Banaraja ruling over Turamaravishya as the king's feudatory. The Nandalapadu inscription,[26] in Anantapur mandal within Telugu language and which is also undated, refers to Banaraja ruling from Pambulige. Likewise, the inscription at Kammavaripalli in Tadipatri taluk is also an undated Telugu record, probably registering a gift of 80 maruttu of land to Bramahana.[27] This inscription, assignable to eighth and ninth centuries wherein Vijayaditya is said to be in all probability was one of the Telugu Chola Chiefs of Renadu. So far as Vikramaditya is concerned, there is only one record available from Chandana[28] in Tadipatri which is in Telugu language. This undated inscription also refers to Vanaraju as ruling over some vishya and registers some gift, the details of the grant is in dilapidated condition.

The last ruler of the Chalukya dynasty of Badami, Kirtivarama II, is represented in three records in the district at Peddapeta and Chandana both in Tadipatri and Nitturu in Gooty mandal. Both of them are undated and the Peddapeta inscription[29] is in Telugu and it registers a gift of 25 maruttu of land at Kudaluru to Duggiya by Ranavijaya.This inscription also speaks about Prithivarma-II. The Chandana record which is available in Kannada,[30] refers to Banaraja as ruling over Ponnavisa to Kanavadi by Dharnappan, who was administering Chenjona, same as Chandana. The Nitturu inscription[31] refers to the region of Kirtivarma II and registers remission of certain taxes due from some gamudas. At Chandana itself there is another undated inscription of eighth century[32] which seems to record a gift of land and refers to some Chalukya king whose name is not clear.

CHALUKYAS OF BADAMI

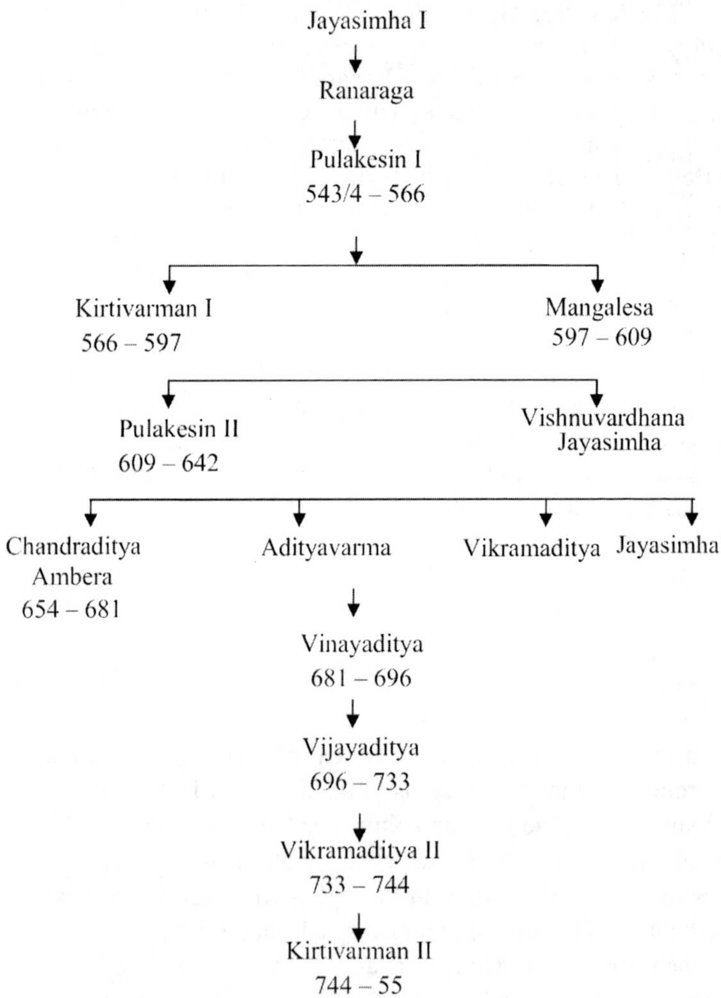

All these inscriptions show that the Anantapur district was part of Chalakuya kingdom. In fact, there are a number of Chalukya records found in Cuddapah, Kurnool and Mahaboobnagar districts indicating that the entire region south of river Tungabadhra was held by the Chalukyas. The Rayalaseema region excluding Chittoor and, even Mahaboobnagar adjacent to Rayalaseema, was under the hegemony of Chalukyas.

Rashtrakutas and Nolambas :

There is no recorded evidence in this district testifying to the rule of the Rashtrakutas who succeeded the Chalukyas of Badami as an imperial power. But during this period (A.D. 757 to 973), a local dynasty called Nolambas or Nolamba Pallavas which owed its allegiance to them held sway over Nolambavadi which included parts of this district. Their principal cities were Uchchangi, Henjeru (Hemavati) and Chitaldurg.

The Nolambas were a major power that ruled Anantapur district. Their records indicate that their kingdom extended over Anantapur and Chittoor districts of Andhra Pradesh and Kolar district of Karnataka. Their inscriptions further indicate that they were descendants of the Pallavas of Kanchi. The meaning of the name Nolamba is not clear. The verbal root 'Nole' in Kannada may be taken to mean 'to penetrate' to go before etc. Their territory called Nolambalige was situated in a strategic position and the invaders invariably had to pass through this region, if they wished to attack each other. Therefore, the word Nolamba may be taken to mean a 'Penetrator' or a group of persons under a leader, who is always at the foremost ranks or frontiers. In Tamil also the verbal root nolai means 'to intrude' or 'to penetrate' which is almost similar in meaning to that of the Kannada root. By the middle of the seventh century A.D., the area that was ruled over by the Nolambas was made over by the Chalukyas of Badami to the Pallavas. This gave an easy access to the Pallvas to intrude into the Chalukya dominion. Nolambavadi or Nolambalige is the name of the region over which these Nolambas ruled. According to the Hemavati inscription.[33] Trinayana was the originator of this family.

But he was more a legendary figure. However, the first historical ruler is Mangala Nolambadiraja, who is assigned a period of rule of 50 years from c.735-85 A.D. The next ruler was Simhapota. His son Charuponnera (c. 785 to 828) also known as Paramesvara Pallavadhiraja, his son Polalchora-I and grandson Mahendra-I also known as Ayyapadeva-I, son of Mahendra-I had all of them entered into marital alliances with the Gangas.

The Kambaduru inscription[34] Paleographically assigned to the ninth century A.D., refers to the rule of Polalchora Nolambadhiraja. This is his earliest record which states that the king bestowed upon Ajjaparuvara Bhidiyereya a bracelet and gave him the title Nolambadodda, in recognition of his having constructed the Beddugonde tank. Likewise, Srimukharama also bestowed upon this individual the title of Srimukhadodda, while Singapotarasa, Ponnerarasa and Dharmamahadeva called him Ponneradodda. This also refers to the construction of a temple for god Mahadeva.

The Madivala inscription[35] states that Nolambadiraja was ruling Ganga-6000, province under Nitimarga, son of Rachamalla I, the Ganga king. Nitimarga himself came to the throne in 837 A.D. Therefore, Polalchora must have been holding the province from some time earlier till 837 A.D. This Nolamba is more familiarly referred to only by the name Nolambadiraja. Prof. Krishnamurthi refers to the Hemavati inscription[36] as the one that refers to Nolambadhiraja by the name Polalchora, but the Kambaduru record under discussion also refers to the Nolambadhiraja as Polalchora Nolambadhiraja. Polalchora seems to have assisted Ganga Rachamalla I, when the latter invaded Kanchi around 830 A.D. In course of this invasion, Polalchora killed Aggalarasa, a chief under Banaraja, who was ruling Gangavadi-6000. Perhaps it is in recognition of his services that Polalchora received Gangavadi-6000. The Hindupur inscription dated 853 A.D.[37] of Nitimarga I, states that the Nolamba chief was ruling the territory as far as Kanchi. It is argued that the Nolamba chief was in a position to extend his territory beyond Ganga-6000, which was confined to the Kolar district of Karnataka. The names of Singapotarasa and Ponnarasa that figure in the Kambadur inscription indicate that these donors had taken the names of the grandfather and father respectively.

Polalchora was succeeded by his son Mahendra I in about 875 A.D. Mahendra I assumes the significant title of Mahabalikula-vidhvamsana indicating that he destroyed the family of the Mahabalis. The contemporary Bana king was Bana Vidydhara, who lived almost upto the end of the rule of Mahendra I, Prof. Krishnamurthi says that by about 878 A.D., Mahendra's kingdom extended over Dharmapuri which was a part of Ganga-6000 and up to Kalyandurg in the north. At Kambaduru there is a record of this Mehandra I dated saka 805 corresponding to 883-84 A.D.[38] This record states that certain gavundas (gamundas) and Brahmanas donated some land to the Aditya (sun god) temple. This shows that the Aditya temple must have been in existence already by then. It is interesting to note that there is an exclusive temple for the sun god. Of course, in this region there are epigraphical references to such shrines for sun god. Mahendra I is referred to as Mayadama in the Hemavati inscription.[39] This damaged epigraph which may be assigned to the later part of the tenth century registers a gift of some land to a basadi and for feeding ascetics (tapasvins) who probably resides in the basadi. The Dharmapuri inscription[40] gives us that Mahendra-I was the son of Jayabbe, wife of Nolambadhiraja, same as Polalchora and daughter of the Ganga king Rachamalla-I and therefore the sister of Nitimarga-I. Mahendra-I was a brave ruler, who made good use of his matrimonial relationship with the Ganga King Rachamalla, the Banas and the Vaidumbas, besides the Telugu Cholas of Renadu–7000 adjacent to Nolambavadi. All these participated against the Chola army at several places like Soremadi. Banavidyadhara Vikramaditya-I was the Bana King also joined with the Ganga King Pritvipati of the collateral branch of the Gangas and his son Nanniya Ganga. There are differences of opinion with regard to the identification of the kings as also the date of battles fought among them. Not much known about the Mahendra's rule in Anantapur district but, Mahendra was responsible for expanding the kingdom is quite clear. Polalchora's alliance with Gangas and later on Mahendra's alliance with the same Gangas strengthened the position of the Nolambas. Gamabbe was a daughter of the Ganga family. Mahendra at a later date attacked Gangavadi itself invading Talakadu. However, he was defeated badly by Nitimarga. Ereyappa, the Ganga, rightly has been described as Tribhuvanadhira in the Kambaduru inscription.[41]

Mahendra I was succeeded by his son Ayypadeva also known as Nolamabadhiraja Nolipaiah. There is one record of this king at Manepalli in Hindupur taluk.[42] This undated record states that Chorayya, son of Sripurasayya beside the gamundas and pannasigas of Eradumura obtained the bittuvatta from the king for the upkeep of tank. This Eradumura may be the same as Eradumkera near Kambadur. The king Ayyapa ruled for about 35 years between c.897–933 A.D. He continued the battle of his father and continued his struggle against the Gangas of Talakadu. To consolidate his position he had to fight incessantly against the Gangas. It was only after Ayyapa's defeat that things somewhat smoothened. Rachamalla II, the Ganga, was in constant fear of invasion from the Rashtrakutas and also the Cholas under Krishna II and Paranthaka I respectively. There was also threat from the Chalukya Bhima of the Eastern Chalukya family. Therefore, the Ganga king thought it was prudent to have cordial relations with the Nolambas. So he gave the Ganga princess Pollabharasi to Ayyapadeva in marriage. Yet, for sometime at least Ayyapa had to acknowledge Krishna II as his overlord. This Rashtrakuta annexed the Nolambavadi region for a short time. The moment Krishna turned his back, Ayyapa declared his independent rule over Nolambavadi. After 918 A.D., Ayyapa virtually freed himself from the clutches of other neighbouring kings and ruled independently. After 897 A.D., the next dated record is available only from 918 A.D. In Hemavathi there is a record of the Nolamba Pallava chief, whose name, however, is not clear. It mentions the death of Edeyanna, son of Haritha, who fought against the Sevuna general. This is dated c. 923-24 A.D.[43]

Ayyapa's eldest son was Anniga Vira Nolamba, who assumed office probably as yuvaraja even by the date of the Hemavathi inscription noted above and his father Ayyapa was ruling right upto 933 A.D. Therefore, his eldest son must have ruled independently only for about seven years. Thereafter he was succeeded by his younger brother Irivanolamba I, also called Dilipa. The Gunimorubagal inscription[44] dated 11th of July 936 A.D., refers to the rule of Vira Nolamba Annayadeva same as Anniga Biranolamba, and that the Hemavathi inscription refers to a king whose name is not clear since it is dated 924 A.D. This may belong either to Ayyapa I or Anniga. It is sure that it refers to a general of the Sevuna king, but it cannot say surely who the Sevuna was. An inscription from Kadabagere[45] states that Ayyapadeva's elder son Anniga, also called Annayya, was holding office as early as 920 A.D. The Rashtrakuta king Indra III was ruling in 922 A.D., in the region around Harpanahalli taluk. His Mahasamanta Bijja was administering Kogali 500 and Masevadi-140, when Madayya fought with Anniga, son of Ayyapa of Nolambavadi at padugallu and died in the battle being victorious against the enemy. Another hero-stone[46] which is in the same place also registers the death of Nakalokka of the Kadamba family, who died victorious after a fight with Anniga, son of Ayyapa Nolambavadi. This shows that although Anniga started to rule independently from c. 930 A.D., he was actually participating in the affairs of the kingdom even from a decade earlier. But, as a ruler, he was in power only upto 940 A.D., when Rashtrakuta king Krishna III finally defeated him, when he was trying to bring Butuga II as the overlord of the kingdom. In Anantapur district there is one record of Biranolamba anniga or Annayya,[47] dated 11th of July 936 A.D. It refers to his rule and states that his Mahasamantadhipati, the learned Varunasivabhatara, who was in charge of Nolambesvara-dasthana together with some gavundas and others made a gift of land for the upkeep of a tank.

Dilipa was succeeded by this brother Anniga Viranolamba about 940 A.D., when his brother was defeated by Rashtrakuta Krishna III. Dilipa also known as Irivanolamba, accepted allegiance of the Rashtrakuta. His kingdom included the districts of Kolar, Tumukur and some parts of Bangalore. However, Chitradurga district which was almost the central Territory of the Nolamba seems to have been lost by him since there is no single inscription of Dilipa in that region. His rule witnessed prosperity and peace. He does not seem to have engaged himself in any serious war. He was more interested in the cultural activities. In his period a number of temples were built, tanks excavated and repaired. In Anantapur district at Madakasira there is a record of this king[48] dated saka 870, Kilaka, corresponding to 948-49 A.D., which states that Kiriya Ponnayya, a servant of the king led an army against Gajankusa Chola and after Dilipanolamba joined it, Gajankusa fought and died in the battle at Ibili. Obliviously, this was not a major battle, but local skirmish, which drew the attention of Dilipa, who came to the rescue of his Mahasamanta.

Some records of this king are available in the district. The first one of them is at Madakasira in the temple of Chola-Raja[49] here in the king is called Irrivinolamba and this record is dated Saka 872, corresponding to 950-951 A.D. It states that both gavunda Gadiyamma and Pallikara Tuvanna were each granted three Khandugas of wet land, when Mallanasivari was administering Chirapai. The gift was made for having repaired the tank at Volagere and it was made in the presence of the inhabitants of Chirapi, Chintakunta, Chiriyavolalu and Vuluvattu. Another record at Madhudi of Madakasira taluk,[50] dated 959-60 A.D., states certain mahajans of the place (names lost) granted some land to a Vishnu temple. The third record[51] from Honneralihalli in the same taluk dated 28th of June 963 A.D., registers an interesting fact that certain individuals of Rolleyanuru, who fought with some thieves when Abbachari died in the fight. They set up this stone in memory of the dead. The Kambaduru inscription[52] states that illustrious Polalchora, grandson of king Irivanolamba, made a gift of bittuvatta for the repairs of the Beldugande tank and ordered the hundred and six gavundas of the village to take care of the tank. Chavundayya, a minister of Polalchoradeva, erected this pillar. This Polalchora as the record itself says, was the grandson of Nanninolamba Ghateyankakara, whose period is dated is from 965-970. Hemavathi inscription[53] of 966-97 A.D., is on a hero-stone registering the death of a certain Ereyamma, who fought in the battle between Mosaleyarasa of Jagalapura and Ayyapadeva, son of Nolambadhiraja's wife Piriyabbarasi. It is clear from the genealogy of the Nolambas, that Ayyappadeva was the son of Nolambadiraja's Dilipayya. He had an elder brother Nanninolamba, who had succeeded his father in about 969 A.D. It is also known that the Ayyapadeva ruled along with his grandfather Irovanolamba when he was a prince and continued to be a prince designate even during the period of the rule of his brother Nanninolamba.

There are six records and all of them refer to the rule of Nolambadhiraja. They are all in characters of the tenth century. All of them are damaged and it is very difficult to make out the details. Two of them[54] refer to the king with the title Ekavakya. The Gollapuram inscription[55] registers a gift of the village Periya Melapi to Balasomabhattara. Likewise, the Agali inscription[56] records the construction of a Vishnu temple and registers a gift of land to the god by Kotayya, a general of the Ballaha, i.e., the Rashtrakuta king, after receiving it from the Nolamba king. The Kalluru inscription[57] refers to the repair of the tank of that village and a gift of land below the tank by the king as bittuvatta. Another inscription[58] is badly damaged, but seems to have been set up in memory of an individual who died by entering into fire. The hero-stone record from Narasingaryani-roppa[59] registers the death of a gavunda after fighting against four regiments of the army. The Phalaram Gollarahatti inscription[60] is engraved on a pillar set up in memory of the death of a hunting dog named puniga after killing a wild boar.

All these records refer to Nolambadhiraja, who is identified with Irivanolamba Nolipayya the same as Nanninolamba I. He ruled from 969 to 975 A.D., and with him the Nolamba rule in Anantapur district appears to have come to a close.

Nolambas

Trinayana
:
Manigala Nolambadhiraja
C. 735-85
:
Simhapota
(Kolinombadhiraja Koliarasa)
C 805 – 828
:
Nalambadhiraja Polalchora
(Jayabhe the Ganga Princy)
C 830 – 875
Mahendra I (Mayindra)
(Mahabalikula Vidvamsna)
C 875 – 897
:
Nannigasraya Ayyapandeva
C 919
:
Nolambadhiraja Nolipayya
C 934
:

Annaga Bira Nolamba C. 940 Iruchora	Irivi Nolamba Dilipa: C 941 - 958 Chaladankakara Nanni Nolamba Polalchora II
Mahendra II (Amoghavakya)	Irivinalamba II (Ghateyaikakara) C. 1010-1037.

It appears that very soon thereafter the later Chalukyas occupied this region by defeating the Nolambas, after which the rule of the Chalukyas of Kalyani commences in this region.

Chalukyas of Kalyani:

The Chalukyas of Kalyani rose to prominence after the Rashtrakuta power declined in about 973 AD. The Rashtrakuta feudatories slowly shifted their allegiance to the Chalukyan dynasty.

Even the Nolambas who were at first siding the Cholas were won over by Taila II (A.D. 973-97) the Chalukyan monarch.

Taila's reign witnessed a conflict between the Chalukyas and the Cholas, with Rajaraja (A.D. 985- 1014), the Chola monarch, disputing the Chalukyan claim to Nolambavadi and Gangavadi. An inscription of A.D. 992 at Kogalx in Bellary district, which then embraced parts of the present district of Anantapur, refers to Taila's victory over the Chola king and his rule over 'Rodda', identified as Roddam in Penukonda taluk. As is evident from some of his inscriptions found in Bellary district, a sizeable portion of Nolambavadi, seems to have remained under Taila's control till his death in A.D. 997. During the reign of his son Satyasraya (A.D. 997-1007) there was recurrence of trouble between the Chalukyan and the Chola kingdoms and this led to the recognition of the Tungabhadra as the boundary between them. After a short and uneventful reign for about eight years by Vikramaditya V (A.D. 1007-15) and Ayvana (A.D. 1015?), nephews of Satyasraya, their brother Jayasimha II (A.D. 1015-42) came to power. His energies were directed against the invasion of the Cholas and the recovery of the lost territory. He was confronted by the Chola monarch Rajendra I (A.D. 1012-44) to whose reign refer several Kannada and Tamil inscriptions found in this district. Some of them also described the exploits of Rajendra's powerful general Araiyan Rajarajan alias Vikrama Chola Cholaiva- varaiyan in the Chalukyan and Vengiwars which earned him several titles such as 'Nalmadi-Bhima,' 'Cholana-Chakra', 'Jayasinghakulakala' etc.[61] The conflict between the monarchs ultimately resulted in Jayasimha's defeat. He was driven beyond the Tungabhadra, although he later attempted to retrieve his position. His successor Somesvara I (A.D. 1042-68) was also entangled in a series of battles of which the one at Koppam fought in A.D. 1054 resulted in his defeat. Five years later Somesvara led an expedition against the Cholas, to which a reference is made by the inscription dated S. 981 (A.D. 1059) at Donekallu (Gooty).

The reign of Somesvara II (A.D. 1068-76) witnessed the unsuccessful seize of Gooty fort by Virarajendra, brother of Rajendra II. But this was followed by the estrangement between the Chalukyan monarch and his brother Vikramaditya leading to the division of the Chalukyan empire between them. Some of the inscriptions of this period at places like Konakondla, Poliki (both in Gooty taluk) and Sangamesvaram (Rayadurg), bearing dates earlier than A.D. 1076, refer to Vikramaditya VI. Even after the death of Virarajendra, the two brothers continued their feud and Somesvara II entered into an alliance with the Chola emperor Kulottunga I and waged a war against his brother. This resulted in the accession of Vikramaditya VI in A.D. 1076.

Towards the close of Vikramaditya's (A.D. 1076-1126) reign, Vishnuvardhana Bittiga, his Hoysala subordinate, revolted against him and defeated Irun gola, the Nidugal Chola chief and captured various places in the district as is testified to by some of his titles like "Scatterer of Henjeru", "trampler of Roddam" and "destroyer of ghats and Roddam". He also occupied Nolambavadi, the Nidugal fort and Tereyur (modern Teriyur), the area situated between the Pinakini and its tributary Jayamangali about 4.5 miles from Hindupur. But his invasion did not last long and Vikramaditya regained the lost territory.

A number of inscriptions relating to Vikramaditya's reign found in this district refer to some of his subordinate chiefs and various offices held during his period. They also testify to the general state of prosperity prevailing in this part of the country. After the accession of Vikramaditya's son Somesvara III (A.D. 1126-38), Vishnuvardhana seems to have recaptured Gangavadi, Nolambavadi and Banavasi and thus established his rule over some portions of this district as well.[62]

It is not known who Somesvara III's successor was although historians refer to him as Jagadekamalla II (A.D. 1133-55). About half a dozen inscriptions referring to his reign and registering grants made by his subordinates have been discovered in this district. The weak rule of Taila III (A.D. 1149-63) that followed witnessed an invasion by Kalachurya Bijala and this resulted in the overthrow of the Chalukyan monarch. The Chalukyan power, however, survived for some time. An inscription at Madhudi (Madakasira) of S. 1091

(A.D. 1169) refers to Pratapachakravartin Jagadekamalla as ruling from Kalyani. The last Chalukyan ruler to ascend the throne was Somesvara IV (A.D. 1184-1200).[63] An inscription at Patasivaram (Madakasira) refers to him as 'destroyer of the Kalachurya race'. It was during his reign that the Hoysala subordinate Ballala II invaded the Chalukyan Empire, defeated the monarch and captured his capital.

Yadavas of Devagiri and Hoysalas of Dvarasamudram:

Yadava ruler of Devagiri Bhillama V, who was also a subordinate of the Chalukyas, managed to inflict a crushing defeat on the Hoysalas and occupy the Chalukyan capital. But this proved only a temporary success as Ballala reorganised his forces and recaptured a number of important fortresses, including Gooty, driving away the Yadavas across the Krishna. Two epigraphs of S. 1100 (A.D. 1178) and S. 1127 (A.D. 1205) at Parigi (Hindupur) and Hemavati (Madakasira) respectively refer to grants made by Ballala. The conflict between the Yadavas and the Hoysalas continued unabated even during the reigns of Jaitugi and Simhana, son and grandson of Bhillama V. A number of inscriptions in this district ranging from S. 1137 (A.D. 1215) to S. 1142 (A.D. 1220) refer to Simhana and his subordinates, of whom the chief were Mahamandalesvara Ranakumara Jagatapu Dandideva Chola Maharaja, Lakshmidhara Pandita,Pattasahanadhipati Malleya Sahini and Mahamandalesvara Jagadala Bhogarasadeva Maharaja.

After Simhana's death, the Yadava empire sustained a defeat at the hands of the Hoysalas, during the time of Mahadeva and his son Ammana. Ammana's cousin Ramachandra, however, attempted to avenge Mahadeva's defeat and sent an expedition under his general Saluya Tikkamarasa in A.D. 1275. A counter-expedition organised after sometime by the Hoysala ruler Narasimha III, succeeded in capturing Nidugal. Mutual conflicts between the Hoysalas and the Yadavas continued long thereafter. In A.D. 1320, Ballala III, son of Narasimha, occupied Penukonda and appointed his son-in-law Macheya Dannayaka as its governor. But in A.D. 1324 the latter was attacked by the ruler of Kampili. This did not bring about any change in the position as Dannayaka emerged victorious in the battle.[64]

Nidugal Cholas:

Nidugal Cholas a branch of the Telugu Cholas claiming descent from Karikala Chola and styling themselves as 'lords of Oraiyur', established itself in Anantapur district about the middle of the eleventh century A.D., and exercised control over the territory round Nidugal and Hemavati. Some inscriptions referring to them are found in this district and also in Tumkur district of the Mysore State. Eleven generations of princes of this family have been enumerated in these inscriptions, and towns like Nidugal, Hemavati and Govindavadi have also been mentioned. Of the chiefs of this line, the most powerful were Mangarasa, Irungola I, Mallideva and Irungola II and they were referred to in a number of inscriptions found in this district. The rule of this family seems to have come to an end with the reign of Ganesvaradeva, the grandson of Irungola II.[65]

Vaidumbas

The Vaidumbas to whom there is a reference in an inscription of S. 1120 (A.D. 1198) at Tadipatri are another family which ruled over the eastern part of this district presumably as the subordinates of the Western Chalukyas. The inscription mentions Udayaditya an important chief of the family and traces his genealogy.[66]

Muhammadan Advance:

About 1310, a year which is one of the great landmarks in South Indian chronicles, the advance of the Muhammadans from the north began to seriously threaten the very existence of all Hindu dominion in the south. Malik Kafur, the famous general of Alla-ud-din of the Khilji dynasty of Delhi, swept into the Deccan with an immense force, captured Orangal (Warangal) in the Nizam's Dominions and took and sacked Dvarasamudra. Two years later his armies again marched south and Devagiri fell. Both the Hoysalas and Yadavas were practically extinguished.[67]

Vijayanagara Kings (1335-1565):

The Vijayanagara Empire was established on the onslaught of

Muslim domination over Hindu territories and to protect Hindu religion from its capital near Hampi and it tried to present for two centuries stemmed the tide of Muhammadan advance.

There are many legends which are related about the foundation of Vijayanagara kingdom. According to Robert Sewell, two brothers of the Kuruba caste, named Harihara and Bukka, who were employed under the king of Warangal, fled from the second sack of that city by the Musalmans in 1323 and took service under the Raja of the fort of Anegundi standing on the northern bank of the Tungabhadra nearly opposite the present village of Hampi. There they rose to be minister and treasurer respectively.

In 1334 this Raja was attacked by Muhammad bin Taghlaq of Delhi sultanate, whose rebellious nephew he had harboured. Seeing defeat to be certain he caused a huge fire to be lit on which his wives and those of his chief men immolated themselves, and then with his followers he sallied forth against the invader and was slain. Muhammad Taghlaq left a local Governor to rule the new conquest and retired northwards. The countryside, however, rose against the new ruler and eventually Muhammad, finding events too strong for him, restored the principality to the Hindus, and raised to be its Raja and minister, respectively, the two brothers Harihara and Bukka who had previously been its minister and treasurer.[68] Harihara, who runs the story, was one day out hunting when a hare instead of fleeing from his dogs, flew at them and bit them. Returning homewards, he met the sage Maddhavachariar, surnamed Vidyaranya or forest of learning who, hearing of this portent, advised the Raja to build a city on the spot and gave him his assistance in doing so. Thus, was founded, in about 1335, Vijayanagar, 'the City of Victory'. The territory subject to the kingdom extended with extraordinary rapidity and Bukka I, Harihara's brother and successor, is said to extension, have ruled over all Southern India. Seeing that the only alternative was despotism of Muhammadans, the Hindus of the south doubtless acknowledged his sway without much demur. Bukka died about 1379 and was followed by his son Harihara II. He was the first of the Vijayanagar kings to assume the imperial title of Maharajadhiraja, or 'king of kings' his predecessors having only described themselves as Mahamandalesvara, or 'great lord'. The extent of his dominions may be gathered from the fact that inscriptions of his time are found in Mysore, Dharwar, Conjeeveram, Chingleput and Trichinopoly.

In 1347, however, the Musalman Viceroy of Daulatabad had revolted against the authority of Delhi, and proclaimed himself independent and founded the Bahmini line of kings whose capital was at Kulburga in what is now the Nizam's Dominions. He soon extended his sway as far south as the Krishna river and for the next 135 years his dynasty constantly and strenuously opposed any northern expansion of the power of Vijayanagar. The details of the many struggles which occurred between these two rivals belong rather to the history of Bellary, in which district many of them took place, than to that of Anantapur. They are related in Ferishta's history and Mr. Sewell's Forgotten Umpire.

It is in Bellary, too, that are to be found the chief permanent traces of the rule of the Vijayanagar kings, such as the remains of their capital and the irrigation channels they led from the Tungabhadra river. In Anantapur-except that they built some portions, not now separately distinguishable, of the fortifications at Gooty and Penukonda and that inscriptions show that here and there (at Tadipatri for example) they endowed or beautified temples—there is little that can be pointed to as their handiwork.[69]

Between 1489 and 1527 the Bahmini kingdom at Kulburga fell to pieces. Several of the most powerful nobles revolted against the Bahmini dynasty and established themselves as independent rulers, and though the representatives of the line continued during this period to be sovereigns in name, their power rapidly declined and was eventually divided between the five Muhammadan kingdoms of Bijapur, Ahmadabad, Berar, Ahmadnagar and Golconda. These five nevertheless continued the relentless opposition to Vijayanagar which their predecessors had always maintained and that kingdom continued constantly at war with one or other of them.

Decay of Vijayanagar:

Vijayanagara Empire reached the height of its power and

magnificence under king Krishna Devaraya, who ruled from 1509 to 1530. His successor, his brother Achyuta Raya (1530-1542) was however, a coward and at the same time a tyrant, and from his reign may be dated the beginning of the end of the empire. He alienated his best friends by his violent despotism and at length his nobles combined against him and took all real power into their own hands.

The leaders of this combination were three brothers named Rama Raja, Tirumala and Venkatidri, of whom the two first were married to daughters of king Krishna Devaraya. Rama Raja was virtually king of Vijayanagar during the last part of Achyuta's reign and throughout that of the next ruler Sadasiva. Ramaraya was a strong man and did much to repair the damage to the prestige of the dynasty. Like his predecessors Ramaraja treated the Musalman kings of the Deccan, as dirt beneath his feet and allowed his troops to practice every description of outrage and sacrilege in their territories whenever he obtained a victory there.[70]

The Musalmans Combine against Vijayanagara :

For a long while their mutual jealousies and enmities prevented the Musalman kings from combining to retaliate upon him, but at against length they patched up their quarrels and formed "a general league of the faithful" against him.

On 25th December, 1564, they began their united advance southward and halted near the town and fortress of Talikota, 25 miles north of the Krishna river. Rama Raja dispatched his brother Tirumala with 20,000 horse, 100,000 foot and 500 elephants to block the passage of the river, then sent off his brother Venkatadri with another large army, and finally marched in person to the point of attack with the whole remaining power of the Vijayanagar empire. His total force is said to have numbered 600,000 foot and 100,000 horses. The Hindus had fortified their side of the ford opposite the enemy's camp, but the latter drew them off by pretending to attempt another passage, and then returning suddenly to the original fort crossed it unopposed. They then marched south towards Rama Raja's camp.

Battle of Talikota-1565:

On the 23rd January 1565, the great battle of Talikota one of the most decisive engagements in all South Indian history, was fought. All the available forces on either side took part in it. Rama Raja, though over ninety years of age, commanded the Vijayanagar centre and his brothers Tirumala and Venkaadri led, the left and right divisions respectively. The Musalmans awaited the attack with their artillery in the centre, opposite Rama Raja's division.

This consisted of six hundred pieces of ordnance disposed in three lines, the heavy artillery in front, then the smaller pieces, and in the rear light swivel guns. Masking all these were two thousand archers. Later they kept up a heavy fire as the enemy advanced and then falling rapidly back allowed the massed batteries to open fire.[71] Their effect was murderous and decisive, and the Hindus retreated in confusion. On the flanks they had, however, been more successful and had driven back the Musalmans, and the centre rallied for a charge upon the guns. At first, their onslaught seemed to prevail, but the Musalmans' heavy guns, loaded with bags of copper coin, were fired into them at close quarters. As a result, 5,000 of them fell, and the Musalman cavalry charged through the intervals of the guns and cut their way straight through the disorganised masses of the enemy right up to where Rama Raja was posted.

Rama Raja had at first superintended operations from a litter. Later, thinking to encourage his men, he had seated himself on a "rich throne set with jewels, under a canopy of crimson velvet embroidered with gold and adorned with fringes of pearls' from whence he distributed money, gold and jewels to those of his followers who acquitted themselves well. Later again, he returned to his litter and it was at this moment that the Musalman cavalry charged up to his position. One of the enemy's elephants stampeded towards him, his bearers dropped him and fled, and before he could mount a horse he was a prisoner in the enemy's hands. He was taken before the king of Ahmadnagar, who immediately had his head cut off and raised on a long spear so that the Hindu troops might see it.

This disaster caused an instant panic among the Vijayanagar forces and they broke and fled. "They were pursued," says Ferishta, "by the allies with such successful slaughter that the river which ran near the field was dyed red with their blood. It is computed on the best authorities that above 100,000 infidels were slain in the fight and during the pursuit".[72]

The King flees to Penukonda:

Their panic was so great that they made no attempt to rally on a fresh position or even to defend the hills and approaches round about their capital at Hampi. Venkatadri had been slain and of the three brothers Tirumala alone remained. He hastily returned to Vijayanagar and fled thence with the puppet king Sadasiva to the hill fort of Penukonda in Anantapur district, taking with him a few followers and a convoy of 550 elephants laden with treasure in gold, diamonds and precious stones valued at more than 100 million sterling, and also the state insignia and the celebrated jeweled throne.

Deserted by their king and the commandant of their troops the people of the capital made no effort to defend themselves, and the very next day the city was looted by the hordes of the wandering gipsy tribes of the country. On the third day the victorious Muhammadans arrived, and for the next five months they set themselves deliberately to destroy everything destructible within the walls of the capital. Vijayanagar as a city was blotted out, and has never since been inhabited by any but the few cultivators who still till the fields that wind about among its deserted streets and temples. The next year Tirumala made an attempt to recapture it but failed, and Penukonda, which had always been one of the chief strongholds of this part of the country, became the capital of what remained of the empire.[73]

The Vijayanagar power now fell rapidly into decay. The nobles who ruled its outlying provinces began to throw off their allegiance and declare themselves independent and much of the country was plunged into anarchy.

Tirumala seizes the throne:

At Penukonda Sadasiva remained king in name, though in reality a prisoner, until 1568 when Tirumala (so it is said) murdered him and seized the throne for himself. Under his orders, the Penukonda fort was repaired and extended. He was succeeded in 1575 by his son Ranga, who shortly afterwards transferred his capital to Chandragiri, in the North Arcot district.

End of the Vijayanagara Empire:

Ranga was followed, in 1586, by his brother Venkata, who ruled for 28 years and died an old man in 1614. During his reign more of his vassals-among them the viceroys of Madura, Tanjore and Mysore-threw off their allegiance. At his death there were widespread revolts, disturbances and civil warfare, and the power of Vijayanagara was virtually at an end.

In 1639, a king of the line named Ranga, who was ruling at Chandragiri, granted to the English the land on which Fort St. George is now built, but in 1646 both Chandragiri and Chingleput, which was also one of his nominal capitals, were taken from him by the king of Golconda and he fled to the protection of the chief of Bednur, one of the few of the former dependents of the empire who continued to acknowledge his suzerainty. Such had been the former prestige of the fallen kings that for many years afterwards grants to temples and the like were declared by loyal descendants of their subjects to be made by their royal permission. But such phrases were merely polite fiction, for the last remnant of their power had long since been torn from them. The representative of this great line is the Raja of Anegundi on the bank of the Tungabhadra in the Nizam's Dominions, who subsists upon a small jaghir and a pension paid him by the British Government.[74]

Muhammadan and others rule over the region:

Meanwhile the Musalman kings had gradually extended their hold over the district. At first their mutual jealousies and animosities had prevented them from reaping to the full the fruits of their victory at Talikota, and some of the strongest of the Vijayanagar fortresses remained in the possession of the local governors of the empire. But eventually the king's of Bijapur and Ahmadnagar agreed to take different lines of conquest, so that their operations should not clash, and the former proceeded to invade the country south of the Krishna, including the Bellary and Anantapur districts.

In 1577, he appeared before Penukonda. The Vijayanagar king, as has been stated, had already moved to Chandragiri, but the garrison succeeded in bribing off part of the attacking army and the siege failed. In 1589 another attempt was made by the king of Golconda, but the king's son-in-law, Jagadeva Raya, the chief of Channapatna, in Mysore, offered a most plucky resistance and drove off his forces. Later, however, the place fell to the Musalmans and with it Gooty, and eventually the whole district, came under their sway. They ruled it by governors of their own appointment or through local chieftains, called poligars, who acknowledged their supremacy and paid them tribute but in all other ways were virtually in independent power.[75]

The Marathas, 1677:

But in the west of the peninsula a new power had been arising—that of the Marathas. In 1677, Sivaji, the famous Maratha chief, took most of the possessions held by the king of Bijapur in the Karnatic and in the next year visited the Deccan. In 1680, the rights held by Bijapur over this part of the country were formally made over to him and the poligars paid their tribute to him.

Aurangzeb, 1687:

In 1687, the emperor Aurangzeb of Delhi marched south to reduce Bijapur and Golconda to obedience to his rule and overthrow the power of the Marathas within the district and added the country to the Mughal Subah of Bijapur.

The Nizam, 1723:

In 1723, the Nizam, the emperor's governor at Hyderabad, while continuing nominally in subordination to Delhi, made himself independent and ruled his province, which included the Anantapur district, as though he were king of it. But his power over it, which had never been absolute, remained very partial, and though he claimed sovereign rights within it the Marathas continued to collect tribute from its poligars. Much of it, indeed, became virtually a

Maratha possession. Morari Rao, the well-known Maratha free-lance, whose exploits fill so many pages of South Indian history, established himself at Gooty about 1746, obtained possession of Penukonda, exacted separate tribute from (at any rate some of) the poligars and made himself arbiter of the destinies of the district.

Haidar Ali, 1761:

Meanwhile, however, yet another power was arising, that of the Hindu kingdom of Mysore. In 1761, Haidar Ali, the famous soldier of fortune, usurped its throne and began to extend its possessions. His first acquisitions in Anantapur district were the forts of Penukonda and Madakasira, which belonged to Morari Rao, and in 1775 he took Gooty itself, and sent Morari Rao into an imprisonment from which he never emerged. These victories established Haidar as suzerain of the district and the poligars paid their tribute (which he usually considerably enhanced) to him. Haidar died in 1782 and was succeeded by his son Tipu.

The Second Mysore War, 1792:

In 1790, Lord Cornwallis, the then Governor-General of India, entered into an alliance with the Marathas and the Nizam to clip Tipu's wings, and it was agreed that whatever territories should be acquired by the allies from that monarch should be equally divided among them. Tipu was reduced to submission in 1792 and by the treaty of that year he ceded half his territories to the allies. The portion of this tract which was included in the present Anantapur district, namely, the then taluks of Tadipatri and Tadimarri, fell to the share of the Nizam.[76]

The third Mysore War, 1799:

In 1799, the three allies again declared war against Mysore and Seringapatam was taken and Tipu was killed. By the partition treaty which followed, the rest of the district (with parts of Cuddapah and Bellary) was given over to the Nizam.

The District ceded to the English, 1800:

In 1800, the Nizam agreed to cede to the English all the territories acquired by him under the two treaties of 1792 and 1799 in return for a subsidiary force to be stationed in his dominions.

Anantapur, thus, passed to the British. The districts which were thus handed over (Anantapur, Bellary, Cuddapah and part of Kurnool) are still known as the Ceded districts.

Colonial Rule:

Soon after ceding the Anantapur district to the Britishers, it became part and parcel of the then Madras Presidency. It continued as a part and parcel of Madras Presidency up to India's Independence in 1947. After Independence the district formed as a part of Madras State up to 1953. In October 1953, the district became part and parcel of Andhra State. In 1956, the district became one of the important districts in the State of Andhra Pradesh.

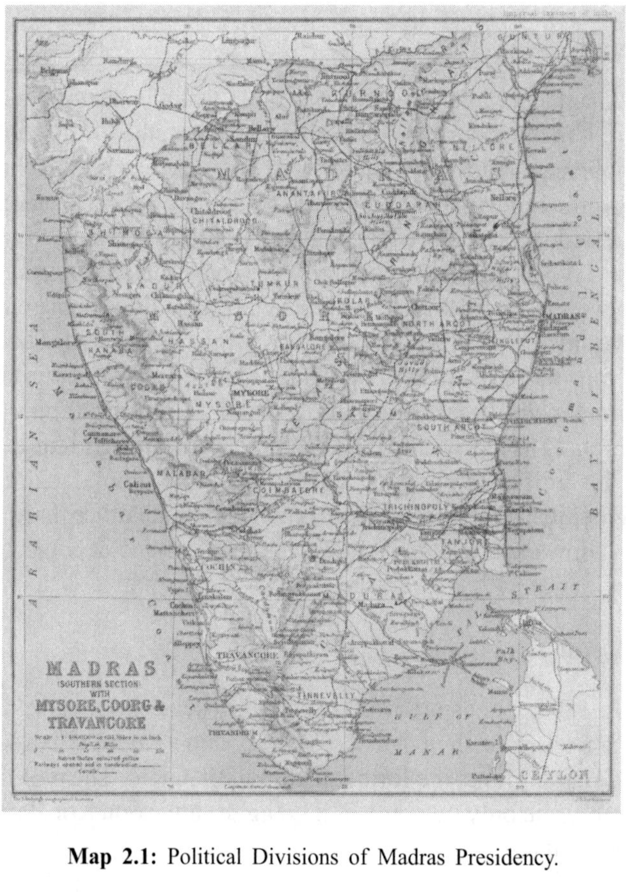

Map 2.1: Political Divisions of Madras Presidency.

Sir Thomas (then Major) Munro was their first (and the most Ingush famous) Principal Collector. He chose Anantapur as his residence and the bungalow he built there is in existence up to 1920s. He held charge of the taluks which now make up the Anantapur district and also of the Rayadurg taluk of Bellary. The rest of the new territory was administered by Sub-Collectors subordinate to Munro who were stationed in various parts of it. Munro went Home on leave in 1807 and the next year the ceded territory was divided into the two collectorates of Bellary and Cuddapah. At the beginning of 1882 the former of these, which had long been recognised to be too heavy a charge for one Collector, was split into the two existing districts of Bellary and Anantapur.[77]

Poligars:

Anantapur gave less trouble to quiet than the rest of the ceded country. In other portions of this, especially on the Cuddapah side, the poligars already referred to, who had survived all the changes of government which had followed so quickly upon one another's heels, frequently required the argument of regular troops to reduce them to order. But in the country which now makes up Anantapur there were none of these chieftains who were formidable enough to give any real trouble. Of the eighty poligars in the ceded country only four-those of Anantapur, Nadimidoddi (in Anantapur taluk), Kammalapadu (near Vajrakaruru), and Talmurlah (apparently Tarimela) - lived within it, and they were all of them at that time insignificant persons. The poligar of Kammalapadu was obstreperous and therefore was expelled and the other three were given allowances in land or otherwise and deprived of control over their villages.

Plot to seize Gooty, 1804:

In 1804, a conspiracy was formed to seize Gooty and Adoni forts and to establish in that part of the country Kudrit Ullah Khan, son of Basalat Jang, the former jaghirdar of Adoni. The plot failed miserably, the only outcome of it being the attack on Konakondla, in Gooty taluk.

Freedom Struggle:

There are not many noteworthy events in the history of the district until we come to the movement launched by the Indian National Congress with whose establishment in 1885, a new epoch began in the history of the country. People of this district, like those in the rest of the country, came under the influence of new political ideas like nationalism and democracy and began to agitate for progressive reforms. District Associations, on the analogy of the Congress, were started and District Conferences also came to be held. Delegates were chosen at these conferences and sent to the annual sessions of the Congress. Among those who were elected was Pattu Kesava Pillai. He along with several other local leaders took a prominent part in exposing the excesses of the British administration and in condemning the offences committed by Europeans against Indians.

The partition of Bengal in 1905 witnessed a tremendous political awakening in the country. The Bengalis vigorously advocated boycott, swadeshi and national education. M. N. Sinha, the Secretary of the society for the resuscitation of the Indian Literature of Calcutta, and his brother, both working under the leadership of Surendranath Banerjea, arrived in this district in 1906 and engaged themselves in the work of securing oaths from the supporters of the Swadeshi Movement. Another feature of the Swadeshi Movement was the visit of several persons to this district either in connection with the collection of contributions in support of National Education or to preach swadeshi. The famous nationalist Kopalli Hanumantha Rao of Machilipatnam (Krishna) collected subscriptions at Gooty for his National College. Another Swami Rao of Bellary, visited Anantapur in 1908 and delivered lectures on swadeshi to large audiences.[78]

The Home Rule Movement launched by Mrs. Annie Besant in 1916 received the active support of Pattu Kesava Pillai, but no more information is available on the evolution of this movement in this district. It, however, led to the holding of a number of conferences. In August 1919, the 25th session of the Andhra Provincial

Conference, under the Presidentship of A. S. Krishna Rao of Nellore and the seventh session of the Andhra Mahajana Conference under the Presidentship of G. Harisarvottama Rao were held at Anantapur. They expressed in unequivocal terms that the reforms proposed by the British were inadequate and demanded that the measures should be modified to ensure complete provincial autonomy and a share in the control of the Government of India.

The year 1920 marked a new epoch in the history of national agitation. Mahatma Gandhi inaugurated a progressive non-violent non-co-operation movement which convulsed the entire district and in particular the taluks of Anantapur, Tadipatri, Kalyandurg, Penukonda and Gooty. As part of this movement, Congress committees were formed in many places, boycott of toddy shops was preached at Kalyandurg and Penukonda by A. P. Kavi, Venkatappa, A, Narayana Reddy and others and meetings were held at Tadipatri and several other centres.[79] A number of students of the graduate and under-graduate classes gave up their studies and some teachers and clerks resigned from Government service at Anantapur. Spinning wheels were also popularised and toddy shops were picketed in the Tadipatri taluk.[80] A National School was started at Anantapur in April 1923 under the aegis of the District Congress Committee, with the money raised through the 'Swarajya Bhiksham Paisa Fund.' The most important of all the events of the period was the visit of Mahatma Gandhi to this district for a day. He arrived on 29th October 1921 at the Tadipatri Railway Station accompanied by Maulana Azad Subhani, Desabhakta Konda Venkatappayya and G. Harisarvottama Rao and was presented with addresses and purses for the Tilak Swarajya Fund. The British Government reacted very sharply to this agitation and adopted repressive measures such as the arrest of the local leaders, and the prohibition of meetings, processions and hartals.

Some of the other important trends during the decade (1922-32) following the non-co-operation movement were the holding of the ninth session of the Andhra Provincial Conference at Anantapur, the picketing of toddy shops and the resignation of Congressmen from the provincial and central legislatures.

A resolution was adopted urging all political parties to boycott the Simon Commission deputed to India to examine whether the people of the country were entitled to a further measure of self-government. In its turn, Government prohibited the students of the Government Arts College at Anantapur from wearing Gandhi caps, a measure which created a stir among the people. In spite of reactionary measures like these the people continued their agitation against Government. They also formed a Temperance Propaganda Committee and propagated picketing of toddy shops.

The Congress which met at Lahore in 1929 called upon members to resign from legislatures and other Government Committees as a prelude to the campaign for independence. In accordance with this resolution, C. P. Obi Reddy, member of the Madras Legislative Council from Anantapur, resigned his membership and several patriots of the district courted arrest and were convicted to varying terms of imprisonment. The Anantapur District Board which met on 31st May 1930 condemned the repressive policy of the Government.[81]

It is not known whether any attempt was made to prepare salt at Anantapur during the nineteen thirties when Salt Satyagraha was launched in the country. The other activities connected with the movement were the defiance of the prohibitory orders issued by Magistrates, carrying of national flags, raising of Congress slogans, distribution of leaflets and propagating swadeshi.[82]

Among the events of 1934 and 1935 were the tours of Mahatma Gandhi and Rajendra Prasad in the district. Gandhi arrived at Gooty on 3rd January 1934 from Cuddapah and visited Peddavaduguru, Ramarajupalle, Timmancherla, Guntakal, Uravakonda, Vajrakarur, Anantapur and Hindupur and was presented at all these places with addresses, purses and miscellaneous articles which he openly auctioned for large sums of money.

During the Individual Satyagraha Movement of 1940, 98 persons were selected from this district for offering satyagraha and were all arrested and sentenced to various terms of imprisonment under the Defense of India Rules.

The Quit India Movement which started in August 1942 took a violent turn in this district. The most important of the incidents connected with it were the removal of rails at two places on the Marmugoa Masulipatam line near Guntakal, damaging the Madras-Bombay trunk road, placing stones and gun-powder bags across railway tracks and in railway stations, setting fire to the office of the Deputy Inspector of Schools and the Board High School at Penukonda, cutting telegraphic wires at several places and felling palmyra trees. Students took an active part in the movement and paralysed the work of educational institutions by organising strikes. To put down the movement Government arrested the satyagrahis and took other repressive measures such as the imposition of collective fines.[83]

The tension continued in this district as in the rest of the country till 20th February 1947 when the British Government declared its intention to quit India by June 1948 and appointed Lord Mountbatten, Viceroy of India to arrange for the transfer of power. This evoked great enthusiasm all over the country. The scheme of transfer of power brought in its wake the partition of the Indian sub-continent into India and Pakistan. The Indian Independence Act, passed by the British Parliament in July 1947, fixed 15th August 1947 for the transfer of power. At midnight on 14th-15th August, a special session of the Constituent Assembly was held at Delhi at which the independence of India was solemnly proclaimed. 15th of August, 1947 marked the end of the long-drawn National struggle against British rule and Anantapur rejoiced over it along with the rest of the country. At present the district consists of 63 revenue Mandals spared in 5 revenue divisions. Map 2.2 gives the present picture of Anantapur district with revenue Mandals.

Map 2.2: Mandals in Anantapur District.

Thus, dwellers in the district of whom any traces now survive are the prehistoric peoples who built the kistvaens found within it and fashioned the rude stone implements which have been discovered on the tops of some of its hills. Traces of palaeolithic settlements occur in Gooty taluk. The existence of rock edicts of Asoka reveals that the district is a part and parcel of Mauryan Empire. The next important rulers of the district are Satavahanas. After the end of Satavahana suzerainty, the Anantapur district became part and parcel of various dynasties like Western Gangas, Banas, Chalukyas of Badami Rashtrakutas and Nolambas Chalukyas of Kalyani, Yadavas of Devagiri, Hoysalas of Dvarasamudram,

Nidugal Cholas, Vaidumbas and Vijayanagara empire. After the decay of Vijayanagara Empire, the district has gone into the hands of Muslim rulers like Aurangazeb, Hyder Ali, Tippu Sultan and Nizam of Hyderabad. At last the district is ceded to Britishers by Hyderabad Nizam in 1800. The rule of Britishers continued up to India's Independence in 1947.

REFERENCES

1. Meadows Taylor's paper in *Journal of Bombay Branch* of R.A.S., iv, 412, 1852, p. 28.
2. Mr. Bruce Foote's paper in J.A.S.B., vi., pt. 2, No. 3,188., p. 108.
3. Nos. 124, 125 and 127 of 1899 in the Government Epigraphist's records.
4. R. Bruce Foote, "*Indian Pre-historic and Proto-historic Antiquities*", p. 21.
5. Aiyangar, P.T.S., *History of the Tamils to 600 A.D.* Madras. 1929, p. 215.
6. Sircar, D.C., *Epigraphia Indica*, Archeoloical Survey of India. 1957-58.
7. Gopal, G.R., *History of Andhra Pradesh*. Part-I. Agam Kala Prakashan. Delhi, 1981. pp. 20-22.
8. *E.I.*, XIV, pp. 153-55.
9. *Ibid.*, I, pp. 2-10. *Ibid.*, 11, pp. 1083-86.
10. Ramamohan Rao, K. (Ed.,), *Directory of Monuments*, Department of Archeology and Museums. Andhra Pradesh, Hyderabad. 1993 p. VI.
11. Ramesh, K.V., *Inscriptions of Western Gangas*. Vol. XXV, pp. 234-39
12. *Ibid.*, XIV, pp. 331-40.
13. Desai, P.B., Ritti, S.H., A History of Karnataka Karnataka University, Dharwad, 1970, pp. 80-83.
14. Rangacharya, V., "*Inscriptions of the Madras Presidency*", Vol. I, p. 28.
15. *SII.*, Vol. IX, Pt. I, No. 46.
16. Ramesh, K.V., *Chalukyas of Vatapi*, Agamkala Prakashan. Delhi, 1984. pp. 76-77.
17. *SII.*, Vol X, No. 24.

18. *Annual Reports on Indian Epigraphy*; 1958-59. No. 268.
19. Indian Archaelogy A Review, (IAR), 1959-60, p. 2. *Epigraphica Indiac*a. XXXVIII, pp. 334.
20. *Ibid.*, 335.
21. *Ibid.*, p. 336.
22. *Ibid.*, pp. 337-38
23. *Ibid.*, 339.
24. *SII*. X. No. 23.
25. *Ibid.*, IX. Pt. I. No. 47.
26. *ARIE*., 1964-65, No. 24.
27. *Ibid.*, No.18
28. *ARIE*., 1958-59, No. 16.
29. *Ibid.*, No. 23.
30. *Ibid.*, No. 17.
31. *SII*., Vol. IX, pt. I, No. 50.
32. *ARIE*., 1958-59, No. 18.
33. Krishnamurthy, M.S., *The Nolambas*, University of Mysore, 1980. pp. 1-5.
34. *SII*., IX, Pt. 1. No. 17.
35. *E.C.*, X, KI, No.79.
36. *Op. cit.*, p. 51.
37. *ARSIE*. 1913, No. 588.
38. *SII*., IX, Pt. I, No. 18.
39. *Ibid.*, No.19.
40. *Ibid.*, No.23.
41. *Ibid.*, No.18.
42. *Ibid.*, No.21.
43. *Ibid.*, No.22.
44. *Ibid.*, No. 24.
45. *Ibid.*, No.57.
46. *Ibid.*, No.58.
47. *Ibid.*, No.24.
48. *Ibid.*, No.25.

49. SII., IX, pt. I, No. 26.
50. *Ibid.*, No. 27.
51. *Ibid.*, No. 29.
52. *Ibid.*, No.30.
53. *Ibid.*, No. 31.
54. *Ibid.*, Nos. 34 and 37.
55. *Ibid.*, No. 32.
56. *Ibid.*, No. 33.
57. *Ibid.*, No. 34.
58. *Ibid.*, No. 35.
59. *Ibid.*, No. 36.
60. *Ibid.*, No. 67.
61. Gopalachari, K., *Early History of the Andhra Country,* p. 52.
62. Yazdani, *The Early History of the Deccan,* Part-6, p. 95.
63. *Ibid.*, p. 1055.
64. Reddy, R. Pattabhi, "1846, Nati Rayalseema Raltangu Thlrugubatu, (Peasant Rebellion of Rayalseema, 1846), in *Kadalika* (a monthly Journal from Anantapur), September, 1985, p. 34.
65. *Ibid.*, p. 37.
66. Beck, F. Brenda., "The Right and Left Division of South Indian Society," in *Journal of Asian Studies*, JAS, 29, 1970, p. 778.
67. *Ibid,*, p. 779.
68. Appadurai, Arjun and Carol Breckenridge., "The South Indian Temple; Authority, Honour and Redistribution" *In Contribution to Indian Sociology, CIS*, 10.2, 1976, pp. 187-211.
69. *Ibid.*, p. 213.
70. Krishnaswamy Ayyar, S., *Sources of Vijayanagar History*, p. 105.
71. Nilakanta Sastry, K.A. and Dr. N. Venkataramanayya, *Vijayanagar History,* Vol. I, p. 15.
72. Venkataramanayya, N., *Studies in the Third Dynasty of Vijayanagar History*, p. 28.
73. Appa Rao, G.V., *The Annals of Handeh Anantapuram,* p. 67.
74. *Ibid.*, p. 289.
75. Abdul Majeed Siddiqui History of Golconda 1946.

76. History of the rise of the Mahomedan power, Vol. III by John
77. Life of Mir Jumla.
78. Gribble, J.D.B., *A History of the Deccan*, Vol. II, p. 28.
79. Yusuf Hasain Khan, *Nizam-ul-Mulk Asaf Jah-I,* p. 32n.
80. Hayavadana Rao *The History of Mysore*, Vol. III, p. 24.
81. Sardesai, G. S., *New History of the Marathas*, Vol. III, p. 17.
82. Rao, Narasimha, *Corporate Life in Medieval Andhradesa*, Secunderabad, 1967, p. 128.
83. *Ibid.*, p. 133.

3

Social Development: Myths and Realities

The British educational effort was very limited to control the myths of the region. During the British raj there were no major changes in the settlement of village society, especially in the caste system and in the status of untouchables. Socially the framework consisted of self-sufficient village communities in groups of contiguous villages and the caste was the typical Indian institution to accommodate various socio-economic strata and nascent classes, binding them together in groups and ensuring such constituents and occupational protection as well. The present chapter presents social development of myth and realities of common people of Anantapur region under the Colonial rule in India.

Demography :

According to the first census of India conducted for Madras Presidency in 1871, Indian population was 31,220,973. Since then, a census has been conducted once in every ten years. In 1941 British India's last census was held and it returned a population of 49,341,810 in Madras Presidency. Of the population of the Deccan as a whole the most striking characteristics are its sparseness, its slow rate of increase, and deficiency in females, its use of Telugu as a vernacular language and its illiteracy and dependence upon agriculture as almost the sole means of livelihood, and the high proportion of Musalmans and the low percentage of Christians in Anantapur district shares all these qualities which comes under the purview of Madras Presidency. The density of its population is just little over half the average density of figure for the Presidency as a whole. As was to be expected from population, Hindupur and Madakasira are the least sparsely peopled; next come Tadipatri and Gooty; then follows Penukonda, Anantapur and Dharmavaram while Kalyandurg brings up the rear. In this last, though it contains few hills or jungles, the density of the people per square mile is only about one-third of the average for the Presidency.[1]

Table 3.1: Population Characteristics of Anantapur District

Sl. No.	Year	Population	Variation	
			Persons	Percentage
1	1871	741,255	-	-
2	1881	599,899	-141,356	-19.07
3	1891	727,725	127,826	21.31
4	1901	1,025,322	297,597	40.89
5	1911	1,053,449	28,127	2.74
6	1921	1,040,166	-13,283	-1.26
7	1931	1,138,081	97,915	9.41
8	1941	1,273,060	134,979	11.86

Source: 1. Anantapur District Gazetteer, 1905.
2. Hand Book of Statistics, Anantapur District, 2010.

According to 1941 Census, the total population of Anantapur district was 12,73,060 but, in 1881 and 1921 the district was registered a negative growth rate. The important reason for the negative growth in population of the district was incessant droughts that occurred before 1881. These circumstances forced the people either to die of starvation or migrate to other places for livelihood. The population recession in the district in 1921 was due to the spread of epidemics in the district. The district ranks eleventh in population in Madras Presidency. In the thirty years ending with 1901 the inhabitants of the district increased only at the rate of six percent. They suffered very severely in the great famine of 1876-1878 and at the census of 1881 their numbers were one-fifth fewer than they had been in 1871 and in Madakasira taluk, it was 30 percent fewer. In the next decade the usual rebound after the famine took place and the population increased at the rate of 17 percent, but in next ten years between 1891 and 1901 it grew at little more than the average in the Presidency as a whole. During this period it was slow rate of advance in three central taluks; in Penukonda and Hindupur, the growth was rapid and in Madakasira, it amounted to nearly 20 percent. Emigration and immigration have affected the figures slightly but, the balance of movement of the people between Anantapur and other districts of Madras is somewhat in its favour and the similar net result of the movement- between Madras and Mysore is a shade against it.[2] The Figure 3.1 gives the clear picture of the population of the district from 1871 to 1941.

Figure-3.1
Population of Anantapur District During 1871 to 1941

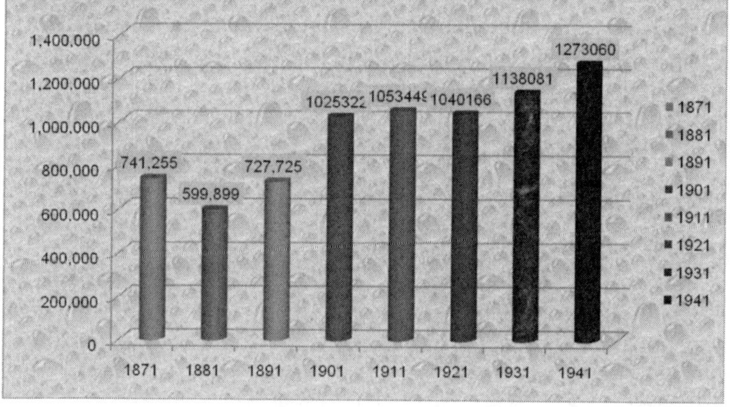

Emigration and Immigration

There are not many instances of emigration from Anantapur district. However, due to adverse seasonal conditions from second half of the nineteenth century to till 1940s, a large number of labour classes from Tadipatri, left their habitations for employment in the Tungabhadra Project. Similarly, emigration of some families also took place in 1942 from Uravakonda to the Mysore State due to a deplorably bad season prevailed in the region. But there are no cases reported from anywhere in large scale and or permanent desertion of villages resulting from epidemics in the district. The movement of population into any of the neighbouring districts or even the Mysore State has been occasional and short lived with most of the emigrants returning to their homes after the crisis.[3] The district does not hold out much attraction to immigrants owing to its poor and extremely precarious irrigation sources and the dearth of virgin land. The 1941 Census reveals that out of every 1,000 persons enumerated in the district, 37 were born outside the district. The number of immigrants from outside the State and from abroad constitutes 13,514 of which 13,283 are from other States of India and remaining from neighbouring Mysore Presidency only and among the Mysoreans, the female outnumbered the male.[4]

Linguistic Analysis of the Population

Under British rule the important languages spoken in the Madras Presidency includes Telugu, Tamil, Kanarese, Malayalam etc. The map 3.1 gives the clear picture of linguistic scenario divisions of Madras Presidency.

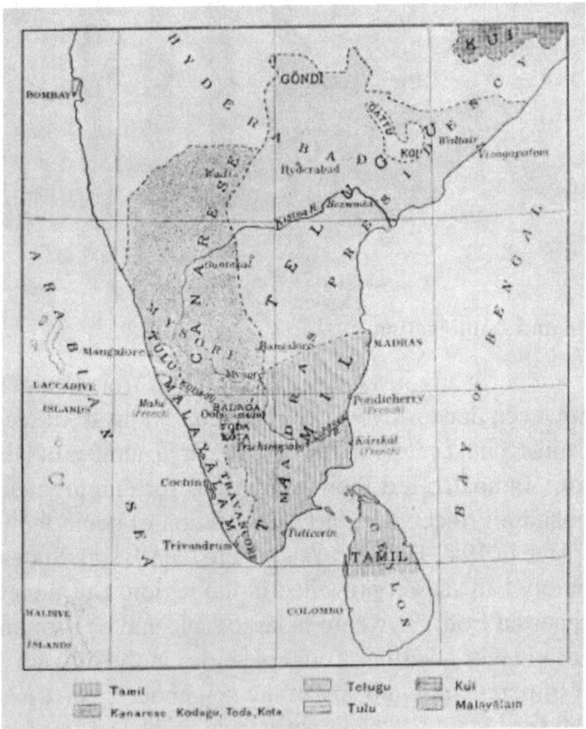

Map 3.1: Linguistic Map of Madras State-1905.

During British rule a linguistic analysis of the population reveals that Telugu is the primary language of the district and that it is spoken by 80 percent of its rural and more than 60 percent of its urban population. Kannada, spoken roughly by 10 percent of the district population mostly in the taluks of Madakasira, Rayadurg, Kalyandurg, Uravakonda and Hindupur, stands second in importance. Hindustani or Urdu is spoken by more than a lakh and half persons in the taluks of Kadiri, Hindupur, Penukonda, Anantapur, Rayadurg and Tadipatri almost invariably by Muslims who constitute about ten percent of the total population of the district. Of the other languages or dialects, Sugali or Lambadi is the one most substantially spoken in the district.[5] Eighty percent of the people speak Telugu, eleven percent speaks Canarese, and six percent speak Hindustani. Canarese is the vernacular language spoken along the western border of the district and two-fifths of the population in Madakasira speaks Canarese. Marathi is spoken by 6,000 Marathas in the district, most of whom are weavers or dyers, and Lambadi and Korava members of the two tribes after which these languages are named comes to the next.

Education: During British rule, Anantapur is educationally the most backward of all the districts in the Deccan. It is only two districts in the Presidency are able to read and write. Only four in every hundred of the total population and only four in every thousand of the women and girls possess this accomplishment. Telugu, the vernacular of the district, is naturally the language which is best known. Tadipatri is the best educated taluk, and is followed closely by Hindupur. Dharmavaram, Anantapur and Kalyandurg (in this order) are the least enlightened. Primary education was not taken very seriously as a government obligation and was financed largely by the weak local authorities. As a result, the great mass of the population had no access to education and, at the independence in 1947, 88 percent of the population were illiterate. But progresses was accelerated from the 1930s onwards, but at independence only one-fifth of children were receiving any primary schooling. As elsewhere, the Christians are far more often able to read and write than the members of any other religion and their pre-eminence is especially marked in the education of their girls. The percentage of the Musalmans, who are literate slightly, exceeds the corresponding figure among the Hindus.[6]

The education department of the Colonial rule is also classed Anantapur as backward district in education. There was no college in any part of the district, and there are only two high or upper secondary institutions established. One of these is the municipal school at Anantapur headquarters. This began in 1882 as a Government middle school was transferred to the council in 1884 and was raised to high school standard in 1885-86. It is at present in a flourishing condition, financially and otherwise. Four lower secondary schools exist in the district. Three of these are at Penukonda taluk board and the Railway schools at Guntakal and Gooty, all the schools are English schools and the fourth, the London Mission boarding-school for Native Christians at Gooty, is a vernacular institution. The other upper secondary school is the London Mission's Anglo-vernacular school at Gooty, which was raised from a lower secondary institution to an upper secondary institution in 1897-98.[7] The training-schools include the Government institution at Anantapur maintained by the London Mission at Gooty opened in 1900-01. There are no schools for girls above the primary level and no industrial or commercial institutions or classes in the district.

Occupations:

The percentage of the people who depend for their livelihood upon agricultural and pastoral pursuits is even higher than usual. The following are the important occupations pursued by the people in the district.

Agricultural pursuit: In Anantapur district, less than three-quarters of the population, depend directly upon agricultural and pastoral pursuits for their daily life. Anantapur along with other territories of Madras Presidency, the British dispossessed many of the old Moghul and Maharatta nobility and big zamindars, and vested property rights and tax obligations on individual peasants. This settlement was known as the ryotwari system (peasant tenure). However, the term peasant is misleading, because most of those who acquired land titles belonged to the traditionally dominant castes in rural villages. The peasants belonging to lower-caste cultivators in villages became their tenants. Thus there was no change in social structure at the village level, except that the new ownership rights gave greater opportunities for sale and mortgage, and the security of the tenant was less than it had been under the previous system. Cattle are bred for sale in considerable numbers at Pamudurti, the retail trade being chiefly in the hands of the Lambadis. Goats and sheep are valued as manuring agents and for their skins; sheep provide in addition mutton and wool. The wool is sold to the people of Kuruba community to make the blankets. Sheep are collected in large quantities at Hindupur and driven for sale every week to Bangalore to be converted into mutton.[8]

Arts and Industries: Out of the total non-agricultural population, the percentage who subsists by handicrafts other than those of the ordinary village artisans is smaller than in almost any district. Such of these callings as exist, moreover, with the single exception of the textile occupations, not only economically unimportant but artistically and industrially insignificant. Weavers are more numerous in proportion to the total population than in any other district except Bellary. They may be divided into weavers of gunny, cotton, silk and wool.

Gunny Weavers: Gunny is made from locally grown sunn hemp (*crotolaria juncea*) in a few villages in Anantapur, among which may be mentioned, Byadigera in Madakasira taluk, Chilumutturu and Hindupur. The hemp is a five months' crop and is irrigated, the fibre is extracted by the usual process of soaking the stems of the plants in water for four or five days and then beating them with a stick. The gunny is woven in strips and then sown into bags. Coloured stripes are inserted by dyeing some of the threads with indigo or turmeric or by smearing them with red earth. The industry is a very small one, less than a dozen families at each of these villages being employed at it. The bags made are disposed of locally.[9]

Cotton-Weaving: The cotton-weaving industry consists mainly in the making of the coarse white sheeting which the average ryot wears and the coloured cloths used by the women. There is in addition some little manufacture of tapes for cots (chiefly by Dudekulas) and of cloths for turbans and bodices, and in Uravakonda five or six families occasionally make striped cotton rugs similar to those woven at Adoni. The coarse white cloths for the men are woven in many villages and mainly by the Malas. Imported mill-made thread is generally employed, but here and there the ryots still spin thread from their own cotton and give it to the Malas to be woven, paying them for their labour. Cotton cloths for women are similarly made in many villages. The chief centres of industry are however Tadipatri, Uravakonda and Dharmavaram, and the castes which are chiefly employed in it the Devangas, Togatas and Sales with a fair sprinkling of Musalmans.[10] The processes and implements employed do not differ from those in use elsewhere and need not be described in detail. As in other districts, the women and children assist in the preparation of the warp and other preliminary steps.

Cotton Dyeing: Practically all the thread used is mill-made and is imported from other parts of India or from Europe. Much of it is bought ready- dyed. Where the dyeing is effected locally it is very usually done by people other than the weavers. The Rangaraja, a Maratha caste, and the Musalman community also do much of it. Except that indigo (either grown in Tadipatri taluk or imported from Cuddapah) is still used for blue, the dyes are almost always imported mineral preparations. Only some half a dozen colours are employed, but the combination of these in the process of weaving produces other tints as indigo warp crossed by a dark red woof making, for example, a cloth of a dull purplish colour. Both the colours employed and the combinations made are, in general, inferior to those of the Bellary weavers.[11]

Silk-weaving: Cloths with both warp and woof of silk are not often made, as they are not only expensive but do not wear well, the best in the district are manufactured in Dharmavaram. Some of these are made of silk 'shot' with two colours and are ornamented with borders nine inches wide woven of gold thread and for some eighteen inches at each end are decorated with patterns in gold thread so lavishly applied that the cloth is quite stiff and heavy. These are worth as much as Rs.50 a piece. Cloths of Kornad and other foreign patterns are also made here to some extent during British rule. Elsewhere the weaving of silk is usually confined to a narrow border, some four to six inches wide, along the edge of the cotton cloth, and in such cases the woof of the fabric is usually of cotton.[12] It is a prevalent fashion to have one of the borders of one colour and the other of another. The chief centres for this kind of silk-weaving are the same as those (already mentioned) for the weaving of cotton, but most of the work is done by Pattu Sales, Padma Sales and Pattegaras (a Maratha caste which is uncommon outside the district), none of whom usually weave cotton. The Devangas, however, weave in both materials. The silk thread is most of it imported from Mysore State, though some comes from the Bombay side or from the retail dealers in Bellary.

Silk-dyeing: Like cotton thread, the silk is sometimes bought ready-dyed and sometimes dyed locally. In Dharmavaram, vegetable dyes are still used for silk and are applied by the weavers themselves and not by any separate castes. Cochineal is employed for crimson and the usual 'kapila' powder for yellow. Only one tint of crimson and one of yellow are employed. A vivid grass-green and a kind of violet are made from mineral dyes and these contrast painfully with the low-toned vegetable dyes.

Condition of the weavers: The weavers of both cotton and silk are largely in the hands of the capitalists who advance them the thread, take the finished cloths and pay them piece-work wages for their labour. These capitalists are often Marvaris and the purchases of yarn and dyes and the sale of the manufactured article are managed by them. The cloths are exported both to the Bombay Presidency and to Mysore and some go, even to Coorg and South Canara. Weavers for piece-work wages can never make large profits. Even where the weavers own their own looms, their returns are very small and in bad seasons the demand for cloths at once falls off and they are left without means when food is dearest.[13]

Cotton-printing: Cotton stuffs are printed in colours by hand at Pamidi and Choulluru and to some extent at Penukonda and Gutturu. Pamidi is the chief centre. The cloths printed there (and at Choulluru) bear a, general resemblance to the well-known palampores of Masulipatam and Kalabasti. The work is done by Maratha Rangaris (Rangarajas).

The cotton fabric on which the cloths are printed is all of it imported from Europe. It comes in large bales. The processes followed in the printing of the designs on this consist of a tedious series of washings in various mixtures to get rid of the sizing in the cloth and render it soft enough to take the printing evenly and well, more washings in other mixtures to render the dyes fast and yet others to make the colours brilliant. But the Rangaris are very chary of affording any detailed particulars of these processes as they say that their industry has already suffered severely from the competition of the machine-printed imitations of their productions and they are afraid of yet further violations of their trade secrets. The printing is usually done in only two colours, a fine deep red (a vegetable dye) and a black made from iron, but in the case of some of the cloths additional designs are super-imposed upon these at the last moment in a yellow made with turmeric and a vivid green alizarine dye, neither of which harmonize in any way with the red of the ground-work.[14] No blue is used in the printing as the Rangaris are prohibited by some odd caste rule from having anything to do with indigo.

The printing is effected by stamping the cloths by hand with teak-wood blocks on which are cut in high relief elaborate conventional or diaper patterns or representations of tigers, camels, elephants, horsemen, parrots and the like. These blocks are made locally by certain members of the community. The designs are bold and good and the deep red colour used is most effective. The manufactures include palampores or bedspreads, canopy cloths, praying cloths for Musalmans and Lingayats, cloths for women's wear copied from Kalahasti, Berhampore, Cocanada and Pondicherry designs, and patterns specially made for customers in Burma and Ceylon. The Pondicherry' cloths consist of delicate white designs on a ground of the aforesaid deep red and are in excellent taste. The cloths for the Burma and Ceylon markets are printed with less conspicuous patterns of the same kind-usually varying arrangements of white dots on the red ground. These are made by stamping the required patterns in melted wax on the un-dyed cloth and then plunging the whole fabric into the vats. The portions of the doth on which the wax has been imprinted are unaffected by the dye and while the rest of the fabric becomes red they remain white.[15]

The market for Pamidi textiles is a wide one, among other places, they are sent to Bangalore, Bellary, Madras, Sholapur, Colombo, Rangoon, Singapore and even Aden. In Burma and the Straits the Rangaris have their own shops. Two or three families in Pamidi and some more in Penukonda and Guttiiru print the gay doths in which the Lambadi women delight.

Blanket weaving: The black woolen blanket (Kambali) of the country, which serves as bed, portmanteau, clothes or umbrella, as need may require, is made from the wool of the black and white sheep by the Kurubas, the shepherd caste. The sheep are first shorn when they are six months old (the shears used are of the same pattern as in England) and thereafter twice a year until they are four years old, after which their wool is worthless and they are converted into mutton. The wool is cleaned and loosened with a bow like that employed for cleaning cotton but smaller, and is then spun by hand. It is never dyed, but fancy grey and white borders or stripes are made by picking out the different colours of the natural wool.[16]

The blankets are woven on a loom designed on much the usual principles but primitive and clumsy in practice. The shuttle is of the ordinary kind but is so badly made that it sticks every second or third time it is passed. After each thread of the woof is added, a long piece of smooth wood is inserted behind it and used to push it dose up to the last thread and is then removed only to be laboriously replaced after the next thread. It would seem possible to improve these methods without much cost or trouble. The warp is stiffened by being dressed with a paste made of pounded tamarind seeds and water. These blankets are made in every taluk-except perhaps Tadipatri where the black and white sheep are few in number-and are exported in considerable quantities to other districts. The best kinds are manufactured along the western frontier of the district and those of Beluguppa and Kaniganapalli in Kalyandurg taluk are noted. Some of these are made from the wool of the first shearing, carefully hand-picked, but none of them approach in fineness the best of the specimens made in Mysore State, and the highest price they fetch is Rs 7 and the cheapest kinds may be purchased for six or eight annas.

Woolen rugs: In one of the hamlets of Kunuturu, four miles north-west of Dharmavaram in Anantapur district, three Dudekula families, who recently came there from the Pulivendla taluk, weave coloured rugs from sheep's wool which they spin and dye themselves. These are not artistic productions.

Cotton cleaning and pressing: Next to the above textile occupations the industries which employ the largest number of the inhabitants of Anantapur are those which are concerned with the preparation for the market of the agricultural products of the district, namely the cleaning and pressing of cotton, the manufacture of jaggery from sugar-cane juice, the making of various oils and the tanning of the skins of goats and sheep. None of these, however, are large industries.[17]

Cotton is only grown in any quantity in the two northern taluks. The crop is generally sold to the presses at Tadipatri, Timmamcherl and Guntakal either through brokers or direct. The presses buy it either just as it is-with the seeds, leaves, dirt, etc., with which it gets mixed-or cleaned. Cleaning is usually undertaken by the brokers, who employ coolies for the work. It is usually done with an instrument called in Telugu a *girike* or a *ruthnam*. This consists of two horizontal wooden cylinders set close to one another in a frame and revolved in opposite directions, towards one another, by a handle.[18] The cotton is fed between the rollers and the seeds and dirt are squeezed out of it. The cleaning done by this machine is imperfect and the cotton comes out in a matted state with the fibres lying in all directions, making it troublesome to card subsequently. When the cotton is required for the local spinning of the coarse cotton cloths referred to above, the Dudekulas clean it further with a bow. The cotton is placed on a bamboo grating. Above it is suspended a bow some six feet long. The string of this is placed in the middle of the cotton and is then continuously struck with a piece of wood shaped like a dumbbell. The vibrations of the string jerk the cotton into the air, free it from the seed, which falls through the grating, and loosen the fibres so that the material is much more easily spun into thread.

Jaggery-Making: The growing of sugar-cane is almost entirely confined to the Hindupur and Penukonda taluks and only in the former of these is it at all an important crop. Iron mills for extracting the juice have now very generally superseded the old inefficient wooden machines. Ryots who cannot afford to buy them, hire them, the usual charge being one rupee a day. The jaggery is made in the usual unscientific manner by boiling the juice in shallow iron pans and afterwards separating the molasses with wet water-weeds. Most of it is exported from Hindupur railway station, whence it goes chiefly to Tadipatri, Adoni and Kurnool district. The profits from sugar-cane cultivation are high but the expenses are also very considerable and the crop greatly exhausts the soil. Near Hindupur a little sugar-candy is made by boiling refined sugar and allowing it to cool and crystallize. The syrup which then remains is also again boiled and converted into soft sugar.

Oil Sellers (Gandla Caste People): Castor is the only oil-seed which occupies any noteworthy proportion of the cultivable area of the district, though in Dharmavaram (and to a less extent in Anantapur) much gingelly is grown. Oil is also made in small quantities from the seeds of the nimippe and kanuga trees, from cocoanut kernels and from safflower. The castor seed is first boiled or roasted and then crushed either with a pestle or mortar or in the common country oil mill. It is next boiled with water until the oil rises to the top. The oil is then skimmed off. In Madakasira an improved iron mill has recently been set up. Castor is the usual lamp-oil of the country. The cake is often used as manure (on wet lands) and is also exported for the same purpose, some of it going to the Nilgiris for use on the coffee and tea estates there. The other oils are all cold-drawn in the ordinary mill. Sometimes the ryots give the Ganigas (the oil monger caste) their own seed to have the oil extracted from it, paying them for the labour, and sometimes the Ganigas buy the seed and sell the oil made from it. In Dharmavaram town, which is noted for its gingelly oil, there is a settlement of Tamil oil-makers. This oil is used for cooking. The cake is given to the cattle and is also eaten with jaggery as a sort of relish by some of the lower castes.[19]

Religious Life of People:

Over nine-tenths of the inhabitants are Hindus. This is a higher proportion than the average for the Presidency as a whole but much lower than the corresponding figure in the other three Deccan districts. Followers of Islam are more numerous in Tadipatri and Gooty than in any other taluks and fewest in the west, in Kalyandurg and Madakasira.

Hinduism: The religious life and attitude of the people of Anantapur differ in one respect in a marked manner from those of the neighbouring district of Bellary. In the latter the 'Lingiyats' are numerous and influential and their creed and their places of worship force themselves prominently into notice. In Anantapur this sect is much less in evidence and the Brahman takes his usual place as the unquestioned arbiter in religious matters. Anantapur, however, resembles Bellary in possessing few temples of special sanctity or renown and in being given much less to the worship of the orthodox Hindu gods than to the cult of Hanuman and the village goddesses.

These latter demand the same bloody sacrifices and the same The village barbaric rites as in Bellary but nonetheless Brahmans are found to deities, make them offerings of the less heterodox kind, such as coconuts, betel, and so on. The priests at these shrines are always (as elsewhere) non-Brahmans—usually carpenters—and the goddesses themselves and the forms of reverence paid to them present no unusual points of interest. The animal sacrifices used often in days gone by to lead to riots owing to the prevalence of the belief that if a man of a neighbouring village could by any means obtain some of the blood of the sacrificed animal and convey it to his own village the religious merit accruing from the sacrifice would devolve upon the people of this latter and not upon those of the place where the sacrifice had occurred.[20] The neighbouring village used to send in a volunteer to endeavour to obtain the blood and then support him in force in his efforts to get it to their habitations. Even now great care is used to see that strangers do not come near the sacrifice while it is proceeding.

Tree and Serpent Worship: Traces of serpent worship survive in the many stones bearing representations of snakes which are to be found in the villages, but these seem to get less attention than they used. As elsewhere, the pipal and the *margosa* trees are held in reverence, and, as in Bellary, the *vanni* (*prosopis spicigera*) takes an important part in the ceremonies at the Dasara.

Connected with the *margosa* tree is the worship of Chaudesvari, the goddess of the Togata caste of weavers, regarding whom little seems to be on record. She is supposed to reside in margosa trees and either the tree itself or a stone representing the goddess and placed at its foot is worshipped by the Togatas at certain seasons, such as the Telugu New Year's Day. Apparently the other weaver castes take no share in the ceremonies. They consist largely of animal sacrifices. Nevertheless a particular class of Brahmans, called Nandavarikula Brahmans, takes a prominent part in the festival. This name Nandavarikula is derived from the village of Nandavaram in Kurnool and doubtless many stories are prevalent there about the people of this sub-division. The account given in Tadipatri, where they are fairly numerous, is as under: Once upon a time a king from Southern India went on a pilgrimage with his wife to Benares. While there he unwittingly incurred a nameless but heinous pollution. Horrified, he applied to some Brahmans there to purify him, promising them half his kingdom in return. They asked for some tangible record of this promise and the king called upon the goddess Chaudesvari,-who had a temple nearby, to witness his oath. The purification was effected and he departed home. Later on the Brahmans came south and asked for the fulfillment of his promise.[21] The king declared that he could not remember having made any such undertaking. The Brahmans accordingly went to Benares and asked Chaudesvari to come south and bear witness to the king's oath. She agreed, on the usual condition that they should go in front and not look back at her as she came. As happens in other stories of the same kind, they are said to have broken the condition. At Nandavaram they looked back and the goddess instantly stopped and remained immovable. A temple was built for her there and the Brahmans remained in the south and still take part in the worship of goddess Choudeswari which the Togatas inaugurate, even though she is one of the deities of Hindu pantheon and delights in animal sacrifice. At Tadipatri other castes besides the Togatas help at the festival.

Ancestor worship: Another uncommon kind of ceremony is the ancestor-worship which occurs in parts of the eastern taluks. In that quarter carefully and strongly built tombs may often be seen, each of them provided with a niche in which a lamp may be placed. At these the Vaishnavites of several castes do regular worship to their ancestors on the date of the annual ceremony of the deceased and on the Mahalaya Amavasya day. The tombs are previously whitewashed and on the date in question, after dark, goats are sacrificed, cocoanuts broken, camphor burnt and a lamp is lighted in the niche on the tomb.[22]

Vows: A peculiarity of the district is the unusual commonness of the well-known practice of taking vows to different deities to induce them to assist the suppliant. A person vows before a shrine that if lie obtains some boon, such as recovery from sickness or success in an undertaking, he will repay the deity by taking a prominent part in its next festival, or by sacrificing a goat or burning a certain quantity of camphor before it. The custom is similar to that which was so common in the dark centuries in Europe of vowing candles to such and such an altar if deliverance from peril or success in enterprise was granted. A form which the vow often assumes is an undertaking to shave the head of a child for the first time at one or other of certain holy places if it is protected during its early years from the many diseases to which infants are peculiarly liable. Among the best known of the holy spots at which this kind of vow is performed are Gampamalla, the hill just north of Singanamala village, Mulakanuru hill in Kalyandurg taluk and Chendrayani Konda, to the north of Bukkapatnam. All of these are just such wild and desolate spots as one would expect to be readily accredited with unusual sanctity. The Jains numbered only 300 in the district, and two-thirds of them are found in Madakasira taluk.

Christianity: The Christians numbers only three for every thousand of the population, a smaller proportion is found in all districts in the Presidency except Ganjam and Visakagapatam. Two-fifths of them are Roman Catholics, about a third belong to the London Mission and the remaining are divided in smaller proportions among other sects. As many as one-half of the total population of this group reside in the one taluk i.e. Gooty. In neither Kalyandurg nor Madakasira taluks are there as many as a score of them.

Of the Christian Missions, those of the Roman Catholic Church come first in point of seniority. Their earliest converts within the district were certain Kapus of Maddigubba, a village about ten miles west of Anantapur. In 1718, the headman of that village, a Kapu who had suffered for two years from an obstinate disease which no native treatment or hymns could cure, insisted on being taken to Father Le Gac, the Jesuit Missionary at Krishnapuram in Mysore, that he might beg him to cure the complaint. Having first had all the family idols thrown down a well lest their influence should in any way counteract the expected cure, he set out for Krishnapuram, accompanied by many of his relations. Father Le Gac had heard of his intention and had sent him word that "his mission was not to give medicines but to instruct in the law of God, but when the sick man arrived he took him into his house and eight days afterwards was prevailed upon to baptise him. At first the invalid rallied, but shortly afterwards, on Christmas Eve, he died. Afterwards many of his relations and fellow villagers were baptised and later its neighbour village Alamuru—became a Christian centre. The greatest opponents of Christian converts were Dasaris, but the palegar of Anantapur, Prasanappa Nayudu, befriended them and with his permission they built a chapel at Maddigubba and in 1720 Easter festival was celebrated with much ceremony at this chapel. The palegar had promised to be there but was too unwell to go. He however sent one of his relations to represent him and also dispatched his own musicians and a quantity of fireworks for the celebration. Later in the year, when he had somewhat recovered, he went to the village in person, accompanied by a mounted guard and soldiers and elephants, attended mass in the morning and joined the procession in the evening. His successor, his brother Pavadappa Nayudu, was also well disposed towards the Christians at Maddigubba and the congregation increased until it numbered some 200 persons. Many of these were wealthy. In 1735, Madu Rayudu, a Maratha Brahman who was at the head of some flying column, was attracted by this fact and attacked Alamuru. The Reddis there defended themselves for three months and the chief of them went into Anantapur to beg the poligar's help. The poligar complimented the envoy on his bravery, had him taken round the town in state on one of his own elephants, but ended up by forcing him to pay 6,000 pistoles (perhaps pagodas) and then declining to assist him.[23]

Roman Catholic Mission: Some of these Reddis were immigrants from "Bouccapuram," which was "80 leagues" from Alamuru, but they were so disgusted with the poligar's treatment of their headman that they resolved to at once return to their own country. They accordingly crept out of the village in silence one night, taking with them their women and children, their cattle and their other moveable property, and set off for their old home. They escaped without being noticed by the besiegers and though the polegar of Anantapur, on hearing of the matter, first begged, and then tried to compel, them to return they shook off the dust of the district for ever from their feet. In 1743, during the internal confusion which occurred while the bigger polegar were away assisting the Nizam at the size of Trichinopoly, the Maddigubba village and chapel were pillaged and the place 'became a wilderness without a soul left in it'. It was doubtless repopulated not long after, for the Christian faith spread from it to Paramatiyaleru, just north of Atmakuru.[24] However, that after the suppression of the Jesuits by Pope Clement XIV in 1773 the little colony of converts received little attention for many years. The chief Roman Catholic settlement in the district during British reign is Paramatiyaleru and here resides the only European Catholic Missionary in the whole of Anantapur.

The London Mission: The Protestant missions are two in number, namely, the London Mission and the Ceylon and Indian General Mission. The former has its officers at Gooty and Anantapur. Active operations in this district were begun in 1881, in which year the Rev. W.W. Stephenson moved from Nandyal in Kurnool district (the London Mission's work at which place was then handed over to the Society for the Propagation of the Gospel) to Gooty. By 1905, Gooty contained four missionaries and in Anantapur there is a fifth and a lady missionary. The Gooty 'field of the mission' includes part of Kurnool, the Tadipatri taluk and the Gooty taluk as far south as the Pennar river, while the Anantapur field is held to comprise the rest of the district. The mission's work is however lest active in Hindupur and Madakasira taluks now that the Ceylon and Indian General Mission has established itself there. There are churches at Gooty and Anantapur and buildings used both as schools and churches at a number of the various out-stations. At Gooty there is a Theological Training Institution in which boys are trained to assist in the work in the villages.

The Ceylon and Indian General Mission, an institution which adheres to the tenets of none of the usually recognised Protestant sects, has been established at Hindupur and Penukonda for the last nine years and has recently extended its operations into the Madakasira taluk. The European and Eurasian staff of the Mission includes one missionary and three ladies at Hindupur;

two missionaries at Madakasira; another and a lady at Maluguru, seven miles north of Hindupur; and two ladies at Penukonda. There are churches at Penukonda and Hindupur, schools (none of them above the primary grade) at these two places and at Govindapuram in the Madakasira taluk and a night school and a home for destitute Christian boys at Hindupur.

The Musalmans: In Anantapur, the Musalmans are much fewer in proportion to the rest of the population than in the Deccan districts generally. As many as thirteen percent, of them are from Dudekula community, the sect of cotton-cleaners who follow indiscriminately both Musalman and Hindu ways and customs. Labbais are very rare. It is said that near Rolla there is a small community of priests to the Labbais who call themselves Muhammadans but cannot intermarry with others of the faith, and that in the south-west of Madakasira taluk there is another sub-division, called the Mondu Tulukar (who are usually stone-cutters and live in hamlets by themselves), who similarly cannot marry with other Musalmans. Perhaps someone with leisure may find it worthwhile to make enquiries regarding these two off-shoots.[25]

Hindu-Muslim Relations: Though in days gone by when (as in Penukonda) Musalmans were wont to turn Hindu temples into mosques, the antagonism between the followers of the two religions must often have been extremely bitter, they now for the most part live on the most amicable terms. Musalmans often dress like Hindus; in many villages the same wells are used by both communities; each contributes to, and even shares in the other's religious festivals; Hindus pay reverence to Musalman fakirs; and Musalmans will break cocoanuts before a Hindu goddess shrine.

Celebration Mohurrum [Hindu-Muslim Unity]: Perhaps the most curious example of the manner in which the two communities have coalesced is the fact that in parts of the district (the east of Anantapur taluk, for instance) the Hindus have annexed the Mohurrum and celebrate it with perhaps more fervour than any of their own feasts. In several villages a permanent 'Mohurrum chavadi,' or building in which the Mohurrum is conducted, has been erected by Hindus. The ceremonies cannot, however, be inaugurated without the assistance of at least one Musalman. In the real Mohurrum, part of the ceremonial consists in carrying in procession the *ullums* or representations in metal of the crests of the martyred Hosain's banner; and at the beginning of the celebration these are taken to the building round which the rites centre and with much pomp and circumstance are set up on end by various devices. In the Hindus' Mohurrum the significance of these representations is misunderstood and they are called the Pirlu or saints, but it is held to be essential that they should be set up by a Muhammadan and if there is no one of that faith in the village one is brought in from elsewhere for the purpose. Curiously also, it is considered essential that this man should consecrate the meat which is to be eaten during the Mohurrum.[26]

At the real Mohurrum, a pit is dug and a bonfire made in it round which lamentations over the death of Hussan and Hosain are made. In the Hindu version of the ceremony, this item is often developed into a regular fire-walking ceremony. Vows are also commonly taken before the 'Peerlu'. For Musalmans the most sacred place in the district is Babayya's darga at Penukonda. This holy place is visited all the people irrespective of caste and religion.

Festivals

Hindu Festivals: The lives of the people of the district are not only enlivened but also chastened by a great variety of festivals. The most important of these common to all Hindu castes are the New Year's Day, Ayudha Pooja, the Deepavali and the Sankranti or Pongal. The New Year's day or Ugadi for Andhras falls generally in the later part of March. The day is marked by great rejoicing when relations are invited and a juice prepared out of margosa flowers, jaggery and new tamarind is distributed.[27] Towards the evening, the Purohit produces the new 'panchangam' (almanac) and reads out the more striking of the passages. Ayudha pooja is dedicated to Saraswati, the goddess of learning and falls in October when Brahmins worship books and others their tools and instruments. Deepavali, which commemorates the destruction of the demon Narakasura by Sri Krishna, is celebrated with great eclat, particularly by wearing new clothes and firing crackers. The Sankranti is the day on which the Sun passes from Dakshinayanam (Sagittarius) to Uttarayanam (Capricorn) and falls in the middle of January. The day following this festival is called 'Kanumu' when domestic animals are washed and garlanded and their horns painted. Besides these, there are several other festivals observed by various communities. Srirama- navami, the birth day of Sri Rama which falls towards the end of March, is celebrated particularly by all Vaishnavites. Sri Jay anti, the birth day of Sri Krishna, is another important festival observed towards the end of August. Vinayaka Chaturthi which follows shortly afterwards and which is dedicated to Ganesa, is celebrated by all Hindus. Navaratri and Vijayadasami which commemorate the victory of goddess Durga over the demon Mahishasura, are generally observed by all Hindus for ten days. They are celebrated in October by the display of dolls and puja to Durga. Both morning and evening the pupils of the pial school, dressed in new apparel holding bows and arrows in their hands, parade through the streets preceded by their teacher reciting and shouting poems and go from house to house seeking presents. Mondays in the month of Kartika which are held sacred to lord Siva, are marked by worship in all His temples. Vaikunta Ekadasi is a day of solemn observance for Vaishnavites. Similarly Mahasivaratri is sacred for all Saivites and it falls in the beginning of March and is observed as a day of fasting and prayer.

Muslim Festivals: Muharram, the first month of the Hijra year, is a festival marked by solemn mourning in remembrance of the martyrdom of the Prophet's grandson, Imam Husain. It lasts for 10 days. Houses called Ashur-Khanas are set apart for the mourning ceremonies. The festival is mainly a Shia one. But Sunnis also take part in these ceremonies while Wahabis, who believe in the letter of the tradition, have nothing to do with it. There is an interesting alam (pir) at Gugudu (Anantapur) ascribed to one Kullayiswami (the saint with a long cap) which is held in great veneration and people of all communities visit it in fulfilment of their vows.[28] One of the principal attractions of the festival is the fire walking ceremony, which takes place on the ninth and the eleventh days of Muharram. In Enumula-doddi (Kalyandurg), Dommaras celebrate this festival with a Dommara as the Mullah (priest).

It was on the last Wednesday of the second month of the calendar, Safar that the Prophet partially recovered from his last illness and he could take a short walk. On the anniversary of this called the Akhiri Chaharshamba, the Muslims, especially women leave their seclusion, go to open places and enjoy it as a sort of picnic. The twelfth day of the third month, Rabi-ul-Awwal called Eed-i-Milad is held sacred as it was on that day that the Prophet was born. This day is marked by a series of lectures and speeches (called Maulud Sharif) delivered in Telugu and Urdu on the life of the Prophet and these are attended by Muslims as well as Hindus and Christians without distinction.[29] The eleventh day of the fourth month, Rabi-us- Sani is observed as the anniversary of the Hazrat Mah- boob-i-Subhani Pir Dastagir and is called Yazda- hum Sharif. On this day those who can afford it provide fare to the poor and the needy. The night before the twenty-seventh of Rajab, known as Shab-i-Mi'raj, is held sacred as the Prophet is said to have had a vision of ascent to the Heavens, and many Muslims consider that he was bodily lifted to the divine abode. The event is celebrated by night long prayers in mosques by devout Muslims.

"Shab-e-barat" is the Urdu version of the Arabic "Lailatu'l-Baraat" meaning the Night of Forgiveness and is the name given to the night preceding the 15th of Shaban.[30] The Prophet announced that on that night God forgave the sins of many sinners and enjoined prayers. But this direction is now mostly forgotten. The "Shab-e-Barat" is celebrated with much merriment particularly by children, by firing crackers and illuminating homes, almost in the same manner as the 'Diwali' is celebrated among the Hindus.

The month of Ramzan is held most sacred and is scrupulously observed in the district by fasting. The 27th day of the month, the Shab Qadr, the night on which the first verse of the Quran was revealed to the Prophet, is marked by night long prayers in the local mosques. The Ramzan and the Baqrid are the two chief festivals, the former at the end of the Ramzan and the latter on the tenth of the last month of the Hijira year. Muslims go to the local Eedgahs dressed in new clothes. The Ramzan Eed, also called the Eed-ul-Fitr is marked by alms giving and feasts, while Baqrid is celebrated with the sacrifice of goats and rams and the distribution of meat among the members of the family, the poor and the needy.

Christian Festivals: The important festivals of the Roman Catholics are the Ash Wednesday, Good Friday, Easter, All souls day and Christmas. Like Hindus they also celebrate Ugadi, Dasara, Deepavali, Sankranti etc. The festivals held sacred by the Protestants are Good Friday, Easter, Christmas and Harvest. Like Roman Catholics they also observe important Hindu festivals. Christmas is the festival day most important for them. It is the day when Jesus Christ was born. Good Friday is preceded by a period of fasting known as Lent. Easter day which falls on the Sunday immediately following Good Friday is a day of rejoicing as it was on this day that Christ's resurrection took place. In addition to these festivals, all Fridays in the week are observed by orthodox Roman Catholics as days of fast when meat is not taken. On Sundays or at Church festivals the entire community assembles and attends Church service.

Status of Village in Anantapur:

The Anantapur village may be said to differ considerably from the type found in Bellary. Bellary was on the frontier of the Vijayanagar empire and so was exposed to constant attack and pillage and the poligars within it were numerous and pugnacious. Consequently in the olden days almost all its villages were fortified and hamlets outside their walls were perilous places of residence and proportionately rare. In Anantapur, fortifications are fewer and hamlets more common. The older parts of the more important towns, such as Gooty and Dharmavaram, still however carry upon them the marks of the turbulent times through which they have passed, the houses in them being crowded closely together within the limits of the old fortifications in a manner which is neither convenient nor sanitary.[31]

Houses: The houses in Anantapur district closely resemble those of Bellary. Their walls are of stone in mud and, as day which will make good tiles is rare, their roofs are usually flat and consist of horizontal rafters upon which are piled faggots and a foot or so of earth, the whole being coated outside with day. Ventilation is obtained through circular openings in this construction which are covered with an earthen pot in wet weather. These roofs usually leak badly in heavy rain. They are often approached by an outside Houses, stairway. In the south of the district, and less commonly in Penukonda, the houses are sometimes provided with watch-towers having a flight of stairs inside them and small windows. One of these towers is a very prominent object from all parts of Dharmavaram town. In the same part of the country many of the houses are faced by lofty verandahs supported on tall wooden pillars which are often tastefully carved and painted. The pial, or outer verandah, is however much less universal than in the southern districts, and so also is the inner courtyard and the 'backyard' of the Tamil country. The reason probably is that, from causes already indicated, the space available was cramped and had to be utilised to the utmost. Cattle are kept in the front room of the house instead of at the back as usual. Few houses of the smaller kinds have a worship room, but a corner of one of the living rooms is often marked off and devoted to the family gods. The sad colour of the stone walls of the buildings, the scarcity of trees and other vegetation, the narrow streets, and the rarity of any form of decoration upon the houses, make the average Anantapur village an unlovely place.[32]

Dress and Ornaments: The pattern of dress varies from one community to another. But the perceptible link that can be discerned is its simplicity. White garments seem to be generally preferred to coloured and gaudy ones. Both in towns and villages, men wear white dhotis of varying counts. The more aged among them wear the long dhoti. The ordinary cultivator dresses himself in the coarse cotton stuff locally woven. Sometimes he spins the yarn himself and hands it over to the local weavers paying them for their labour. Some ryots wear short trousers reaching the knee. The 'Kambali' (blanket) is almost invariably carried by them. The turbans worn are generally white and are very large. The labourers wear short cotton drawers, while agriculturists wear dhoti and 'Sella' (upper cloth). Others simply wrap the short dhoti called 'Addapancha' round their waist. 'Jubba', a collarless shirt, is another item of popular wear. Some young men take a fancy for wearing the long dhoti in a somewhat different style usually referred to as 'cyclekattu'. Some of the villagers, especially in Madakasira taluk, still wear a 'Puttagochi', a small strip of cloth passed between thighs and attached at the front and the back to a string tied round the waist. Muslims usually wear fez caps while young boys put on shirts and shorts.

Women generally wear handloom sarees of varying colours and patterns, six to nine yards in length. The mode of wearing the saree varies among the various Brahmin sects. Madhwa and Desastha Brahmin women pass the saree between their legs, while all others bring it again round the waist. Brahmin widows wear red sarees and cover their heads with a portion of the saree, Kapu widows don white sarees. Among others the saree is passed once round the waist and a knot is tied to keep it fixed and then folds are made in front. The saree is then tied tightly round the waist and its end is thrown over the left shoulder. Generally women wear 'Ravika' (short tight jacket) and an underwear called 'Langa'. Traditionally some of the women among 'Oddes' (Odderas) and 'Gollas' do not wear 'Ravika' although in recent years a short jacket is put on by the young women. Those accustomed to chew pan, carry with them a cloth bag containing three or four pockets in which are kept the betel leaf, arecanut, lime and dried tobacco leaf or dust. Muslim girls wear 'Pavada' and 'Kurtha'. In towns, the grown up girls put on pyjama, kurtha and vodni. 'Duppata' is universally carried by all women observing 'gosha'.[33]

Due to the impact of western lifestyles, sartorial fashions are fast changing. A more or less uniform pattern of dress is being adopted by all irrespective of distinctions of caste. The ward-robe of modern men and women excels in its variety and consists of coats, waist coats, pants, neckties and hats in the case of the former and cholis, blouses, jumpers, brassieres, petticoats and sarees of five to six yards in that of the latter. A pair of trousers along with a shirt or bush coat or bush shirt or American slack forms the usual out-fit of young men. The shirt is usually tucked underneath the trousers and the sleeves are rolled up above the elbow. The Scheduled Tribes in the district, however, adhered to their traditional style of dress. Some like the Sugali women wear a petticoat, patchy and of bright colour. They have also a tight fitting jacket and their arms are covered up to elbows with bangles and bracelets.

All Hindu women except widows wear "bottu" of 'Kumkum'. Tattooing was formerly common but now-a-days it is fast disappearing. Women are fond of jewellery, the married treasuring the 'tali', earrings, bangles and toe-rings. The higher classes go in for a variety of ornaments ranging from necklaces, pendants and girdles to bangles, ear-rings and nose- screws made of gold and often studded with precious stones. Others take to a cheaper variety of jewellery mostly of silver. All women love flowers and all except widows use them on almost all occasions. Christian (except Roman Catholic women) and Muslim women do not put on Kumkum. The favourite ornaments of the Sugali women are bangles of ivory from the wrists to the elbows. These are sometimes dyed red. They also wear ear, finger and toe rings and necklaces. Their hair is usually dressed in plaits or put up in a knot to a side, bulging out with an artificial chignon of wool or hair. Teen aged girls of all communities use an ornamental bunch of balls called *Kuchchulu*. Golla women wear on the right wrist 'Kadiyams' made of brass bearing the image of Krishna. In addition to ear-rings, they also wear silver ornaments called 'Bundi' on the upper arm and a 'Dabu' round the waist. They are also accustomed to wear necklaces of beads. A gold chain with a large pendant embedded with stones called 'Nanupathakam' is usually worn round the neck by Kapu and Kamma women. Vaisya families possess a variety of gold ornaments, now mostly out-dated, like Vaddanam, Vanki, Rettakadi-yam, Nagottu, Kasuladanda, Nagara, etc. An ornament which commonly arouses some curiosity is 'Tiri-pam Kante' a plain silver wire-ring worn round the neck made out of charitable money doles and supposed to ward off evils, Muslim women wear necklaces, earrings, bracelets and anklets, while men mostly put on silver rings.[34]

Fashion has now come to be associated with wearing as few ornaments as possible. Men generally do not wear ornaments except for some finger rings, gold chains and wrist watches. Women wear a gold necklace and some bracelets or bangles made of gold. A pair of 'Kammalu' (studs) also adorns their ears. Children generally wear anklets. On important occasions like marriages women display most of their ornamental wear. They also use cosmetics. The educated use footwear made in towns while shoes made locally are worn by cultivators and others.

Food Habits: Rice constitutes the staple food of the people both in towns and villages. Korra, cholam, ragi and sajja are also consumed in places where they are grown. Brahmins and some other castes abstain from eating meat. Madigas and Malas are the only classes among the Hindus who eat beef. Pork is eaten by the Yerukalas. Christians and Muslims generally take mutton, fish and the flesh of ordinary edible birds. The former also consume pork and the latter sometimes beef. The older among the Brahmins and the other higher classes take only two meals' a day, one at mid-day and the other after sunset. But now-a-days they supplement these by some light refreshments and coffee in the morning and coffee or tea in the afternoon. Their meal commonly consists of rice, ghee, dhal, rasam, sambar made of vegetables, appalams, pickles, curds or butter milk. On festive occasions these are supplemented by a few sweet and savoury dishes and some fruits. Orthodox Brahmin widows do not take a regular meal at night but are content with light food consisting of cakes of rice or fried and pounded rice called 'Atukulu'. The labour classes subsist on three meals, a breakfast of cold rice in the morning, a lunch of porridge at mid-day and a dinner of hot rice, meat, soup or curry at night. At breakfast, cold rice is now-a-days widely replaced by coffee. To an average ryot, rice is a delicacy taken usually on festival days. Most of the ryots consume half the meal with a 'chatny' made of tamarind, chillies and salt with an occasional admixture of dhal and the other half with curd or buttermilk. Porridge made of cholam or ragi flour is their principal food. In the northern taluks, korra is used at night while in parts of Rayadurg rice is used instead. The usual food of the labour classes is Cholam and Ragi.[35] In Gooty, Tadipatri and Anantapur, Cholam and Korra are the staple foodgrains while in the southern taluks, Ragi is their chief source of sustenance. It is only the richer classes who regularly eat rice. Borugulu, rice cooked in sand and Atukulu, rice fried and pounded, are considered delicacies. Vegetables are not regarded as an invariable necessity except in towns. Some use buttermilk and ghee, the latter being more often sold than consumed. The popular items of breakfast of the upper and the middle class families are preparations like 'Dosa', 'Idli', etc., prepared from dough rice and black- gram and cholam-cake and those from wheat like 'Chapati', 'Upma' and 'Puri'. Pickles of mango, lime and tamarind form part of lunch and supper. The consumption of wheat 'Parota' or 'Chapati' and 'Kichidi' made of rice and dhal or plain rice is usually confined to Muslims. Groundnut oil generally figures in all culinary preparations and the condiments used include pepper, turmeric, ginger, cardamom, cloves, spices, chillies, mustard, onion and garlic. To most curries is added coconut in some form or other. In towns there are a number of hotels and restaurants catering to various categories of people and serving hot beverages like tea and coffee besides food. During summer cool drinks, sherbets, aerated waters like soda or orange squash are largely in demand. Smoking, 'pan' chewing and use of snuff are also common.

Amusements: The boys and girls have a number of games and amusements and these are often curiously similar to those of the children of western nations. Hide and seek, games of the fox-and-geese variety (played with cowries), and the universal *kolattam* are the chief amusements of the girls. The boys play with marbles and tops and also have rougher amusements such as varieties of tip-cat, prisoner's base, rounder's and cricket, the last being played with a brick for a wicket.

The elders of the lower classes play primitive games of cards in which much gambling goes on (the upper castes also play cards for small stakes), toss for coppers, indulge in cock-fighting, attend the shows given by strolling players and now and again get up a beat for pig. Cock-fighting often leads to gambling and quarrels and is therefore actively discouraged by the police. It is in consequence generally managed unobtrusively. The combatants are fitted with very long and sharp spurs. Strolling players are usually Killekyatas by caste. These people travel round the villages and give a performance wherever they can secure sufficient patronage. Contributions take the form of money or of oil for the footlights. Scenes from the 'Ramayana and the Mahabhrata, and the story of 'Desing *Raja*' of Gingee are perhaps the favourite plays. Sometimes the men and women of other settled castes, such as the *Oddes, Kamsalas and Kammaras* get up a performance among themselves. The *Dommaras* also travel round and give gymnastic and acrobatic displays and the Jogis sing songs to the accompaniment of a drum and a sort of tambourine. The Telugu New Year's Day is the great occasion for driving pig and the Boyas are the chief organizers of the beats. Young and old join in them and since to have good sport is held to be the best of auguries for the coming year the excitement aroused is often almost ludicrous in its intensity.[36]

Social Life: Within village society the social structure was probably similar to that in Moghul India, with the two top economic groups corresponding to the old dominant castes, the next group to peasant castes, and the bottom group consisting largely of untouchables.

Conditions of different Castes: The most numerous castes are the Kapus, the great land-holding body in the Telugu districts. They number nearly a sixth of the total Hindu population. They consist, of course, of many subdivisions with differing social customs (some, for example, are strict vegetarians) but these distinctions are but little understood and they are generally spoken of as though they were a homogeneous unit.[37] They are held in much respect as substantial, steady-going yeomen, who next to the Brahmans are the leaders of Hindu society. Close after them in numerical importance come the Boyas (or, in Canarese, Bedars) the old fighting caste of this part of the country whose exploits are so often recounted in the history books. The polegars' forces and, Haidar's famous troops were largely recruited from these people and they still retain a keen interest in sport and manly exercises. It is said that in the south-west of Kalyandurg taluk the Myasa sub-division of them, like their fellows round Rayadurg in Bellary district, practice circumcision, but I had not time to personally verify the statement.

After Boyas, rank the Madigas and Malas, the leather-workers and coolies of the community. They eat beef and drink heavily and are thus unclean and lived in hamlets called *Madiga geris* (streets inhabited by Madiga communities), outside the villages. Like other of the lowest castes, they cannot enter the Hindu temples, nor may they use the wells of the upper Hindu castes. In other districts they have to act as their own barbers and washer men, but in Anantapur this disability is somewhat relaxed, as the barbers make no objection to let them use their razors for a consideration and the dhobis wash their clothes as long as they themselves first unroll them and dip them into the water. This act is held to remove the pollution which would otherwise attach to them.[38] After Madigas next comes the Canarese Kurubas, the shepherd community and the weavers of the woollen blankets which are such an indispensable item in the average ryot's wardrobe. Below them in numerical importance come the other castes usual to all Telugu districts, such as the Balija and Komati traders, the Golla neat-herds, Kamma cultivators, Odde ('Woddah') stone- workers, the Malas who weave coarse cotton stuffs and work as agricultural coolies, the washermen (Tsakalas) and barbers (Mangalas), the Upparas who used to live by making earth-salt and are now usually petty cultivators, the Idiga toddy-drawers, the Kamsala and Kummara artisans, and the weaving castes such as the Devangas, Togatas and Sales of all kinds. Among the weavers may be mentioned the Pattegaras. They number only a few hundred but are rare outside the district. They are Marathas by origin and speak a corrupt Marathi among themselves.

Beggars: A noticeable point in the constitution of the Anantapur population is the frequency of the various beggar castes. *Bhatrazus* tour round the villages, make extempore verses in praise of the principal householders in them and are rewarded by gifts of old clothes, grain and money. *Budubudukalas* live by a less artistic form of the sanie method, travelling from village to village and getting similar recompense by prophesying good fortune to the various inhabitants. The *Killekyata* play-actors, the *Dommara* acrobats and the *Jogi* musicians have already been referred to.[39]

The beggars who are most in evidence are the *Dasaris*. This community is recruited from several castes, such as the Kapus, Balijas, Kurubas, Boyas and Malas, and members of it who belong to the two last of these (which are low in the social scale) are not allowed to dine with the others. All Dasaris are Vaishnavites and admission to the community is obtained by being branded by some Vaishnavite guru. Thenceforward the novice becomes a Dasari and lives by begging from door to door. The profession is almost hereditary in some families. The five insignia of a Dasari are the conch-shell which he blows to announce his arrival; the gong lie strikes as he goes his rounds; the tall iron lamp which he keeps lighted as he begs; the brass or copper vessel suspended from his shoulder in which he places the alms received; and the small metal image of Hanuman which he hangs round his neck. Of these the iron lamp is at once the most conspicuous and the most indispensable-A Dasari without his lamp would not obtain few contributions. It is said to represent Venkatesa, and it must be burning, an unlighted lamp being inauspicious. Dasari's also subsist by doing puja at ceremonial and festival occasions for certain of the Hindu castes.

The status of women: In this region, as in the rest of the country, economic dependence of women is almost proverbial in the case of all communities. The burden of maternal duties is considered to be too heavy to impose additional responsibilities on them. But this is getting gradually changed and women have come to assume a fairly dominant role in various spheres of activity. By and large a good number of them are employed as teachers, nurses, midwives, clerks, typists and receptionists in offices. Some among them are also lawyers and doctors.[40] These are signs of a promising trend of a section of population slowly liberating itself from its past state of dependence. Among the poorer classes, women work in large numbers as agricultural and industrial labourers and as unskilled workers in industrial establishments. Cases are also not rare of men, relying on the earnings of their womenfolk. It must, however, be conceded that a large proportion of women is unemployed primarily due to lack of opportunities. The natural disabilities associated with women are also a factor to be reckoned' with.

Dancing girls: The Anantapur temples do not each maintain a corps of dancing girls as do so those of the temples in the south. The few women of this class in the district, who are called Bogams by caste, are quite independent of the temples. The custom of dedicating Basavis, which is so common further west in Bellary, Mysore and Dharwar, prevails to a limited extent in the western part of the district. Apparently the only castes who practise it are the Boyas, Malas and Madigas. A girl who is dedicated at a temple as a Basavi does not marry but lives in her parents' house under the protection of some man of her own or an equal or higher caste who is expected to maintain and clothe her. Her children belong to her father's and not to her temporary husband's family and she herself is treated as, and inherits like, a son instead of a daughter.[41]

During 1871-1901 the inhabitants of the district only increased at the rate of 6 percent. The people of the district suffered very severely in the great famine of 1876-78 and at the census of 1881 their numbers were one-fifth fewer than they had been in 1871. In the next decade the usual rebound after the famine took place and the population increased at the rate of 17 percent., but in the ten years between 1891 and 1901 it grew at little more than the average pace in the Presidency as a whole. Emigration and immigration have affected the figures but slightly. The population continued to grow up to 1941 with minor variations. Eighty percent of the people speak Telugu, 11 percent Kannada, and six percent Hindustani. Kannada is the vernacular along the western border and in Madakasira two-fifths of the population talks it. In case of education Anantapur is the most backward in the whole Madras Presidency. The occupations of the people reveal that the percentage of the people who depend for their livelihood upon agricultural and pastoral pursuits is even higher than usual. Over nine-tenths of the inhabitants are Hindus. Around 7 percent are Musalmans. The percentage of Jains and the Christians is negligible. The pattern of dress varies from one community to another. But the perceptible link that can be discerned is its simplicity. White garments seem to be generally preferred to coloured. Women generally wear handloom sarees of varying colours and patterns. Rice constitutes the staple food of the people both in towns and villages. Korra, cholam, ragi and sajja are also consumed in places where they are grown. Young and old, people of all castes and communities play a variety of indigenous games.

REFERENCES

1. Appa Rao, G.V., *The Annals of Handeh Anantapuram,* p. 7.
2. Krishnaswami, S.Y., *Rural Problems in Madras*, Monograph, Madras, 1947, p. 31.
3. Inter-District Migrations—1951 Census Returns, p.5.
4. *Ibid.*, p. 6.
5. Guha, Nikhiles, *Pre-British State System in South India, Mysore 1761-1799*, Calcutta, 1985, p. 8.
6. Epstein, Scarlett, "Customary System of Rewards in Rural South India," in Dalton George ed., *Economic Development and Social Change*, New Delhi, 1971, p. 109.
7. Bhattacharya, S., *Financial Foundations of the British Raj*, Simla, 197, p. 33.
8. E. Thurston, *Castes and Tribes of Southern, India*-Volumes I, p. 89.
9. *Ibid.*, p. 99.
10. _______. "Weavers, Merchants and Company: The Handloom Industry in Southeaster India, 1750-1790." *Indian Economic and Social History Review*, 17, No. 3 (1980) pp. 257-258.
11. Rao, P. Raghunadha, *History of Modern Andhra*, Sterling Publishers, New Delhi,1983, p. 120.
12. *Ibid.*, p. 121.
13. *Ibid.*, p. 121.
14. Chatterjee, Partha, *Nationalist Thought and the Colonial World: A Derivative Discourse*, London: Zed, 1986, p. 46.
15. Ramakrishna, V., *Social Reforms in Andhra (1848-1919),* Vikas Publishers, Delhi 1983, p. 128.
16. Vaikuntham, Y., *Education and Social Change in South India: Andhra, 1880- 1920*, Madras, 1982, p. 11.

17. *Ibid.*, p. 26.
18. Gopalachari, K., *Early History of the Andhra Country*,: University of Madras, Madras 1976, p. 75.
19. *Ibid.*, p. 76.
20. Arnold, David, *Police, Power and Colonial Rule, Madras, 1859-1947*, New Delhi, 1986, p. 26.
21. Iyengar, P. T. S., 'Misconceptions about the Andhras', Indian *Antiquary*, 42, 1913, p. 281.
22. *Ibid.*, p. 282.
23. *Ibid.*, p. 301.
24. Subba Rao, B., *The Geographic Factors in Andhra History and Archaeology*', BDCRI, Poona, No. 12, 1948, p. 183.
25. Tejaswini, Yarlagadda, *Social History of the Deccan*, Bharatiya Kala Prakashan, Delhi, 2003, p. 25.
26. _____. *The Nation and Its Fragments: Colonial and Postcolonial Histories*, Princeton: Princeton University Press, 1993, p. 46.
27. Kumar, Prasanna & Murthy, V. Linga & Ravi, K. (ed), *Government & Politics in Andhra Pradesh,* S.Chand Co., New Delhi, 1982, p. 210.
28. _____, A Socio-Economic History of Modern Andhra", in Social Science Probings, Vol.2, No.l, March 1985, pp. 39.
29. Mangalam, S. J., *Historical Geography and Toponomy of Andhra Pradesh*, Sundeep Prakashan, New Delhi, 1986, p. 52.
30. *Ibid.*, p. 54.
31. Mudaliar, Chandra, *State and Religious Endowments in Madras*, Madras, 1976, p. 22.
32. Ramakrishna, V., *op. cit.* p. 132.
33. Sundaram, K., *Studies in Economic and Social Conditions of Medieval Andhra (AD 1000- 1600 AD)*, Triveni Publishers, Machilipatnam, 1969, p. 68.
34. Hanumantha Rao, B. S. L., *Religion in Andhra*, Department of Archaeology and Museums, Government of Andhra Pradesh, Hyderabad, 1993, p. 92.
35. *Ibid.*, p. 93.
36. Rami Reddy, G. 1989, "Caste, Class and Dominance in Andhra Pradesh." Francine R. Frankel and M.S.A. Rao, eds *Dominance and State Power in Modern India*. Vol.1, pp. 265-321. Oxford University Press, Delhi, p. 76.

37. *Ibid.*, p. 77.
38. Hanumantha Rao, B. S. L., *Social Mobility in Medieval Andhra*, Telugu University, Hyderabad, 1995, p. 54.
39. *Ibid.*, p. 55.
40. Chandra, Satish, *Medieval India: Society, the Jagirdari Crisis and the Village*, Macmillan, Delhi, 1982 p. 32.
41. Singh, A.K., 1990, *Devadasis System in Ancient India*. H.K. Publishers and Distributors, Delhi, p. 13.

4

Economic Development of the People Under British Rule

British imperialism was more pragmatic than that of other colonial powers. Its motivation primarily based on its economic interests. At first the main purpose was to achieve a monopolistic trading position. Later, it was felt that a regime of free trade would make India a major market for British goods and a source of raw materials, but British capitalists who invested in India, or who sold banking or shipping services there, continued effectively to enjoy monopolistic privileges. The Britishers relied on market forces to deal with problems like famine. They did nothing to stimulate agriculture or protect industry. In the light of the above the present chapter deals with the economic development of the region under colonial regime.

Agriculture Development:

Anantapur region is economically very backward and frequent drought conditions keep the people in distress. Soil and climatic conditions of the district are adverse and the ryot, the farmer, is ignorant of modern technology and industries other than rural are almost non-existent during the British regime. In 1871, Anantapur district had a density of population of only 152 to the square mile, as against 226 of the Madras Presidency. The distress in 1877-78 was probably severest in Anantapur and Bellary districts; hence the pressure of population on an area was not the cause of famine, but the pressure upon the existing means and methods of getting a livelihood and raising crops. Capital will not descend from the sky (though it can arise out of the earth) and it seems that there is no way of making the district regularly maintain itself other than by acting on the ryot in the matter of education in rural economy.

The colonial government made institutional changes in agriculture by transforming traditionally circumscribed property rights into something more closely resembling the unencumbered private property characteristic of Western capitalism. The beneficiaries of these new rights varied in different parts of India. The jagirdari system was abolished and the bulk of the old warlord aristocracy was dispossessed. Their previous income from land revenue, and that of the Moghul state, was now appropriated by the British as land tax. In the Madras Presidency, of which Anantapur is a part, the British dispossessed many of the old Moghul and Maharatta nobility and big zamindars, and vested property rights and tax obligations in individual 'peasants'. This settlement was known as the *ryotwari* (peasant tenure) system. However, the term peasant is misleading, because most of those who acquired land titles belonged to the traditionally dominant castes in villages. Lower-caste cultivators became their tenants. Thus, there was no change in social structure at the village level, except that the new ownership rights gave greater opportunities for sale and mortgage, and the security of the tenant was less than it had been under the previous system.[2] The change in legal status was limited by several factors. First of all, illiterate peasant did not always understand the new situation, and there were strong social ties in the joint family and the caste *panchayats* to prevent major deviations from old habits. Secondly, the new administration was rather remote from individual villages (with a district officer responsible for over a thousand villages), and many British administrators had a personal bias in favour of customary tenant rights because by maintaining them they could avoid political trouble. At a later stage, the government itself introduced a good deal of legislation to protect customary rights in response to peasant disturbances. The British were more concerned with arrangements which would guarantee their revenue and not provoke too much political disturbance rather than in increasing productivity or introducing capitalist institutions. The class of landless agricultural labourers grew in size under British rule. Little was done to promote agricultural technology. There was some improvement in seeds, but no extension service, no improvement in livestock and no official encouragement to use fertiliser.

With the object of helping the farmer with latest ideas on agriculture an Agricultural Society was started at Penukonda by the government in 1901. The society is still active and members are on its rolls belonging to the District and 200 members are from outside of the district. The district Collector is its President. The society publishes a periodical, which is mainly devoted to agricultural matters, and organizes lectures on these subjects. It also conducts crop exhibitions motivating some of its members to experiment with ground-nut and potatoes in a piece of wet land under the Penukonda tank which serves as a trial ground and model farm.

Early Industries:

Prior to Independence, Anantapur was not particularly well known for any industries although some places seem to have specialised in manufacturing of certain types of products which have now almost disappeared.[3] There is no proper record of evidence to show that the district was rich like some of its neighbouring districts in iron ore smelting or the manufacture of earth salt, salt-petre and or even indigo dye etc. However, casual references were made in the old records about some of these industries, which, in course of time, failed to survive. Of these to mention some, the making of bangles at Gutturu (Penukonda), and of handmade paper at Nyamaddala (Dharmavaram), the hand printing of cloth at Pamidi (Gooty), the manufacture of candles at Gooty and the preparation of indigo dye at a few places in Tadipatri taluk deserve mention. Again, the first three among these have almost disappeared while there are now no traces of the other two. The production of the synthetic dye rendered the manufacture of indigo un-remunerative while the local candles could not withstand competition from those of the foreign variety.

Earth Salt: Earth salt, however, used to be extensively manufactured in this district almost till the close of the nineteenth century. Whatever saline efflorescence was available in the district was utilised for manufacturing earth salt in what were known as 'Modas' which were largely in vogue in the taluks of Tadpatri, Gooty, Rayadurg, Dharmavaram, Penukonda, Hindupur and Madakasira. In fact, as many as 3,553 'Modas', spread over 979 villages in Tadpatri, Gooty, Rayadurg and Dharmavaram. Penukonda, Hindupur and Madakasira taluks, were reported to have been in existence by 1823. A heap of earth was piled up and on the top of it was hollowed out one or more circular basins, of about five feet in diameter and two feet deep. From the bottom of these basins channels lined with 'hunam' ran down to one or more reservoirs- similarly lined. Salt-earth was collected in the places where it effloresced naturally in the dry months and taken to the 'Moda' on pack buffaloes. It was thrown into the basins and then a quantity of water was poured upon it. The brine so obtained flowed through the channels at the bottom of the basins into the reservoirs. From these it was baled with chaities into a set of masonry evaporating pans where it was allowed to be converted into salt by solar evaporation. Each lot of earth salt which was thus lixiviated was taken from the basins and thrown outside. This process constantly repeated, gradually raised the level of the 'Moda' and the basins which were perpetually being remade on the top of it. Some of the 'Modas' gradually grew to be as much as 20 feet in height. When they became too high for the buffaloes to carry the salt- earth upto their summits with ease, they were abandoned and others started elsewhere.[4]

The salt was largely used by the poorer classes for domestic consumption and by the richer ryots for their cattle. But the industry was suppressed in 1880 as it interfered with the profits of the State monopoly established in 1805. The owners of the 'Modas' were, however, paid reasonable compensation. Later, the northern taluks of the district obtained their salt supplies from the 'Bombay

Presidency and the southern ones from the salt factories at Nellore and Chingleput. There are now no vestiges of the manufacture of earth salt nor any signs of the 'Modas' and the district obtains its requirements of salt from Nellore and Guntur.

Bangle Making: Bangle making must have once been a flourishing indigenous industry in this district. This can be inferred not only from the pieces of broken bangles and beads found by Bruce Foote in the pre-historic caves in the district but also on the testimony of Havellf (1887) to a few families manufacturing glass bangles at Gutturu. In 1880, Mr. Gamble found in the villages of Penukonda taluk no less than 93 bangle kilns of which 75 were abandoned and 18 working. The kilns which were found to be not working were chiefly those lying beyond the reach of wood. Even during the seventies of the last century, quite a number of villages between Bellary and Gooty seem to have specialised in this manufacture. It was reported to have been carried on in almost all the taluks except Tadpatri. With the introduction of the Madras Forest Act of 1881, this industry started declining, as illicit felling of trees was restricted and fuel could not be obtained free of cost. The centers particularly noted for this industry were Gutturu, Madakasira and Ganginenipally. Of these Gutturu once known as 'Gajula Gutturu' (Gutturu of bangles), continued to be an important centre of manufacture employing at its zenith as many as 700 workers.[5] But by 1928, only one household was found to have been engaged in this enterprise. The reasons for this sharp decline were mainly the poverty of the workers, the inability of the local variety of bangles to compete with those of Ferozabad which were superior in point of finish and design, the crude nature of the black glass made locally and the generally disorganised state of the industry. The bangles manufactured were of a coarse variety and of different colours like green, black, blue and red and were disposed of mostly in Mysore, their chief market. With a view to rejuvenate this industry a pure Glass Bangle Training Centre was set up at Gutturu in 1955 and it functioned for nearly six years. Attempts made during 1960 to form an industrial Co-operative with the trainees of the centre as members, did not seem to have met with any success. Many of the artisans earlier engaged in this industry have now taken to the manufacture of aloe fiber.

Handmade Paper: The manufacture of handmade paper made rapid strides even by 1872 and places like Nyamaddala in Dharmavaram taluk had earned great reputation. The old Bellary Manual (1872) records that "coarse paper was made in the Bellary district from old gunny but the manufacture was not an important one. The process was in all essentials the same as was followed at 'home' in the manufacture of handmade paper. This paper was much used by merchants for account books."[6] By about 1900 it was found that there were 24 karkhanas (factories) engaging 40 families at Nyamaddala while its neighbouring village, Chindapalle, ran four factories employing 10 to 12 families, and that all those engaged in the industry were Balijas. Some attempts were made during the twenties of this century to resuscitate this industry but they did not succeed.

Dyeing and Printing: In Anantapur region the centres noted for dyeing and printing were Pamidi, Chowluru and Gutturu. Of these, Pamidi held the pride of place although it is not known how the industry actually originated at this centre. What is, however, interesting is the fact that the local artisans were Rangaris who, according to Kaifiyat of Pamidi, had migrated to this place during the reign of Aurangzeb, the Moghul Emperor, and engaged themselves in dyeing and printing. The work of printing was done by cutting out patterns on wooden blocks, which were locally made. The dyes used in colouring the prints were indigenous. But what is really interesting is that some of the 'palampores' (upper cloth) with mythological designs made here are reported to have attracted almost world-wide attention. Even by the seventies of the last century, the Chintzes of Pamidi found a market all over the country and even beyond, at places like Rangoon, Singapore and Aden. The manufacturers had their own emporia in Burma and Singapore. The cloth printed here bore such a striking resemblance to the well known palampores of Masulipatam (Krishna) and Kalahasti (Chittoor) that it brought into currency the common aphorism that 'one Pamidi is seven hundred Bunders', to stress the superiority of Pamidi Printing over that of Bander.[7] Havell found towards the close of 1880, that 200 workers were employed in this industry at Pamidi, the articles manufactured being mainly printed handkerchiefs and turbans and a rather tastefully designed 'Pardha' or screen cloth used in marriages. The cotton fabric for printing was originally imported from Europe, but subsequently from Bombay and Sholapur. The designs were mostly conventional representations of tigers, camels, elephants, horses, parrots and the like. The manufactures included bed spread, canopy cloth, praying cloth for Muslims and Lingayats and cloth for women's wear. They were also specially designed to cater to the needs of customers in countries like Burma and Ceylon. Apart from the Chintzes, gay cloth of the handloom type used by the Lambadi women was also manufactured. The Rangaris supplied 10 to 12 counts yarn to the weavers of Reddipalle, Khaderpeta and other neighbouring villages and got in return the cloth woven. By 1928 the only types of hand-printed cloth were those either used by Lambadi women or woven for the markets of Burma, Penang, Singapore, Southern India and Bombay. Subsequently, the increasing production of Chintzes and mill made voiles at a comparatively lower cost rendered the local manufacture of printed cloth un-remunerative. Added to this was the unhealthy competition from abroad which closed the overseas market. The artisans have now taken to the production of readymade apparel and there are hardly a few families which still carry on the industry.

Handloom Weaving: Handloom Industry occupied an important place in the economy of the district in ancient times, having absorbed a considerable proportion of the workers of the district. The principal types of weaving in vogue were those of cotton, silk, wool and gunny of which the most important was the weaving of cotton cloth. The inscriptional evidence goes to show how the financial incentives were provided to facilitate the development of the industry. A Canarese record from Chola-samudram in Hindupur taluk mentions a tax fixed on each loom (Magga). Another inscription, dated 1536- 37 A.D. informs that the weavers at Anantapur paid half rupee per loom, indicating a flourishing textile industry in the district. According to Atharvana Tanthram cotton fabrics were manufactured largely in Dharmavaram, Tadipatri and Gooty. The groups chiefly engaged in this profession were Togatas, Devangas and Sales and a fair sprinkling of Muslims and Dudekulas.[8]

Indigo: Indigo dye used to be manufactured at places like Varadayapalle Kadavakal and Amalladinne around Putlur in Tadipatri taluk of Anantapur district. But the local dye unlike, in Cuddapah, did not enjoy international reputation as it was of an inferior type. The advent of synthetic dyes, which Germany brought to the market in 1891, led to the decline of this industry.

Among other industries, mention may be made of manufacture of gunny and wood carving. Gunny was made from a locally grown sun hemp (Crotolaria juncea) in Byadigera, Chilamatturu and Hindupur. It was woven into strips and then sewn into bags. Coloured stripes were also inserted by dyeing threads with indigo, turmeric or by smearing them with red earth. The wood carving was another art practiced by Jinjgaras, especially in the southern parts of the district, where they were cutting ornamental jambs and Jintels on doorways. But in Tadipatri and elsewhere they also made small wooden toys.

Power: The dissemination of power in Anantapur district was gradual. The first town to be electrified was Hindupur. A licence was granted in January 1929 to the Hindupur Municipal Council for the supply of electrical energy within its jurisdiction. The appointment early in 1929 of an electrical engineer and the installation of machinery in 1930 resulted in the immediate supply of power. The generating capacity of the station was 60 KW. The station was a D.C. Station generating current of 460/230 Volts supplied by two diesel oil engine of 25 KW's and one of 10 KW capacity. The tariff for the supply of power being more than 6 annas per unit for lighting and fans was in those years considered high in the town. As the capacity of the station was limited, a ban on the connection of further loads was imposed on it in the middle of the thirties. In 1939-40, the tariff in the Hindupur station was reduced. By the middle of the forties, just about the close of the war, it was reported that the 'Hindupur local authority electric supply undertaking has been working unsatisfactorily financially'. And in 1946-47, Government sanctioned the 'Hindupur distribution scheme' contemplating the taking of bulk supply of electricity from Mysore and distributing it at Hindupur and around, consequent to which a 33 K.V. line from Mysore border to Hindupur sub-station was laid' during 1949-50. The scheme was estimated to cost Rs 4.92 lakhs which in the course of 10 years increased to Rs 9.75 lakhs. A 11 K.V. line from the Hindupur substation to the Municipality and all K.V. line to Mulagavati were also erected. The lines could not be charged in the same year for want of transformers.[9]

The next town to be electrified in the district was *Anantapur*. The Municipal Council at the place proposed a scheme for the electrification of the town in 1934. The proposal secured the sanction of Government and consequently supply was commenced on 16th October, 1938 with an installed generating capacity of 125 KW from 2 generators of 50 KW's. and one of 25 KW's. The Anantapur municipal electricity undertaking was acquired by Government on 15th July, 1949 at the request of the municipality. At the time Government took over the undertaking, the supply position in the town was reported to be extremely unsatisfactory.[10]

In 1946-47, Government sanctioned the 'Ceded Districts Scheme' at an estimated cost of Rs 75.78 lakh whereby power generated at Jog falls was to be purchased in bulk from Mysore and distributed to the Ceded Districts. This power was also to be supplied for meeting the needs of the proposed Tungabhadra dam construction. The survey and alignment of a 66 KV line from Mysore State border to Guntakal *via* Tungabhadra dam site were completed in the same year. By 1950-51, a 66 KV, line from Tungabhadra dam site sub-section to Bellary sub-station inclusive of the sub-stations at Sokki, Kudligi dam site (Bellary district) and Guntakal was completed.

Mining and Heavy Industries: In spite of the comparative pre-eminence of Cuddapah and Kurnool in mineral production, Anantapur can still be regarded as a district of minerals. Thus, steatite which Cuddapah does not produce and gold which is mined neither in Cuddapah nor Kurnool are found in this district on a substantial scale. Prior to the advent of the British, the district seems to have witnessed considerable mining activity. Diamond and gold mining were carried on at Vajrakarur even during Tigu's time at the close of the eighteenth century. But the former has lost its importance, while the mining of the latter was revived in the first decade of the twentieth century only to disappear two decades later. Of the minerals still mined, iron ore, steatite and limestone are the most important.

Diamonds: The Brihat Samhita alludes to the existence of diamonds in Matanga (the land between the Krishna and the Godavari) even in sixth century A.D. Diamonds have been worked till the middle of the last century in the present Cuddapah, Kurnool and Anantapur districts. An epigraph at Gadekallu in Gooty taluk of Anantapur under Vijayanagara king Achyutadevaraya dated Saka 1453, Khara, Magha, ba, 14 Sivarathri alludes to the existence of a diamond treasury ('Vijra Bhandara') at Vajrakarur in the 'Uravakonda sima'. The Bellary Manual (1872) records that the most celebrated diamond mines were at Munimadugu, then in Tadipatri taluk and now in Kurnool district, and also at Wajrakarur in Gooty taluk of this district. It further observes that diamonds were found in the sand stone breccia and conglomerate and about the period it was written, the mines were no longer worked systematically although diamonds not of very great value were occasionally met with. The old method of working the mines in these areas was to excavate pits about twenty feet square and four feet deep. The earth taken out was washed in pans and the diamonds were found at the bottom with the sediment. Prior to the advent of the British, the conditions imposed on the working of these mines were that all diamonds of the weight of one pagoda and upwards were to be the property of the Government and on all others a royalty of two percent was to be paid to Government in addition to a monthly nuzzur of one Madras pagoda for each mine. In conformity with these conditions a sum of half a lakh of rupees was annually paid as nuzzerana.[11]

In 1836, Captain Newbold recorded that diamonds were found at Vajrakarur while towards the close of the eighteenth century, Heyne referred to their existence in 'Guti' or 'Gutidroog' (obviously Gooty). The source of derivation of the diamonds at Vajrakarur appears to be a neck of blue rock which bears a strong superficial resemblance to the Kimberly blue ground. This rock is softer than the formations surrounding it and has consequently weathered more rapidly. Thus, a small hollow has been formed and it is in this hollow that prospecting has been made.

The first organisation which initiated regular prospecting operations at Vajrakarur was a syndicate in which R. G. Orr of Madras and others enjoyed a substantial interest. They engaged the services of a practical diamond miner with much experience at Kimberly and put in 1884 and 1885 steam winding and washing gear, and sunk shafts in the neck and examined the rock extracted from them. About this time, a diamond was found in a field next to the road close to the village which M/s. P. Orr and Sons, of Madras, purchased for undertaking operations. The diamond was reported to have been cut at Amsterdam and was valued at over £10,000. A couple of years later, 'The Madras Presidency Diamond Fields Co. Ltd.,' was floated to continue the operations initiated by Orr and his associates. This company seemed to have met with considerable opposition from the diamond interests in Hatton Garden as many of the London diamond merchants who had appreciable interest in the South African mines were apprehensive of the large quantities of the Indian gems which have more 'fine' than the African stones stealing the market. The company bought outright 250 acres of Patta and Enam lands in the neighbourhood of Vajrakarur and acquired mining rights over another 400 acres. Shallow surface pits were excavated in this area and the spoil washed. But they suspended this work in 1895 and diverted their attention to the shafts in the neck. Later, the greater part of the land which had been purchased was sold again and eventually the Company disposed of its interests to the 'Indian Exploration Company Limited'. This company continued the sinking of one of the principal shafts and extracted from it a sizable quantity of the blue rock. There is, however, no evidence of this company having extracted any diamonds of value. About 200 labourers were engaged the removal and washing of the conglomerate which was mined'.[12]

Gold: Modern underground mining for gold was carried out during the period from 1905 to 1927 with the help of M/s. John Taylor and Sons, who, prior to nationalisation, were connected with the Kolar Gold Fields (Mysore). The Anantapur Gold Fields Ltd., started in 1905 with a capital of £30,000, was the first venture to undertake the mining of gold in this region. In 1908, it transferred a portion of its lease, pertaining to the Buruju Block in which the Chennabhavi mines were located, to a new company called the North Anantapur Gold Mines, Ltd.[13] The other portion, relating to the south Jibutil Block was transferred to the Nundydroog Mines of Mysore under option. Subsequently the North Jibutil Block was also transferred to it and the mines worked under the name of Jibutil Gold Mines of Anantapur Ltd.

The North Anantapur Gold Mines Ltd.. sank five shafts upto 1913. The capacity of the mill was 30 stamps treating 3,000 tons per month. This Company practically discontinued its mining operations in July, 1922. However, small quantities of gold were extracted by the Company till June, 1925 when further mining was completely discontinued. During the course of its prospecting operations, the company discovered some old workings in Gooty taluk about 25 miles north of its mines. Exploration work was carried on in this area and in 1926 the North Anantapur Mines Ltd., applied for a mining lease near the villages of Ramapuram and Venkatampalli. Gold was extracted in 1926 but the workings ceased in August, 1927. The Jubitil Gold Mines also abandoned its operations in September, 1924.The output and value of gold produced from the field during the period 1910-1927 is presented in the following Table 4.1.

Table 4.1: Output and value of gold produced during 1910-1927

Year	Output Oz*	Value £
1910	2,332	10,120
1911	5,284	20,835
1912	7,269	28,499
1913	11,019	43,194
1914	19,873	82,959
1915	23,870	101,324

Year	Output Oz*	Value £
1916	11,371	94,789
1917	20,529	87,066
1918	17,831	67,219
1919	11,018	616,934
1920	13,645	803,535
1921	10,108	721,359
1922	8,388	608,673
1923	1,519	101,016
1924	3,646	238,603
1925	288	16,517
1926	930	53,219
1927	2,395	137,320

Source: Report of the Ceramic Survey of Madras Presidency, 1934.
*OZ is an abbreviations Ounce which is equal to one-sixteenth of a pound or approximately 28 grams.

As per Table 4.1, the output as well as value of gold produced in the district is erratically distributed. The output of gold produced in 1910 is 2,332 ounces. But by 1915 the production reached to 23,870 ounces. Thereafter the production declined and by 1927 it stood by 2,395 ounces. This is graphically presented in Figure 4.1.

Figure-4.1
Production of Gold in Anantapur District During 1910-1927

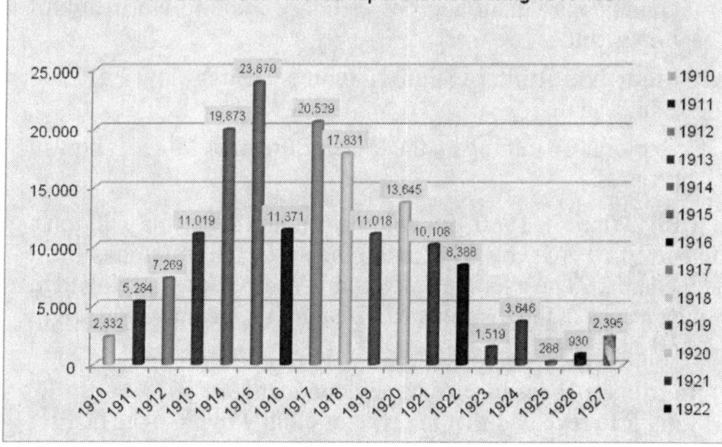

Silver

Along with gold, silver was also extracted and the relevant production figures were given in the following Table 4.2.

Table 4.2: Output of Silver produced in the district during 1910-1927

Year	Output Oz
1916	1,362
1917	1,281
1918	1,169
1919	753
1920	8680
1921	619
1922	554
1923	103
1924	249
1925	NA
1926	59

Source: Report of the Ceramic Survey of Madras Presidency, 1934.

The number of workers employed in these mines, on an average, ranged from 1,186 in 1910 to 308 in 1926. The following were the important mines identified now by local names:

1. Chennabhavi mine in North Anantapur block,
2. Omprathama Ghani, Yapamana Ghani and Ramagiri Ghani, Gantalappa Ghani and power house mine in North Jubitil mines, and
3. Main Jubitil mines, Superintendent, Bungalow East and South Shafts.
4. Exploratory mining by the Indian Bureau of Mines is now in progress.

Ruby Mica: In 1936, the volume produced was only 40 tons, which fell to 1 cwt. by 1942 and since then, no mica has been produced at all. The average daily number of persons employed in the mica mines in the district was 12 each in 1936 and 1940, 18 in 1941 and 21 in 1942.[14]

Handloom Weaving: A survey conducted in 1927 by Sri D. Narayana Rao revealed that the type of cloth woven in the district had not changed over the years since the turn of this century. The only addition was the manufacture of cloth for turbans and bodices. Sarees of less than 40 counts were mostly woven. Uravakonda was producing coarse sarees of 20 counts with coloured borders heavily dyed in indigo. These were exported to Malnad (Mysore) for use by the labouring classes working in the coffee plantations. The mercirised yarn had also come into use. Uravakonda had developed the use of warping machines. A Weavers' Co-operative Society started at Uravakonda in 1922 with 150 members on a limited liability with a share capital of Rs 9,000 and Rs 30,000 as working capital, was wound up after a few years.[15]

A survey of cotton handloom industries conducted in 1939 revealed that in this district besides Togatas and Devangas, Adi-Andhras also continued to engage themselves in weaving, particularly in Tadipatri area. In Gooty area, however, Muslim weavers took their place along with Devangas, Togatas and Padma-sales. The preparatory work, involving processes like winding, warping and sizing was done by weavers in their houses with the help of the members of their families. Statement showing the steady decrease in the number of Kurubas in the district, primarily engaged in blanket weaving and also as shepherds from 1891 to 1951.

Table 4.3: Year-wise Number of Blanket Weaving Communities in the District

S. No	Description	1891	1901	1911	1921	1931	1951
1.	Blanket weavers and Sheller's	6,796	...	...	2,204	2,550	781
2.	Woolen yarn spinners and sellers	384	4,577	11,289	...	...	...
3.	Wool carders	9	...	...	162	...	...
4.	Wool sellers	17	...	...	...	...	...
5.	Sheep and Goat Breeders	4,531	3,715	7,701	3,302	9,152	1,958
6.	Shepherds	11,311	6,028	...	...	...	...

Source: Anantapur District Gazeteer-1970.

The ruin of the indigenous industry in the district as in the other parts of the district is evident from Table 4.3. The blanket weavers and sellers reduced from 6,796 in 1891 to 781 by 1951. The Sheep and Goat Breeders also reduced from 4,531 in 1891 to 1958 by 1951.[16]

Banking System

Indigenous Banking: Anantapur is one of the poorest districts in the entire State. Its poverty and general economic backwardness are least conducive to the growth of any banking institutions, indigenous or organised. Epigraphical and other historical evidence does not also allude to the existence of either banking institutions or banking traditions in this district in the past. Whatever banking activity there is in the district is confined to its towns and chief marketing centers like Guntakal, Tadpatri, Hindupur and Anantapur. The only indigenous bankers in the district are the Marwaris at these places engaged in money lending and wholesale business and their operations are mostly restricted to traders and other sections in urban areas.

Among the other indigenous financing agencies in the district are the 'nidhis', which came into existence in the erstwhile Madras Presidency about the year 1850 for rendering financial assistance to their members. The Madras Provincial Banking Enquiry Committee, 1930, recorded the existence, at the end of 31st March, 1929, of ten nidhis registered under the Indian Companies Act in this district with a paid-up share capital of Rs 4.41 lakhs.

Table 4.4: Nidhis registered under the Indian Companies Act

SI. No.	Name and location	Date of registration	Authorised share capital Rs.
1.	Hindupur Mutual Benefit Permanent Fund Ltd., Hindupur	12-12-1918	90,000
2.	Dharmavaram Mutual Benefit Permanent Fund Ltd., Dharmavaram.	21-5-1920	99,990
3.	Madakasira Mutual Benefit Permanent Fund Ltd., Madakasira	29-6-1920	50,000
4.	Penukonda Maruti Benefit Permanent Fund Ltd., Penukonda..	29-7-1922	49,995
5.	Anantapur Sri Satyanarayana Nidhi Ltd.,Anantapur	11-1-1927	99,990
6.	Anantapur National Fund Ltd., Anantapur	11-1-1927	1,19,980

Source: Madras Provincial Banking Enquiry Committee, 1930.

In addition to their share capital, these nidhis raise their working capital by accepting fixed, current and recurring deposits from their members and they are quite popular in the district. Another type of indigenous financing associations were the credit sanghams started at places like Pamidi (Gooty taluk) and Yadiki (Tadpatri) but they are now no longer in existence.

Chit Funds also constitute another significant category of indigenous finance in the district. They are quite numerous and are particularly popular among the middle and the lower classes in the urban areas. Among them, the Popular Chit Funds and Loans Private Ltd., Tadipatri and the Sree Kanyaka Parameswari Chit Funds and Loans Ltd., Gooty are the only registered institutions on record. They were engaged for sometime in chit fund business but were dissolved in 1964.

The banking genius of the professional money lenders, mostly Vaisyas, has found expression in the establishment of 'Financing Corporations' which of late have been becoming increasingly popular in the district. Registered under the Indian Partnership Act, 1932, these corporations are partnership concerns commanding a working capital of about two lakhs of rupees. The first among them was started at Anantapur in 1961 and about fourteen of them are now functioning at Anantapur, Hindupur, Dharmavaram and Kadiri, These are more or less indigenous banking institutions accepting savings, recurring and fixed deposits, conducting chit fund business and advancing loans against time bills, discounting hundis and providing hire purchase loans for motor vehicles falling under the Motor Vehicles Taxation Act. The Reserve Bank of India does not exercise any control over their business as they do not come under the purview of the provisions of the Banking Companies Act, 1949.[17]

Role of Private Money Lenders and Financiers:

The inert state of the money market in the district manifests itself in the small number of money lenders and the small amounts of money in which they deal in. In the urban areas of the district and in its important marketing centers, the business of money lending is mostly in the hands of Vaisyas and Marwaris who were the professional money lenders. These classes combine trade with money lending and advance money to ryots and see that the crops,- mostly the commercial ones like groundnut and cotton, pass through their hands. The groundnut decorticating and oil mill owners, at places like Kadiri, Mudigubba and Nallacheruvu, also lend money to the agriculturists so that the latter might in turn bring their groundnut stocks during the harvest season to them for sale in settlement of their debt. The traders and factory owners benefit from these transactions as they not only charge interest at high rates but also procure the agricultural produce at the low prices prevailing during the harvest season. There are very few registered money lenders in the district—two at Guntakal and one at Rayadurg in 1965—but even they meet only the urban credit requirements.

Rural credit requirements, therefore, continue to be catered to mainly by the agriculturist money lender. It can be said that he practically dominates the sphere of rural credit in the district. The Resettlement Report of 1920 covering the Tadipatri and the Gooty taluks reveals the economic status of the different castes in the forty villages surveyed and shows how money lending was confined mainly to cetrain classes of people.[18]

Table 4.5: Caste-Wise Money Lenders and Indebted Ryots as per Resettlement Report of 1920

Caste	Money Lenders		Indebted Ryots	
	Number	Amount	Number	Amount
Kapu	492	2,33,812	414	2,20,666
Kamma	215	1,38,573	193	1,24,899
Vaisya	174	1,15,751	26	46,442
Balija	44	14,365	114	55,215
Boya	14	3,416	131	25,175

contd...

Caste	Money Lenders		Indebted Ryots	
	Number	Amount	Number	Amount
Brahmin	53	28,009	55	45,394
Rangaraju	32	16,975	12	5,335
Lingayat	38	13,535	9	10,500
Golla	29	15,748	62	19,835
Kuraba	13	8,780	23	7,414
Idiga	21	7,179	23	9,800
Musalman	17	21,882	86	22,853
Others	102	20.858	177	45,355
Total	**1,244**	**6,38,883**	**1,325**	**6,38,883**

Source: Resettlement Report of 1920.

Most of the classes which ran into debt were either peasants or landless labourers and a few of them were village artisans. Among the money lending classes Vaisyas, Kapus, Kammas and Lingayats played an important role. The Figure 4.1 gives clear picture of Caste-wise Money Lenders and indebted ryots.

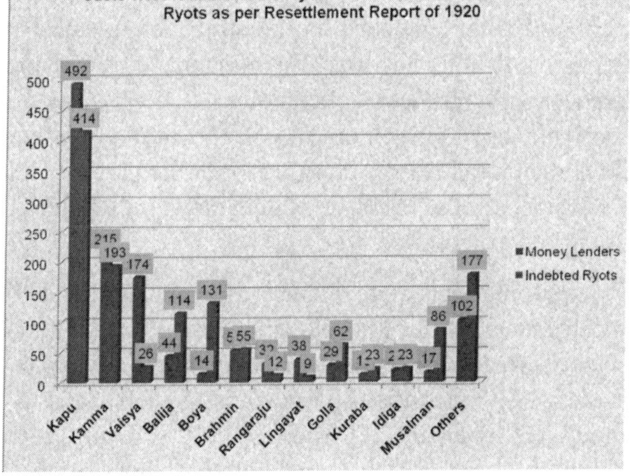

Figure 4.2
Caste-Wise Number of Money Lenders andNumber of Indebted Ryots as per Resettlement Report of 1920

Even now the Reddy, Kamma and Lingayat land-owners are the chief money lenders in villages. Loans are usually given on pronotes, against the pledge of gold ornaments or on the mortgage of landed property at comparatively high rates of interest. Traders and middle men also lend money at similar rates to agriculturists generally for meeting cultivation expenses. Loans in kind like 'nagu' (grain loan) are also resorted to in the district. These loans fetch fantastically high rates of interest ranging from 25 to 50 percent per annum. These are generally short-term loans repayable in three to twelve months and are collected either at the thrashing floor during the period of harvest or at the houses of land-holders.

The problem of protecting the debtor against the usurious methods adopted by the money lender received considerable attention in the past decades. Legislative measures were also undertaken although they touched only the fringe of the problem. The Usurious Loans Act of 1918 authorised the courts, when they found that the interest was excessive and the transaction between the parties substantially unfair, to reopen the transaction and relieve the debtor of all liability in respect of any excessive interest. This enactment was, however, found ineffective as it did not define what constituted an excessive rate of interest or an unfair transaction. Similarly, the Madras Debtor's Protection Act, 1934, the first legislative enactment intended for the protection of small debtors borrowing less than Rs 500 was also found inadequate to meet the problem. The Madras Debt Conciliation Act, 1936, providing for voluntary and amicable settlement of debts through the medium of Debt Conciliation Boards constituted for the purpose, failed to achieve any substantial results in scaling down rural indebtedness. The Boards were abolished in 1942.[19]

The first bold legislative attempt at compulsory reduction of rural indebtedness was the Madras Agriculturists Relief Act, 1938. It cancelled all arrears of interest outstanding on agricultural debts on 1st October, 1937, (defined as post depression debts) and fixed for the future a maximum rate of £ 6 percent interest for all agricultural loans. But the unfavourable reaction of the creditors coupled -with the judicial decisions on the question rendered the Act almost ineffective. The Madras Pawn-Brokers Act, 1943, required the money lenders in pawn broking business to obtain a license and charge a rate of interest not exceeding the statutorily fixed rate. Even this Act did not succeed in regulating money lending business as it did not require all those engaged in money lending to be registered, its provisions covering only the pawnbrokers. It is, therefore, evident that legislative action did not effectively curb the activities of the money lenders or reduce the volume of rural indebtedness. The only alternative appeared to be the strengthening of institutional, credit through co-operatives and commercial banks and rendering the process of obtaining loans from them simpler and the rates of interest lower.[20]

Joint Stock Banks: The proportion of borrowings from commercial banks is very low in Anantapur district. The All-India Rural Credit Survey conducted in the neighbouring districts of Kurnool and Cuddapah revealed that the proportion of borrowings from commercial banks in these districts was 0.4 percent and 0.3 percent respectively as against 0.9 percent for the country as a whole. In fact, the modern bank is of comparatively recent origin, the earliest of the branches of commercial banks having been opened in this district only during the late 1930's. The State Bank of India (then known as the Imperial Bank of India), the Vysya Bank, the Syndicate Bank (till recently known as the Canara Industrial and Banking Syndicate) and the erstwhile Rayalaseema Bank were the first to extend the sphere of their activities to this district in the years preceding the Second World War. The other banks opened their branches in the district only after 1950. Till its amalgamation with the Indian Bank during 1961, the Rayalaseema Bank had its registered office at Anantapur right from the date of its incorporation in 1939. None of the commercial banks has now its main or registered office in this district. The branch offices of the banks are spread all over the district and except Kalyandurg and Madakasira, all the taluks have at least one branch office of a commercial bank. All the offices of these banks are, however, located in the urban areas. The following is the list of banks established in the district before independence:

1. Anantapur
   - (a) Indian Bank (1939)
   - (b) State Bank of India (1937)
   - (c) Syndicate Bank (1941)
2. Hindupur
   - (a) Syndicate Bank (1937)
   - (b) Vysya Bank (1935)
3. Kadiri
   - (a) Vysya Bank (1943)
4. Tadpatri
   - (a) State Bank of India (1935)
   - (b) Syndicate Bank (1936)

More than half the total numbers of branches are functioning at Guntakal, Anantapur, Hindupur and Tadpatri, which are the most important commercial centres of the district. But their field is only confined to commercial and trade sectors as the degree of industrial development in the district is not very high.

Co-operative Credit Societies and Banks: Anantapur is one of the earliest districts to take advantage of the co-operative movement as a remedy for rural indebtedness. The history of the movement in the district dates back to 1905, the year following the enactment of the Co-operative Credit Societies Act of 1904. The earliest society to be started was the Bukkapatnam Co-operative Society registered on 29th July, 1905. By the end of the Co-operative year 1906-07, there were six societies in the district. Most of these early societies came into existence for providing credit facilities and it was only after the passing of the Co-operative Societies Act of 1912 that the noncredit side of the movement secured recognition. The evolution of the movement in the district falls into six broad phases. From 1906-07 to 1917-18 there was a gradual rise in the number of societies registered. During this period, Anantapur alone accounted for 197 out of 354 societies in the entire Rayalaseema and this was mainly attributed to "the enthusiasm of a few Revenue Officers."[21]

From 1918-19 to 1928-29 there was a rapid expansion of the movement largely as a result of the rise in the level of agricultural prices after the close of the First World War. The total number of societies in the district at the end of this period rose to 525. Most of them were unlimited liability agricultural credit societies with inadequate share capital. They were, therefore, borrowing from some of the bigger societies like the Madras Provincial Co-operative Bank. The necessity for a district financing institution was realised and the Anantapur District Co-operative Central Bank was started in 1919 for financing the primary societies.

The third phase extending from 1929-30 to 1936-37, coincides with the great economic depression. Prices of agricultural commodities fell sharply during this period and many of the co-operatives became victims to the prevailing crisis. Several of them were either working at a loss or had become dormant. Many were liquidated as a result of the policy of consolidation and reconstruction then pursued by the Co-operative Department. Their total number therefore declined to 481 by 1936-37. It was during this period that the Madras Co-operative Societies Act of 1932 was passed to remedy the defects in the Act of 1912. As the rural credit societies could not provide long term finance, the co-operative land mortgage banks came on the scene during the twenties of this century. A separate Act for regulating the working and development of land mortgage banks was passed in 1934. It was in 1935 that the first land mortgage bank was started in this district.[22]

The next phase extending from 1936-37 to 1947-48 was marked by a gradual increase in the number of societies. This was mainly due to the rise in agricultural prices caused by the Second World War. However, the credit side of the movement suffered a setback and it never recovered from the throes of depression of the earlier quinquennium except for a short span of three years from 1936-37 to 1938-39.

Between 1938-39 and 1944-45, the number of agricultural credit societies declined from 414 to 382. The business of the remaining societies (98) had, however, showed a marginal improvement their loan disbursements having slightly increased. The Government of the erstwhile Madras Presidency appointed in

1945 the Rayalaseema Co-operative Enquiry Committee to examine and report inter alia on the working of the cooperatives in the Rayalaseema area and to make suggestions for their improvement. Following the recommendations of the Committee there was a large scale conversion of credit societies into multipurpose societies. The central financing agency in the district was strengthened by grants and subsidies besides other forms of State aid.

The Anantapur District Co-operative Central Bank [established on 3rd February1919], is the premier co-operative institution in the district. During the early decades of its existence, the bank had a rather chequered history. It started functioning with 76 individuals and 160 society members and a paid-up share capital of Rs 22,965. It made steady progress till the onset of the great economic depression which not only hampered its further expansion but also adversely affected the financial position of the societies affiliated to it. Even in the post-depression period, the bank did not make any marked strides in regard to the expansion of either its internal resources or its loan operations. By 1940, there was deterioration in its working owing to the accumulation of over dues and the administration of the bank, which till then was vested in an elected board of management, was entrusted to a nominated board. But even this did not remedy the situation and the bank continued to be under a cloud. In 1944, its management was superseded and a special officer was appointed. The normal constitution of the bank was restored in 1946 and since then an elected board of management has been administering its affairs.

Consequent on the recommendations of the Rayalaseema Co-operative Enquiry Committee, 1945, lump sum grants were provided to the central banks in Rayalaseema to wipe off their unrealisable debts from both living and liquidated societies. The policy of reorganisation and development of the co-operatives continued after independence.

Primary Agricultural Credit Societies: The primary agricultural credit societies are the most wide-spread type of co-operatives in the district under colonial rule. They obtain their funds chiefly by way of borrowings from the Central Bank. Each society is organised on the collective guarantee of its members on the basis of unlimited liability and limited dividends. Credit is obtained on the joint security of members who are generally the residents of one village. These societies issue loans and undertake several multipurpose non-credit functions such as the supply of agricultural, industrial and domestic requirements of their members. During the Second World War, when rationing and controls were in force, some of these societies undertook the purchase and distribution of essential commodities. The co-operative credit society at Bukkapatnam is the earliest to be started in the district. The rates of interest for borrowing and lending money are $4^{1/2}$ and $6^{1/2}$ percent respectively. Figure 4.3 presents the growth of Primary Agricultural Credit Societies in Anantapur district.

Figure-4.3
Growth of Total number of Agricultural Cooperative Societies

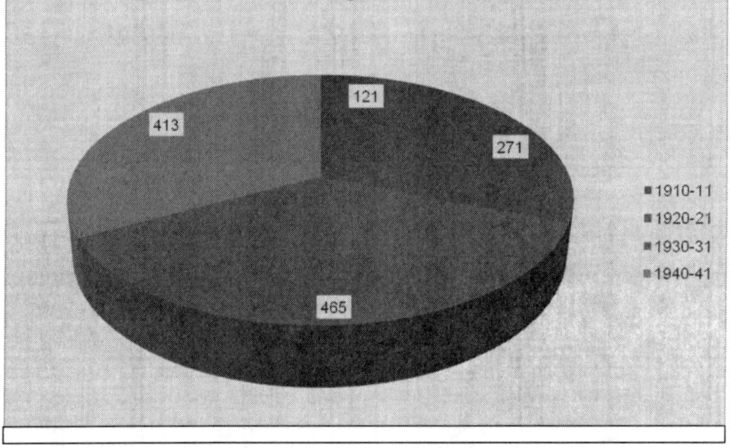

The details connected with the regard to financial position of primary agricultural credit societies in the district from 1910-11 to 1940-41 are given in Table 4.6.

At the end of June, 1941, their total membership was 18,000 while their paid-up share capital was Rs 2.67 lakh. The volume of loans issued by them was about Rs 0.79 lakh, while an amount of Rs 10.55 lakh was outstanding from members. They have borrowed from the Central Bank to the tune of Rs 2.05 lakh. The net profit they earned was Rs 70,0.27 lakh.

Table 4.6: Financial Position of Primary Agricultural Credit Societies (Unlimited Liability) in Anantapur District

(Amounts in lakhs of rupees)

Year	Total number of members	Paid-up share capital	Loans from Central Bank	Total working capital	Amount of loans disbursed during the year	Amount of loans outstanding against members	Profit earned	Loss incurred
1910-11	N.A.	0.12	1.59	N.A. '	2.4	4.02	0.08	Nil
1920-21	15,725	0.78	4.7	11.09	3.51	9.26	0.07	0.26
1930-31	23,803	1.96	1.02	20.12	1.72	16.45	0.25	1.19
1940-41	18,000	2.67	2.05	15.14	0.79	10.55	0.27	N.A.

Source: Report of the Economist for enquiry into rural indebtedness, 1946.

Land Mortgage Banks: The land mortgage banks, started in 1925, are the primary co-operative agencies for the disbursement of long-term finance to agriculturists. Their development in the early years was confined largely to areas in the Presidency which were either wet or irrigated dry. No attempt was made for many years to start any land mortgage banks in this district as it was considered to be a predominantly dry unirrigated tract. The first of the banks to be established was the one at Dharmavaram registered in 1935. Five primary land mortgage banks were functioning in the district in clearly demarcated areas at the end of June, 1964.[23]

Currency and Coinage: Little is known about the coinage of the ancient kings and chiefs who held sway over this district. The numerous political changes that have convulsed this part of the country led to the circulation of a variety of coins. Among the coins discovered are the golden 'pagodas' and 'half pagodas' of the Vijayanagara rulers and their subordinates known as the 'Krishnaraya', the 'Achutaraya' and the 'Venkatapathi' pagodas. The Venkatapathi pagoda was in circulation in the Rayadurg taluk even at the time of Munro. During the period of the Muslim rule in the district, the Mohammed Shahi, the Alamgir and the Jammalamadugu pagodas came into circulation. The Maharatta conquerors had also introduced their own coins known as the Gooty Mohammed Shahi, the Subbarayi and the Tadipatri pagodas. During the conquests of Hyder and Tipu, the district was flooded with the Mysore currency of Bahaduri and Sultani pagodas from the mints of Srirangapatnam and Mysore. The former in particular minted pagodas at Gooty in imitation of the coin of Murari Rao Ghorpade as a reissue of the earlier Mughal pagodas. Whether the Vijayanagar rulers issued silver and copper coins is not known but those that were in circulation before the advent of the British consisted almost entirely of rupees and fanams made of silver and introduced from the Nizam's dominions, Mysore and Arcot. Sir Thomas Munro noted that in 1806 the currency consisted of 32 different kinds of pagodas and 15 of Rupees. They are chiefly local, having been issued by Nawabs, Rajas and Poligars. Their value is constantly fluctuating, sometimes 12 percent is lost on taking them to a neighbouring taluk. In Rayadurg the Venkatapati Pagoda is commonest, while in Gurramconda the ryots will not look at it. This of course obstructs commercial dealings and imposes a heavy tax on the country."[24] Even during Munro's time, the jamabandi was settled in 'Kantarayi Pagodas' in the absence of a single coin in general circulation. The rupee became the standard unit of value and the medium of exchange under the British and its value came to be reckoned in terms of shillings and pence in this district as in the rest of the country.

Trade and Commerce: The district had a hoary past in the field of trade and commerce. Goods of various kinds were exported to distant places and even countries far beyond. The Athavana Tantram records that ghee, oil and tobacco were exported, obtained in large quantities from Dharmavaram in this district, to neighbouring countries. Similarly cloth, silk fabric manufactured at Dharmavaram, Tadpatri, Gutti etc., and black pulses growing in these localities were also sent to places like Srirangapattanam in the South where they were sold at relatively higher rates.

The pattern of trade and commerce in the district is mainly agro-biased. Its manufactures are few, meant mostly to meet local demand. Commerce sustains only about four percent of the total population of the district whereas over seventy-five percent depend on agriculture. Whatever trade is carried on in the district is mostly in the form of collection of its agricultural produce for purposes of export and in the distribution of the imported commodities in which it is deficient. Commercial crops like groundnut, cotton, jaggery and tamarind are of great importance in the economy of the district from the point of view of its export trade. The district is usually deficient in food grains and their imports are vital especially during years when crops suffer due to failure of rains. But in years when rains are timely and sufficient it even exports food grains. A real impetus is given to its trading activity by the sale of its commercial crops which bring the cultivator liquid funds all the year round. It is this aspect of its commercial life that gives a monetary character to its economy. Most of the big traders of the district are Vaisyas. Many of them are also engaged in retail trade. People belonging to other castes like Kapus, Balijas and Lingayats and some Muslims are also found engaged in wholesale and retail trade. The important commodities of export from the district are groundnut (kernels, oil and cake), cotton and cotton seed, tamarind, jaggery, horsegram, handloom and silk cloth, hides and skins and onions. The principal imports into the district are food grains, pulses, sugar, chillies, wheat, cotton textiles, coffee seeds, turmeric, coconuts and coconut oil, salt, coal, petroleum and its products, machinery and spare parts thereof, hardware goods, timber, cosmetics and consumer goods.[25]

Weights and Measures: Very scanty information is available about the ancient system of weights and measures. The little we gather from the inscriptions of the district is also not very helpful because of our ignorance of the equivalent values for the measures mentioned. Some area measures such as 'maruttu', 'mattar', 'khanduga', 'kolaga', 'hala', 'putti', 'edumu' and 'tumu' were adopted but it is now difficult to specify their corresponding modern equivalents. The custom in ancient days was to define an area of land in terms of the quantity of grain that was needed for sowing it or the quantity of produce it was expected to yield.

As regards the weights and measures that were in use about the year 1905, W. Francis gives the following account in his Anantapur District Gazetteer.

"The weights and measures in popular use frequently differ in a bewildering manner from taluk to taluk and even from village to village, and consequently all that will here be attempted is to give some account, based on a report kindly furnished by the Collector of the values of them which are more generally accepted."[26]

Table 4.7: The ordinary table of weights

21 tolas (of .4114 of an ounce)	= 1 seer.
11/2 seer	= 1 sava seer.
2 sava seers	= 1 adi seer (3 seers).
2 adi seers	= 2 panch seer (6 seers).
12 Seers	= 1 dhadiyam,
4 dhadiyams	= 1 maund (25.92 lbs),

Source: Anantapur District Gazetteer-1905.

It is said that the reason is, why a weight of six seers is called panch seer, which literally means 'five seers', is that the old maund weighed 40 seers instead of 48 as at present. The panch seer was then equal to five seers or one-eighth of a maund. In 1812 the Collector changed the weight of the seer from 2-5 to 21 tolas and that of the maund to 48 seers, and one-eighth of this new maund was still called 'panch seer', though it now weighed six seers. The same explanation accounts for the names adi seer and sava seer. There are also the chatak, or one-sixteenth of a seer, the ara pavu, or one-eighth of a seer, the pavu, or one-quarter of a seer and the a Vaseer, or half seer. A seer of gold or silver weighs, as elsewhere, 24 tolas.

Transport and Communication Development:

Roads: The roads of the district are a creation of the last half of the nineteenth century. Writing in 1852 Major R. Henderson, C.B., then Civil Engineer in charge of this part of the country, said that

"Roads there none deserve the name. There certainly are tracks through some parts marked out by aloe and milk-bush hedges, but from want of bridges and drains these tracks are divided into isolated portions by the rivers that intersect them. There is not a single arched bridge throughout the district, though it is intersected by rivers and streams in every direction. The District is actually locked up from the surrounding provinces and without means either for the export of its produce or for the introduction of European articles of commerce."[27]

The state of even the main lines of road was so execrable as to compel the use of bullocks generally for the transport of traffic. For the minor roads throughout an area of nearly 13,000 square miles the maintenance allowance was only Rs 650, or about nine pies per square mile, per annum. The carts in use had small solid wheels, made of flat circular pieces of wood or stone, and the axles revolved with the wheels. Even in 1855 it was stated that wheels with spokes were only just 'coming into general use'. Solid stone and wooden wheels are now restricted to the temple cars and the carts used for transporting stone, and the axles of these latter are usually of iron and no longer revolve with the wheels.

Extension during famines: The construction of roads received a great impetus during the famines of 1866 and 1876. In a district which contained so few tanks or irrigation channels the making of roads formed almost the only possible relief-work. In the 1876 famine alone, Rs 56 lakh was expended on new roads and Rs 12 lakh on repairs to existing lines in the Bellary and Anantapur districts. Owing to circumstances which prevail in every famine, the worth of the work obtained for these large sums was, however, much less than if it had been expended 10 under normal conditions, and it has been calculated that the value of roads. the labour on the new roads was only eleven lakhs and of that on the repairs only three lakhs.[28]

Conditions in 1930: The provisions of the various Local Funds Acts prescribing the Levy of a cess for the upkeep of communications have rendered it possible to find funds to more or less regularly maintain the roads which were then, and have been since, constructed. The principal difficulty is the scarcity of water for the consolidation of the metal and gravel applied to the roads. In Hindupur and Madakasira taluks additional obstacles are the inferiority of the metal available and the high rates of wages which obtain.

The south of Tadipatri and the west of Dharmavaram taluks are still inaccessible in wet weather and the road from Anantapur to Kalyandurg is dilapidated. Generally speaking (thanks in a large measure to the hardness of the surface soil in most of the taluks) the roads are in a better condition than in neighbouring districts, but the drawback to them as means of communication is the absence of bridges over the rivers and the many nullahs and streams which cross them.

Scarcity of the bridges: Just as the strength of a chain is that of its weakest link, so the possibility of a road depends much upon the condition of its worst parts. The exertion required to pull carts through sandy or swampy stream beds and up the steep approaches which often lead to them is not made up to the bullocks by the fact that the roads on either side of them are in good condition, and it is little consolation to a driver whose cart has upset, to the complete ruin of its contents, in one of these sloughs of despond, to find that the road beyond the obstruction is in excellent repair. The Penner runs through the district for about 130 miles, but it is nowhere either bridged or provided with a causeway, and except along the Secunderabad-Bangalore road culverts over the lesser water-courses are rarities. The only ferry which is at all regularly maintained is that across the Penner at Tadipatri. During the rains cart traffic is consequently often entirely stopped for days together, while foot-passengers have to cross the bigger streams by the hazardous method of placing their clothes and possessions in a large earthenware pot and then swimming over clinging to the top of this vessel.[29]

Chief Metalled Roads: The map shows the various lines of communication in the district. The three chief metalled roads are (a) that which runs across the whole of its northern portion from Bellary through Gadekallu, Gooty and Tadipatri and on into Cuddapah; (b) the Secunderabad-Bangalore road which traverses the district from north to south from Kurnool district through Gooty, Anantapur, Penukonda and Kodikonda to Mysore State; and (c) the road which crosses it from north-west to south-east, entering it from Bellary near Vidapanakallu in Gooty taluk and running past Uravakonda, through Anantapur and on into the Kadiri taluk of Cuddapah district. No other roads are metalled throughout. Along some of them the worst portions are given a certain amount of metal but the others are repaired with gravel alone.

Avenues: There are fewer miles of avenues along the roadsides in Anantapur than in any other district but Bellary and the exceptional case of the Nilgiris. A good deal has been done in recent years, but the want of water is a great obstacle in many places and though the heat of the sun in the hot weather is probably as severe in the Deccan as in any other part of the Presidency more than half the roads maintained are without avenues and there are long stretches with only a few self-sown babul trees on their margins, under which insufficient protection the cart men may be seen trying in vain to shelter themselves and their animals during their midday halt.

There is also a marked scarcity of topes at the regular halting places, especially in the northern half of the district and at many of these cart-drivers have to halt in the open and there are no good trees under which a tent can be pitched. Guntakal, Uravakonda, Pamidi, Dharmavaram and Nayampalle are a few cases in point. The Local Boards keep up fifteen choultries for, the use of native travellers. Except the Munro choultry at Gooty, none of these have any endowment. No fees are levied in any of them, except that at the Jubilee chattram at Tadipatri a charge of one anna a day is made for the use of certain rooms which are of a class superior to the others.[30]

Railways:

The western portions of Anantapur have still to depend upon roads. The north and centre of Anantapur are traversed by two railways which meet at the important junction of Guntakal in the north-west corner of the district. From this point other lines radiate to Bellary and the south of the Bombay Presidency, to the Nizam's Dominions and Bombay itself and to Bezwada. This last railway is especially useful in time of scarcity as it connects the district with the fertile deltas of the Krishna and Godavari. The western part of Anantapur is not connected with railway lines but still depends on road transport only.

The Madras Railway: The railway which traverses the northern part of the district is the North-west line of the Madras Railway. It runs from Madras through Tadipatri and Gooty to Guntakal junction and is on the standard gauge. The section as far as Tadipatri was opened to traffic in September 1868. In the next year the line was carried on to Gooty and in 1870 to Guntakal and beyond. It crosses the Penner on a bridge of thirteen spans of 131 feet each.[31]

The Southern Mahratta Railway: The line which passes through the centre of the district is a branch of the Southern Mahratta Railway. It runs from Guntakal junction southwards through Pamidi, Anantapur, Dharmavaram, Penukonda and Hindupur and thence through the Mysore State to Bangalore. It is on the metre gauge and was opened as far as Dharmavaram in March 1892 and up to the Mysore frontier in September 1893. Some of the earthwork for it was done as a relief work in the famine of 1884-85. The section is altogether 119 miles in length. The Penner is crossed near Pamidi on a bridge of eleven spans of 150 feet each.[32]

The South Indian Railway: At Dharmavaram the railway line is joined by the branch of the South Indian Railway which runs from Pakala in North Arcot through the upland western taluks of Cuddapah. This is also on the metre gauge and it was opened on the 1st March 1892, the same date on which the Guntakal-Dharmavaram railway section started working.

The native industry in the district was ruined by massive imports of cheap textiles from England. Home spinning, which was a spare-time activity of village women, was greatly reduced. A large proportion of village hand-loom weavers were displaced, though many switched to using factory instead of home-spun yarn. British imports entered India duty free, and when a small tariff was required for revenue purposes Lancashire pressure led to the imposition of a corresponding excise duty on Indian products to prevent them gaining a competitive advantage. This undoubtedly handicapped industrial development in the district. The banking system gave little help to industry and technical education was poor. Foreign banks held over three-quarters of total deposits, Indian Joint Stock Banks less than one-fourth. The indigenous banking houses were largely pushed out by British.

REFERENCES

1. Venkanna, Agricultural Implements Allied Publishers, New Delhi, 1975, p. 89.
2. Captain, R. V. Littlewood, Livestock of Southern India, N.D.A., D.A.S. A. I. R.C, p. 23.
3. Rao Narayana D., Survey of Cottage Industries in Anantapur District by p. 41.
4. Havell, E.B., Report on the Arts and Industries of certain districts of Madras Presidency p. 18.
5. *Ibid.*, p. 72.
6. Dutt, N.V.B.S., Mineral Resources in Ceded Districts of Andhra Pradesh, p. 15.

7. Ball, "Economic Geology of India", Cosmos book limited, 1987, p. 30.
8. Narayanaswamy, S., Report on the preliminary investigation of Ramagiri Gold Fields 1958, p. 2.
9. Thurston Monograph of the Silk Fabric Industry in Madras Presidency p. 19.
10. *Ibid.*, p. 21.
11. Vcnkatararaanayya, Studies in the History of the Third Dynasty, p. 71.
12. *Ibid.*, p. 74.
13. Report of the Madras Provincial Banking Enquiry Committee, 1930, Vol. I, p. 32.
14. Report of the Rayalaseema Co-operative Enquiry Committee, 1945-46.
15. Report of the Economist for enquiry into rural indebtedness, 1946.
16. Report of the All India Rural Credit Survey, Vol. I, p. 51
17. Krishna Swami, S.Y., Rural Problems in Madras, 1939, p. 21.
18. Statistical Altas Madras Presidency, 1940-41, p. 59.
19. Routes in the Madras Presidency 1879 and 1904, p25.
20. Venkataramanayya, N., *op. cit.,* p. 73.
21. *Ibid.*, p. 74.
22. Srinivasa Raghavachariar, Memorandum on the Progress of the Madras Presidency during the last forty years of British Administration 1893, p. 9.
23. *Ibid.*, p. 10.
24. *Ibid.*, p. 11.
25. *Ibid.*, p. 12.
26. Boag, G.T., The Madras Presidency, 1881-1931, p. 17.
27. Vipen, A., Scheme of Road Development for the Madras Presidency. 1935, p. 28.
28. Proposals for the Economic Development of the Rayalaseema, 1948, p. 62.
29. Times of India Year Book, 1894, p. 2.
30. Bayley's Memorandum on Weights and Measures (1857), p. 23.
31. Papers from the Records at the East India House, Vol. I to IV.
32. Appa Rao, G.V., The Annals of Handeh Anantapuram, p. 82.

5

Development of Local Self-Government

The concept of Local Self-Government was age old governing system. Even before the rule Vijayanagara dynasty, the local assemblies called as "Urs" transacted all public business on behalf of the people inhabiting the villages. In the 'Brahmadaya' villages or 'agraharams', however, assemblies known as the 'Sabhas' were functioning not merely as agencies for collecting taxes but were also redressing public grievances and exercising judicial powers. But the pattern of Local Administration in the Madras Presidency did not receive any statutory basis till the enactment of the Towns Improvement Act X, 1865 and the Local Funds Act IV, 1871. However, a fund was raised in 1854 for being spent on district roads by the Collector and the District Engineer under the supervision of the Board of Revenue. To augment the fund, rents on ferries; carts and grasses and the proceeds of avenue tree clippings were added to it. The surplus proceeds of the cattle pound fund raised from 1860, and tolls and fishery rents collected from 1864 were also credited to it. The Education Cess Act VI of 1863, passed for the maintenance of schools, failed completely in its object as adequate funds could not be raised and it was realised that it was impossible for Government to bear the burden of maintenance of schools and construction and repair of roads all over the Presidency without recourse to local taxation.

Local Fund Boards:

The Towns Improvement Act X of 1865 and the Local Funds Act of 1871 created Municipalities and Local Fund Boards respectively in the Presidency. They were essentially designed to establish a common fund to meet the expenditure on Roads, Education and Public Health and Sanitation. The Local Funds Act of 1871 which provided for such taxation, divided the whole Presidency into a number of Circles and constituted a Local Fund Board for each of them. It repealed the Education Cess Act of 1863 and the District Road Cess Act of 1866 and transferred the existing funds and the charges appertaining to roads and schools to the newly constituted Local Fund Boards. It also provided for the levy of house tax, of a cess similar to the district roads cess limited to a maximum of one anna in the rupee on the annual rental value of occupied lands and of tolls on roads. Local Fund Boards were authorised to spend the proceeds of these taxes on the maintenance of roads; upkeep of schools; construction and repair of hospitals, dispensaries, choultries, markets, tanks and wells; training and employment of vaccinators; carrying out of sanitary inspection; and cleaning of roads and streets.[1]

The district of Bellary of which Anantapur was then a part was divided into three Circles. Tadipatri, Gooty, Anantapur, Alur and Adoni taluks (the last two now in Kurnool district) constituted the first Circle; Hindupur, Penukonda and Madakasira formed the second; and Rayadurg, Bellary and Hospet constituted the third. Kadiri was then a part of the Madanapalle Circle in Cuddapah district. On the formation of the Anantapur district in 1882, the three Local Fund Circles were converted into two, one coterminous with Bellary and the other with Anantapur. The Anantapur Circle Board consisted of 40 members—nineteen officials and twenty-one non-officials. The resources of the Board during this period were very limited as would be evident from the fact that, on the day of its formation, it opened with a credit balance of Rs 54,396 under

Road and Rs 20,270 under General Funds.[2] The income of the Board consisted chiefly of land cess, ferry rents, tolls, bungalow fees, income from the sale of rubbish, etc., besides provincial grants and the contributions for specific purposes. Revenue from fishery rents, the sale of clippings from avenue trees, and fines and penalties were the other sources of income.

To strengthen the non-official element of the local bodies, the Madras Local Boards Act V of 1884 was passed repealing the Act IV of 1871. It provided for the constitution of a District Board at the district level, a Taluk Board at the taluk or divisional level and a Union Board for a village or for a group of villages. The District Board so formed, consisted of a President and not less than twenty-four members, wholly appointed by the Governor-in-Council or partly appointed and partly elected by the members of Taluk Boards. Their term of office was three years. The Collector and the Revenue Divisional Officers were ex-officio members of the Board. The number of official members appointed by the Governor-in-Council together with the ex-officio members should not exceed one-fourth of the membership of the Board. The President of the Board might be elected from among its members whose term of office was three years. The Board was empowered to levy any of the taxes authorised by the new Act with the approval of Government. The Anantapur District Board was constituted in 1885 with 24 members, six of whom were officials and the rest non-officials. All the members were initially appointed by Government. The receipts of the Board in that year amounted to Rs 1,10,635 of which Rs 1,00,278 was derived from land cess, Rs 3,072 from tolls, Rs 5,078 from market rents, Rs 2,050 from choultries and the balance from other sources. Its expenditure was chiefly on the execution of new works and repairs to existing works amounting to Rs 50,209 followed by Rs 27,820 on hospitals and dispensaries, vaccination, sanitation markets, choultries and bungalows, Rs 12,239 on education and Rs 14,320 on administration. There were three toll gates at Gooty, Penukonda and Kalyandurg. The length of village roads maintained by the Board was 253 miles.[3] It ran a Normal School and two Middle Schools (one at Penukonda and another at Tadipatri). The Board also maintained seven dispensaries one each at Gooty, Tadipatri, Kalyandurg, Uravakonda, Penukonda, Hindupur and Dharmavaram. Besides, there were 14 chatrams and sixteen bungalows under its management.

Taluk Boards:

Taluk Boards were formed for each taluk or a group of taluks with a President and not less than twelve members, partly appointed and partly elected by the members of the Union Boards or by the tax-payers themselves. Their term of office was three years. The jurisdiction of these Taluk Boards coincided with that of the Revenue Divisional Officers who were made ex-officio members and Presidents of these Boards. The funds of the Taluk Boards consisted of one-half of the proceeds of the land cess levied by the District Board in the Taluk Boards area, fees such as license fee for markets and rents on choultries, fisheries and ferries. With the approval of Government, the District Board could transfer a portion of its funds to the Taluk Board. The Taluk Boards were formed in this district in October, 1886. They maintained 37 markets and seven dispensaries and of the 16 endowed institutions in their charge (of the Local Boards) 15 were markets. Again, Union Boards were constituted for single villages or groups of villages called Unions, with not less than five members, wholly appointed or partly elected, the headmen of the villages constituting the Union being ex-officio members. One of these headmen was to be the Chairman of the Board and the term of office of its members was three years. The proceeds of the house-tax levied within the area of the Union, varying from four annas to five rupees, constituted the main source of revenue for these Boards.[4] Nine Unions were ordered to be formed in the district in December, 1885 and they started functioning in October 1886. The Unions so formed were those at Gooty, Uravakonda, Tadipatri, Kalyandurg, Dharmavaram, Bukkapatnam, Penukonda, Hindupur and Madakasira. Pamidi was constituted into a Union in 1887 and Yadiki in 1889.

Till 1920, the history of local boards in the district is one of changes in the jurisdiction of Taluk Boards, an increase in the quantum of elected representatives and the creation of more Unions. But there was no change in the functions of these Boards. In practice provision was made to elect one-half of the members of the District Board by means of executive orders. By 1889, there were five non-official members on the District Board elected from the Taluk Boards of Anantapur, Gooty and Hindupur. Three were ex-officio members and 12 (three official and nine non-official) were nominated. In 1891, Government which had hitherto encouraged the Boards to maintain Teachers' Training Schools veered round to the view that Government should maintain these institutions in the interest of efficiency. In 1895-96, the Taluk Boards of Penukonda and Anantapur were reconstituted the former with Penukonda, Hindupur, Madakasira and Dharmavaram taluks and the latter with Anantapur and the newly formed Kalyandurg taluk. Consequently, the Hindupur Board ceased to function. By 1896, all the Unions were levying house tax at fth of the maximum rates prescribed. The imposition of this tax was the subject of popular resentment. The people of Dharmavaram were reported to have protested against its levy and its collection was consequently hampered. The Unions had what was known as a 'Ward system' for supervising sanitation and enforcing other health measures. In 1898, the Local Boards Act was amended as a result of which the Governor could nominate a non-official as the President of a Local Board. The responsibility for the opening and maintenance of relief works in times of famine and scarcity also devolved on the District Board. By 1900, the District Board was levying a land cess of one anna per rupee of assessment. Its income was derived from land cess, house tax, tolls, market rents, sale proceeds of avenue tree clippings and the contribution from provincial funds. It utilised its receipts for starting new works, and for looking after communications, education, medical services, vaccination, sanitation and the maintenance of markets and choultries. In 1900, it maintained five hospitals and five dispensaries.[5]

The average local taxation was two annas and six pies per head in 1900. During this year the Local Boards Act was amended prescribing a procedure for the removal of the President, Vice-President or any member from office. In 1902-03, the Presidents of the respective Boards were declared to be members of the Boards over which they presided. During the next year the rate of house tax in Unions was raised to the maximum permissible under the Act. In 1905- 06 the strength of Kalyandurg Union Panchayat was reduced from 12 to 10. The Royal Commission on Decentralisation whose report was published in 1909 recommended that the village panchayats should be wholly elective and that there should be elected majorities in both the Taluq and' District Boards. In 1909, the privilege of having an elected Vice-President was conferred on the Gooty Taluk Board. In 1909-10, the number of members constituting the taluk boards of Anantapur and Gooty was raised from 13 to 15. Consequent on the addition of the Kadiri taluk to the Anantapur district in 1911, the strength of the District Board was raised from 25 to 32. The Taluk Boards were also regrouped and their number was raised to four in place of the existing three. They were located at Gooty, Anantapur, Dharmavaram and Penukonda. The Dharmavaram and Penukonda Boards had a strength of 15 each, while the others had a strength of 13 each. In 1912, the maximum elective strength of Taluk Boards was raised from 1/3 to 1/2 and the total number of elected seats in all of them became 30.[6]

For the first time a non-official was appointed in 1914 as the President of the Anantapur Taluk Board. During the same year, Amarapuram was constituted into a Union. In 1916, Guntakal and Timmancherla were constituted into a single Union. In 1918, a resolution was passed by the Government of India declaring that the local bodies should have a substantial elected majority and the system of nomination should be restricted only to secure the necessary representation of minorities. During the same year, Konakondla, Singanamala and Yellanur were also constituted as Unions and Beluguppa in 1919. It was in this year that the Penukonda incomplete Secondary School and the first grade Elementary Schools at Uravakonda, Kalyandurg and Tadipatri were upgraded into high schools. In the next year the Penukonda Taluk Board took over the incomplete Edward Coronation Secondary School at Hindupur and upgraded it to a high school. The principle of election was employed on a larger scale in the Local Boards during the year 1919-20. The number of elected seats on the District Boards was raised from 16 to 24 and two-thirds of the strength of the Taluk Boards was made elective. In 1919, a nonofficial Vice-President was appointed to the District Board and non-official Presidents to the Gooty and Penukonda Boards. In the next year the Anantapur Taluk Board was given the right of electing its President and the strength of the Gooty Taluk Board was raised from 15 to 24 to make provision for the representation of minorities and depressed classes. There were in this year 18 Unions in the district, of which nine were classified as major Unions. The right of electing their Chairman was extended to the Unions at Uravakonda, Guntakal, Bukkapatnam, Dharmavaram and Kadiri. The financial position of the District and Taluk Boards, on the eve of the enactment of the Local Boards Act V of 1920, is given in the following table:

Table 5.1: Financial Position of the District and Taluk Boards

Particulars	**Receipts during 1919-20 (Rs)**	**Total receipts including amounts from the Previous Year (Rs)**	**Charges**
District Board	1,80,457	3,63,072	2,46,555
Gooty Taluk Board	1,04,884	1,85,040	1,73,045
Anantapur Taluk Board	66,411	1,09,643	1,08,236
Dharmavaram Taluk Board	56,233	1,02,474	1,00,348
Penukonda Taluk Board	1,34,505	1,99,356	1,47,279

Source: The Madras Presidency, 1881-1931, by G.T. Boag, p. 28.

The District Board spent Rs 1,87,753 on education and Rs 83,834 on sanitation. It maintained five secondary schools, 359 elementary schools, four hospitals, eight dispensaries and 895 miles of roads.

The passing of the Local Boards Act XIV of 1920 constituted the next important landmark in the sphere of Local Administration. This Act gave an independent status to different classes of local boards and enhanced not only their strength but also the proportion of their elected members, their resources and their powers. The strength of the District Board was fixed at a maximum of 52 and a minimum of 24, that of the Taluk Board at a maximum of 24 and a minimum of 12 and that of the Union Board at 15 and seven respectively. The proportion of members to be elected in all these boards was to be not less than three-fourths of their total strength. Their tenure was fixed at three years. The Collector and the Revenue Divisional Officers ceased to be Presidents and ex-officio members. The Presidents of the District and the Taluk Boards became ex-officio members of the District and the Taluk Boards respectively. The Presidents of the Taluk Boards also became ex-officio members of the District Board. In addition to the land cess of one anna in the rupee shared equally by the District and the Taluk Boards, they were also given the option to levy an additional land cess of three pies in the rupee. The imposition of three new taxes—the profession tax, the companies' tax and the pilgrims tax—was also authorised. Local Boards became autonomous and interference by Government was confined only to cases of emergency or mal-administration. Inspectors were appointed to supervise the work of Local Boards and Municipal Councils.

The Local Boards Act of 1920 was brought into force from 1st April, 1921 in Anantapur District Board. Consequently, the number of elected and ex-officio members of the Board was raised from 24 to 28 while the number of nominated members fell from 12 to eight members. The President who was nominated is from nonofficial and there was no direct election to the District Board. The District Board was maintained and supervised 1,040 miles of roads, five rest houses, 281 Boys' and 61 Girls' Elementary Schools, five Secondary Schools, two hospitals and 10 dispensaries, 27 weekly markets, a cart-stand, 11 slaughter houses and 17 main and two sub-toll gates. Land cess was levied at one anna in the rupee of assessment and the District Board levied an additional cess of two paise per rupee. During 1923-24 the strength of the District Board was fixed at 36 consisting of 28 elected and eight nominated members. In the subsequent year, the strength remained the same but there were 24 elected, four ex-officio and eight nominated members. The District Board was granted the privilege of electing its president in 1926. Diwan Bahadur P. Kesava Pillai was not only the first non-official nominated as President but also he was the first elected President.[7]

The reconstituted Taluk Boards came into being in July, 1922. There were four Taluk Boards namely Anantapur comprising

Anantapur and Kalyandurg taluks, Gooty including Gooty and Tadipatri taluks, Penukonda extending over Penukonda, Hindupur and Madakasira taluks and Dharmavaram covering Dharmavaram and Kadiri taluks. The jurisdiction of these Taluk Boards corresponded to the revenue divisions of the district and their members were directly elected. All the Boards had elected Presidents except the one at Dharmavaram whose President was nominated. The Penukonda Taluk Board levied an optional cess of three paisa on land. All the Taluk Boards except Gooty levied the education cess at three pies in the rupee under, the Elementary Education Act of 1920. The Taluk Boards maintained the medical and the educational institutions within their areas and also attended to sanitation, water supply and drainage. But as a result of the condition imposed by Government that they should limit their expenditure to their own resources, they suffered from considerable financial difficulty. During the years 1923-24, this restriction led to the unhappy situation when they were not able to pay the salaries of the Elementary School teachers for some months at a stretch. The work of the Penukonda Taluk Board was marred by the 'development of party spirit and faction' which led to its dissolution in 1927.

The Local Boards (Amendment) Act XI of 1930 made the office of Presidents elected and brought about provincialisation of services. It also provided for the appointment of a District Panchayat Officer and the formation of a Village Development Fund. It abolished the system of nominations, introduced direct election and extended the franchise to every income-tax assess. Women were made eligible to stand for elections. All Unions were designated as Panchayats and provision was made for the removal of Chairman and Presidents by a vote of no-confidence.

Consequent on the introduction of the amending Act, the strength of the Anantapur District Board underwent a radical change. Nine Taluk Boards were created, one for each Revenue Taluk. Table 5.2 gives the particulars of the composition of the various Boards:

Table 5.2: Composition of Taluk Boards in Anantapur District

Name of the Board	Strength	Pattern of Reservation of seats
District Board	52 (9 Reserved and 43 non Reserved)	3 for Mohammedan 1 for Indian- Xions 1 for Women 4 for Adi-Dravidas
Gooty Taluk Board	20	2 for Mohammedan 1 for Indian- Xions 1 for Women 1 for Adi-Dravidas
Tadipatri Taluk Board	16	1for Mohammedan 1 for Indian- Xions 1 for Women 1 for Adi-Dravidas
AnantapurTaluk Board	16	1 for Mohammedan 1 for Indian- Xions 1 for Women 1 for Adi-Dravidas
Kalyandurg Taluk Board	12	1 for Mohammedan 1 for Adi-Dravidas
Dharmavaram Taluk Board	13	1 for Mohammedan 1 for Women 1 for Adi-Dravidas
Kadiri Taluk Board	20	2 for Mohammedan 1 for Women 1 for Adi-Dravidas
Penukonda Taluk Board	12	1 for Mohammedan 1 for Women 1 for Adi-Dravidas
Hindupur Taluk Board	12	1 for Mohammedan 1 for Women 1 for Adi-Dravidas
Madakasira Taluk Board	12	1for Mohammedan 1 for Adi-Dravidas

Source: Administration Reports of Anantapur District, 1882 to 1945.

Some of the significant changes made after 1930 were the abolition of tolls and the levy of the tax on motor vehicles. The Boards were compensated by Government for the consequential loss of revenue. All Taluk Boards were abolished in 1934, and their main functions were taken over by the District Board along with their assets and liabilities.

The Village Development Fund was also abolished and the balance to its credit was placed at the disposal of the District Board. The reserved and non-reserved members of Talik Boards are presented in Figure 5.1.

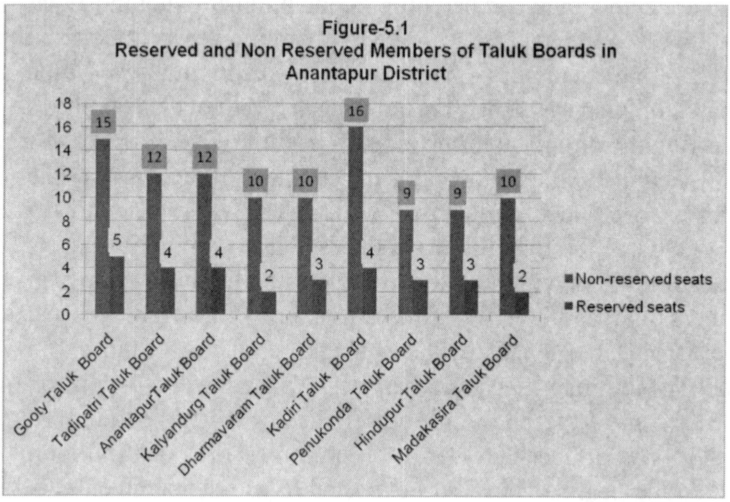

In 1950, Land cess was raised from one and a half annas to two annas per rupee on the annual rental value of all occupied lands and the additional cess so raised was given entirely to the District Board, except in Panchayat areas where one-fourth of it was credited to the Panchayats. Local Boards were authorised to levy a surcharge on stamp duty payable under the Indian Stamp Act of 1899.[8]

By about 1934 the taxes levied in the District Board area were the profession tax at maximum rates, house tax on the capital value of houses in some Panchayat areas and on annual rental value in certain others, and education tax ranging from 12.5 to 25 percent of house tax and profession tax realised by Panchayats. During 1936-37 the Anantapur District Board was in receipt of a moiety of the Government of India's grant for village communications and for rural water supply, if was superseded from November 1941 to April, 1942 for "persistently exceeding the powers conferred on it". In 1946, the roads of military and other importance were transferred to the Highways department for maintenance.

Gram Panchayats :

The Unions created by the 1884 Act were artificial units made up of a number of large and small villages without much of common interest among them. In practice the smaller villages came to be neglected. The Unions came to be regarded as mere tax collecting agencies without any **quid-pro-quo** to the tax payers. They were also not democratic and had little freedom, functioning mostly as agents of Taluk Boards. Although Government permitted from 1912-13 the election of Chairman and members in a few Union Boards, opinion was slowly crystallising in favour of their abolition. The Royal Commission on Decentralisation whose report was published in 1909 recommended the abolition of the Unions. The Central Government's resolution on Local Self-Government of 1915 also favoured their abolition and the establishment of Panchayats in selected areas with permissive powers and limited authority in matters of taxation. In 1915, the district authorities were required to organise Panchayats in villages with a population of more than 3,000 and informal Panchayats in selected villages with a population of 3,000 and less. These informal Panchayats had no statutory authority to collect taxes or to enforce measures of sanitation and public health. They were expected to use their influence in raising public subscriptions for the works they intended to carry on. Towards the end of 1918, there were 23 such Panchayats in the district, 35 having been dissolved between September, 1917 and December, 1918. A good deal of persuasion was found necessary to constitute these informal Panchayats. A sum of Rs 11,000 was allotted as grants to them, but they evoked very little popular enthusiasm. Although a large number of these Panchayats were reported by local authorities to have been started, "it was found, however, on a closer scrutiny that 35 out of the 37 Panchayats said to have been started in **Kalyandurg** taluk did not exist in reality".[9] The Collector reported that 'the experiment, cannot be said to have taken root in this district'.

In 1920, the Village Panchayats Act was passed making it possible for any village to have a Panchayat exercising statutory powers in all matters relating to sanitation, medical relief, education etc. The Panchayat was an elected body consisting of not less than seven and not more than 15 members. All residents of the village aged not less than 25 years were entitled to vote and also to stand for election. The Panchayats were empowered to lay and maintain village roads, construct culverts and bridges; provide lighting in streets and public places; construct drains and dispose of drainage water and sullage; clean streets and remove rubbish; provide public latrines; maintain burning ghats and burial grounds; construct and repair wells, ponds, tanks; control cattle sheds, threshing floors, chatrams and village pounds; and provide vaccination and register births and deaths. The District or the Taluk Board concerned was authorised to empower the Panchayats to exercise other functions, such as the construction and control of markets, provision of sanitation during festivals, control of ferries and fisheries, planting and preservation of avenue trees, establishment and maintenance of elementary schools and provision of medical relief. Government was authorised to transfer village forests, village irrigation works or any institution to a Panchayat. The Panchayat was empowered to levy a tax on the capital value of buildings; profession tax; fees for cattle stands, threshing floors; and such other items as were indicated in the Act. The Inspector of Local Boards was made the Registrar-General of Panchayats. From 1925-26 Government aided the Panchayats with grants for the maintenance of schools and libraries and for the improvement of village communications and water supply. During the decade 1920-30 about 120 Panchayats were set up in the district.[10]

The Local Boards Amendment Act XI of 1930 repealed the Village Panchayats Act of 1920 and brought the Panchayats within the scope of Local Boards. At the same time Union Boards were also converted into Panchayats or Panchayat Boards. Under the amended Act, the 13 Union Boards functioning at Kalyandurg, Gooty, Uravakonda, Konakondla, Guntakal, Pamidi, Yadiki, Yellanur, Dharmavaram, Kadiri, Penukonda, Bukkapatnam and Amarapuram were classified as Panchayat Boards. But each of them formed a separate entity in administration providing the requisite civic amenities. A District Panchayat Officer was appointed for supervising the work of the Panchayats in 1933. In 1937-38,

Amarapuram, Kalyandurg and Konakondla were converted into minor Panchayats as a result of the revised classification of the Panchayat Boards into 'Major and 'Minor' based on their average income. By the end of March, 1946, there were 16 major Panchayats and 188 minor Panchayats in the district. Figure 5.2 gives the clear picture of Class-I Panchayats in Anantapur district during 1890-91 to 1940-41.

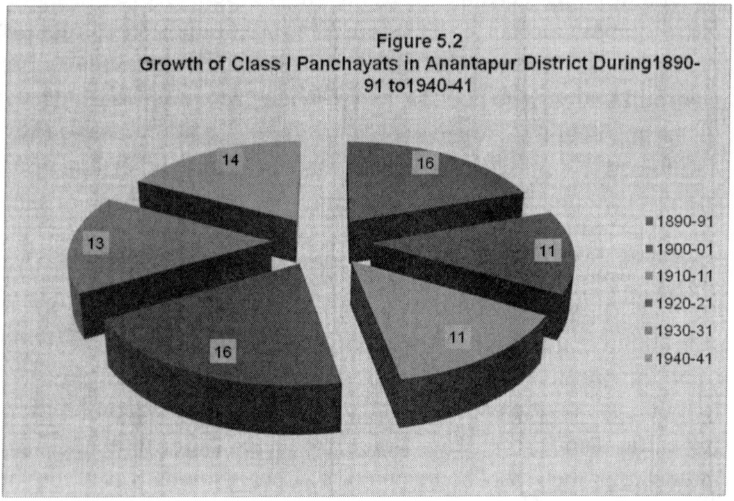

The details with regard to financial position of Class-I Panchayats is furnished in Table 5.3.

Table 5.3: The Financial Position of Class-I Panchayats in Anantapur District

Year	Number of Class-I Panchayats	Opening Balance Rs	Receipts Rs	Total Rs	Expenditure Rs
1890-91	16	974-00	15,793-00	14,819-00	13,691-00
1900-01	11	6,446-00	19,977-00	26,423-00	21,313-00
1910-11	11	3,476-00	24,825-00	28,310-00	24,569-00
1920-21	16	13,500-00	60,251-00	73,751-00	68,678-00
1930-31	13	17,958-00	89,584-00	1,07,542-00	85,318-00
1940-41	14	31,447-00	96,685-00	1,28,132-00	88,342-00

Source: Administration Reports of Anantapur District, 1882-1945.

It is evident from Table 5.3 that the receipts of Class-I Panchayats during colonial rule is gradually increasing. In the same way the expenditure of these Panchayats is steadily increasing. It is pertinent to note that the expenditure of Panchayats never crossed the total amount available with these Panchayats.

From 1940, it became increasingly clear that the dual control exercised by the President of the District Board and by the Inspector of Municipal Councils and Local Boards over the Panchayats was ineffective. During the period of the Second World War it was felt that the Panchayats could be excluded from Local Boards and placed under the Collector. An Act was passed for this purpose in 1946, but was not brought into operation. The National Government introduced fresh legislation in 1950.[11]

Municipalities:

The passing of the India Act XXVI of 1850 marked the first attempt at the creation of Municipalities in the districts. The Act authorised the Government to constitute any town into a municipality if its inhabitants were desirous of making better provision for public health and other amenities. The Executive authority was vested in Commissions consisting of the Magistrate and a certain number of persons appointed by the Governor-in-Council. Government contributed a sum equal to that raised by the inhabitants for this purpose. Anantapur was one of the few places in the Presidency to which the act was applied.

In pursuance of the report of the Royal Army Sanitary Commission of 1863 which made several recommendations for the improvement of conditions of health in towns, Government undertook more extensive measures for the betterment of municipalities. The Madras Towns Improvement Act X of 1865 was consequently passed and applied to all towns with a population of 5,000 and more. According to this Act, Commissioners were appointed to manage municipal affairs and were authorised to levy certain taxes for meeting the charges on 'police' establishments, the construction of roads and the improvement of sanitation. The Commissioners were empowered to raise further funds for purposes such as lighting and water supply. Provision was made for the appointment of not less than 5 inhabitants as Commissioners with the District Magistrate as the President. The District Magistrate, the Local Magistrate and the P.W.O. Officer were Ex-Officio Commissioners. The Act was extended to Gooty in 1869.[12]

The Towns Improvement Act III of 1871 replaced the Act of 1865. Under this Act, Municipalities were no longer required to contribute to 'police' charges. On the other hand, they were authorised to devote municipal funds for the promotion of education and the establishment of hospitals and dispensaries and other institutions of a local character not covered by the earlier Act. Some relaxation was made in the qualifications prescribed for the members of the Municipal Commission and their term of office was extended from one to three years. Under the Act, the Commission consisted of not less than three non-official members with the Collector and the Revenue Divisional Officer as ex-officio members. The Government was empowered to appoint any official in the district as Commissioner on the condition that the number of such official members did not exceed one-half of the total strength.

The Madras District Municipalities Act IV of 1884 was passed on the recommendations of the Local Self- Government Committee constituted in accordance with Lord Rippon's resolution of 1882. This Act Superseded the Towns Improvement Act of 1871. It introduced the term 'Municipality' for the first time and also the word 'Council' and 'Councillors' for 'Commission' and 'Commissioners' respectively. The Municipal Council was to consist of not less than 12 members whose term of office was to be three years. The Revenue Divisional Officer was to be an ex-officio Councillor. All other Councillors might be wholly appointed or partly elected at the discretion of the Governor-in-Council and the elected members should normally be three-fourths of the total strength of the Council. Not more than one-fourth of the total number of Councillors, unless elected were to be Government officials. Each Council was to have a Chairman appointed by Government or elected by the Councillors and an elected Vice-Chairman. The Chairman was responsible for carrying out the purposes of the Act. The main sources of revenue of the municipalities consisted of a tax on lands and buildings levied at 7.5 percent of their rental value, water tax at two percent, a tax on vehicles and animals, tolls as prescribed in the schedule of the Act and licence fee on offensive or dangerous trades. Other sources consisted of rents for the use of choultries, markets, slaughter-houses and cart-stands; fines and forfeitures, payments for municipal services; and grant-in-aid from State funds. The revenue so raised was to be spent on the maintenance and' repair of streets and bridges; construction and maintenance of hospitals and dispensaries, choultries, markets, tanks, wells, drains, sewers, etc.; training and employment of medical practitioners, vaccinators and sanitary inspectors; registration of births and deaths; lighting and cleaning of streets; expansion of education; construction, repair and maintenance of school buildings; and inspection of educational institutions and training of teachers. The only municipality then constituted under the Act was Anantapur. Hindupur and Tadipatri were constituted into municipalities in 1920 under a new Act.

The pattern of municipal administration remained unchanged till 1920. The Madras District Municipalities Act V passed that year provided for a larger proportion of elected members and an increase in the powers and resources of municipalities. An Inspector was appointed to supervise and working of Local Boards and Municipal Councils. The strength of a Municipal Council was fixed on the basis of population at a maximum of 36 and a minimum of 16 and the term of Councillors was three years. The Chairman was to be elected unless Government directed otherwise, but the Vice-Chairman was to be invariably elected from among the members. Not less than three-fourths of its members were to be elected and adequate representation was to be afforded to minority communities by means of nomination. The Revenue Divisional Officer ceased to be an ex-officio member. A paid executive authority known as 'Commissioner' could be appointed for a municipality at the discretion of Government. The Act provided for the levy of the Education tax for the expansion of elementary education.[13]

The term of thc Councils was extended under the transitory provisions of the District Municipalities Act (Amendment) of

1930. This Act modified the earlier Act of 1920 by dispensing with nominations and providing for the election of all the Municipal Councillors. It also removed the disqualification of women to stand for elections and extended the franchise to every tax payer. It provided for the reservation of seats for women and for minority communities such as Muslims, Indian Christians, Scheduled Castes, Europeans and Anglo-Indians. It made the offices of the Chairman and of the Vice-Chairman elective and provided for the provincialisation of municipal services. There was also provision for the passing of a vote of no-confidence against the Chairman and the Vice-Chairman and for the adjudication of disputes between various local bodies by Government. The Municipal Chairman and Vice-Chairman who might be removed from office were debarred from standing for election for a period of six months.

Subsequent legislation, particularly relating to the sphere of municipal finances, followed a pattern similar to that of Local Boards. The Motor Vehicles Taxation Act, 1931 abolished the levy of tolls. The tax on motor vehicles was provincialised and Municipalities were compensated for the loss of revenue. Municipal Councils, which levied a low rate of property tax, could be directed to increase it. In 1945, they were also permitted to levy a surcharge on stamp duty payable under the Indian Stamp Act in respect of the instruments of sale, gift and mortgage registered in municipal areas.

Owing to the conditions of emergency created by the Second World War, elections to municipalities were postponed from time to time till 1947. The new elected Councils came into office in October, 1947. The first elections to Municipalities on the basis of adult franchise were conducted in 1952.

Anantapur Municipality:

Anantapur came first under the India Act XXVI of 1850, the first of the mufassal municipal enactments which permitted towns voluntarily to tax themselves for their own improvement. The Government contributed a sum equal to that raised by the inhabitants for this purpose and the amount raised in the town reached a modest sum of only Rs 40 per month. The Act was introduced in the town in 1864 and continued to be in force for four years until 1869 when it was replaced by the Towns Improvement Act X of 1865. Later it came under the Towns Improvement Act III of 1871 which repealed the previous enactment. Its area was nine square miles and its population was 4,907. During the period 1865-71, its income was derived from tolls, taxes on vehicles and animals, house tax, fees for plying dangerous and offensive trades, magisterial fines, endowments and contributions from Government. It looked after the maintenance of sanitation and ran an elementary school in the town. In 1872, it took over the management of the local hospital. Though the Act of 1884 provided for an elected Chairman, the Anantapur Municipality came to have its first elected Chairman only in 1888, but its Councillors were all nominated by Government. Between 1894 and 1903 the Municipality had again a nominated Chairman as the privilege of electing a Chairman was withdrawn owing to the failure of the Council to elect one at three consecutive meetings. Towards the close of the nineteenth century, the Council levied under the Act of 1884 a tax on buildings based on the rental value of lands, a tax on arts and a tax on carts. The income of the Municipality in 1899-1900 was Rs 18,820 and its expenditure Rs 16,271. A substantial portion of this expenditure was on Education and Public Health.[14]

Till 1920, the sanctioned strength of the Municipality remained at 12, of which four were elected. In 1907, the first step towards providing protected water supply to the town was taken up, but it was only in 1924 that the scheme was completed. In 1908, the municipality set apart a site for extending the town and provided it with roads and wells. In 1916, it placed the high school building, constructed by it in 1915, at the disposal of the newly opened Ceded' Districts College, and provided a scavengers' settlement with the help of a grant of Rs 8,900 received from Government. In 1918, the majority of the Councillors, eight out of 12, came to be elected, the rest being nominated. Towards the beginning of 1920-21 the Council maintained a market, a high school, and seven elementary schools and made provision for lighting, sanitation and public and private conservancy.

The introduction of the Act of 1920 accentuated factions in the Council. Government consequently retained in office the Chairman elected under the old Act for sometime* and this led to the neglect of civic affairs. A Vice-Chairman was elected in 1922 for the first time. In the same year the Councillors failed to take the oath of allegiance to the Crown and the municipality was superseded for about three months. At 'the commencement of the nineteen-thirties the official element among the Councillors was withdrawn. In 1935, a Commissioner was appointed to the Municipality. In 1938, it started its own electrical undertaking to supply power to the town.[15] In 1939, for the first time in the annals of the municipality a no- confidence motion was passed against the Chairman and he was removed. In 1944, the Council was superseded for a period of one year. In 1950, the municipality was classed as second grade and a post of an Engineer was also sanctioned. Elections were conducted in 1952 with the help of electoral rolls prepared on the basis of adult franchise.

Gooty Municipality:

The provisions of the Towns Improvement Act, 1865 were extended to Gooty in 1869. Twelve Non-officials were appointed as Commissioners in addition to the District Magistrate of Bellary and a P.W.D. official in executive charge of the range. The strength of the police to be maintained in the town was fixed at six with a Deputy Inspector in charge of it. The amount to be raised towards police charges was fixed at Rs 4,626 of which a quarter was contributed by Government. The Commissioners were authorised to levy a tax on houses and buildings, tolls, taxes on vehicles and fees for the registration of carts. From the time of its inception the municipality was faced with a chronic financial deficit. In 1874, it was in a state of insolvency and had to be assisted from provincial funds. The up-keep of conservancy establishment, the supply of medicines to the dispensary and the cost of supervision and management exhausted a large proportion of its resources. In 1876, the Municipality was recommended to be closed. Again in 1879, Mr. H. T. Ross, the Sub-Collector and Vice-President of the Council wrote a graphic account of the impecuniosities and ineptitude which had throughout distinguished the proceedings of the Council and the next year it was abolished.[16] Its property was transferred to the Local Fund Board of the Gooty Circle and since then it has been a Class-1 Panchayat.

Hindupur Municipality:

Hindupur was constituted into a municipality from 1st May, 1920, in spite of much opposition from the town. The Chairman and 11 Councillors of the first Council were all nominated by the government. In August, 1921, the strength of the Council was raised from 12 to 16, out of which 12 were elected and four were nominated under the new Act. During 1921-22 the Council was reported to be 'torn with faction'. In 1922, four Councillors had to vacate their seats for failure to take the oath of allegiance. In 1926-27, a Second Class Health Officer and a Revenue Officer were appointed to the Municipality. In 1928, the local hospital till then managed by the Municipality was taken over by Government. The Municipality started an electrical undertaking in 1930 in order to supply power to the town. In 1933, arrangements were made for supplying drinking water to some parts of the town and a library was opened. In 1934, a Commissioner was appointed as the Executive authority of the municipality. In the same year Mahatma Gandhi visited the place and switched on the lights in the main bazar square now known as the Gandhi Chowk. In 1935-36, the municipality was superseded on grounds of maladministration. In 1936-37, a new high school building was constructed.[17] By 1937-38, most of the roads in the town were black-topped. The Council was again superseded in 1944-45 for over 17 months.

Tadipatri Municipality :

Tadipatri was constituted into a municipality in 1920 with a nominated Chairman and 11 Councillors. The first election to the Council was held in 1921-22 but the elected Councillors failed to take the oath of allegiance and walked out of the body leaving the nominated Chairman to carry on the administration. The Council was permitted to elect its Chairman the next year. In 1924-25, the municipality started a hostel for boys studying in the middle school run by it and a Baby Nursing Home. In 1926-27, the Council was superseded for a period of three months owing to its strained' relationship with the Chairman. In 1926, a no-tax campaign was launched by the Vysyas and Marwadis of the town who formed an association called the "Pura Sangham". In 1927, the .Council was superseded for a period of five months. The financial position of the municipality was by that time so unsatisfactory that it was unable to pay even the salaries of its establishment. In 1928, Government took over the management of the hospital till then maintained by the municipality. In 1931, the municipality introduced three full fee and 17 half fee concessions to the students of the high school which were granted on the basis of a competitive examination. In 1933, a Commissioner was appointed and the town came to have protected water supply. In 1935, the municipality constructed a new building for the high school. In 1937 the Council was superseded for two years as the finances of the municipality constantly ran into deficit.[18] It was reconstituted in 1938. The first attempt to have dustless surfacing of roads was made in 1946-47.

Town Planning:

Town Planning, as now understood, had naturally made little impact on the development of the district in the past. While some of its towns like Penukonda, Rayadurg, Kalyandurg and Gooty are reminiscent of the old science of Town Planning (Stapathyam), most of the other towns and villages have not been constructed according to any definite pattern. A striking feature about some of them is their ribbon development. Some of the commercial centres like Hindupur, Guntakal and Tadipatri are heavily congested. None of the towns in the district has any Master Plan. But some attempts were made to survey the Anantapur town during 1871-72. The surveys conducted in 1892 and in 1903 were, however, confined only to the old town. A preliminary survey was taken up by Government in 1953-54, but its report has yet to be finalised.

Efforts to introduce Town Planning were first made in 1909, when the Anantapur Municipality selected a site for the extension of the town, laid out some roads and had some wells dug. A Municipal Committee was appointed during 1932-33 to draft the town planning scheme for Anantapur.[19] None of the other towns in the district except Guntakal, Tadipatri and Hindupur formulated any town planning schemes. In respect of Guntakal, only the preliminary work on the three detailed town planning schemes drawn up is in progress. The general town planning schemes for Tadipatri and Hindupur are still under preparation. The Hindupur High School Extension Town Planning Scheme was, however, approved in 1943 and over a lakh of rupees was spent on it.

The provisions of the Town Planning Act are enforced in the Municipalities in the district through the Town Planning sections specially attached to them. These sections deal with the approval of layouts, the formulation of building plans both for new constructions and the improvement of old ones, and the removal of encroachments.[20]

The first of the House Building Co-operative Societies was established at Gooty in 1925. By 1965, their number rose to ten and they were located at Gooty (1925), Tadipatri (1926), Anantapur (1928), Hindupur (1946), Dharmavaram and Guntakal (1941), Kadiri (1948), Rayadurg (1949), Uravakonda (1959) and Guntakal Bharat Sevak Samaj House Building Society (1961). Of these, the societies at Rayadurg, Gooty and Uravakonda are reported to have become dormant. The first of the colonies constructed for the Low Income Groups was the Scavengers' Settlement established in Anantapur in 1916-17 with a grant of Rs 8,900 from Government.

During the colonial rule, apart from the regular administrative apparatus headed by Collector and District Magistrate, there were institutions like Village Panchayati, Taluk Boards and District Boards. Except in the single municipality of the District, local self-government is in the hands of the District Board and the three Taluk Boards of Anantapur, Gooty and Penukonda, the control of the District Board over the Taluk Boards being the same as elsewhere. The Anantapur board controlled affairs in the Anantapur and Kalyandurg taluks, the Gooty board managed Gooty and Tadipatri and the Penukonda board looked after the remaining four taluks in the south of the district. The income of these bodies is chiefly derived from the house tax, which is levied in all of them at three-quarters of the maximum rates permissible under Act V of 1834 and amounts to just over ten annas per house taxed, against about thirteen annas in the Presidency as a whole.

There was hardly any other institutional set up which could be compared favourably with the present day Panchayati Raj set up. This institutional set up in the post constitutional period was an administrative corollary of development planning and allied nation – building programmes.

REFERENCES

1. Venkatarangaiya, M., "Development of Local Boards in Madras Presidency", p. 72.
2. Manual of Administration in Madras Presidency, 1885, II, p. 14.
3. Manual of Administration Volume I, 1885, p. 38.
4. Boag, G.T., The Madras Presidency 1881-1931, p. 63.
5. Srinivasa Raghavachariar, Memorandum on the Progress of the Madras Presidency during the last forty years of British Administration 1893, p. 57.
6. *Ibid.*, p. 59.
7. *Ibid.*, p. 63.
8. M. Venkatarangaiya, *op. cit,* p. 87.
9. G. T. Boag, *op. cit,* .p. 91.
10. Gadgil, D.R., The Industrial Evolution of India in recent times, 1860-1939, Delhi, 1988, p. 36.
11. Dewey, C.J. and Hopkins, A.G. ed., The Imperial Impact: Studies in the Economic History of Africa and India, London, 1978,p. 108.
12. Karashima, Noboru., South Indian History and Society: Studies from Inscriptions, A.D. 850-1800, Delhi, 1984, p. 59.
13. Maclean, C.D., Manual of the Administration of the Madras Presidency, Madras, 1885, Vol. 1, p. 129.
14. Administration Reports of Anantapur Municipality, 1884-85 to 1886-87, 1888-89, 1889-90, 1891-92 to 1927-28, 1929-30 to 1944-45, 1946-47 to 1964-65.

15. *Ibid.*
16. Administration Reports of Gooty Municipality, 1869-70, 1871-72 to 1879-80.
17. Administration Report of Hindupur Municipality, 1920-21 to 1922-23, 1925-26, 1927-28 to 1941-42.
18. Administration Reports of Tadipatri Municipality, 1920-21 to 1935-36, 1937-38 to 1941-42.
19. Administration Reports of the Director of Town Planning from 1938-39 to 1940-41.
20. *Ibid.*

6

Public Grievances and the Response of Government

The Anantapur district is unfortunately vulnerable to famines. It lies in the heart of the famine zone with an exceedingly light rainfall, poor soils and precarious irrigation sources. Being far away from the east coast and cut off by the Western Ghats, it does not derive the full benefit of either of the monsoons and thus no year passes without hardship to the agriculturist. The rainfall of Anantapur is lighter than that of any other district in the Madras Presidency except Bellary, and the difference between these two is only a matter of few centimeters. The annual average rainfall in both of them varies between 22 and 23 inches. Anantapur lies midway between the two monsoons but receives the full benefit of neither. It is too close to the Western Ghats to be benefited greatly by the south-west monsoon and the north-east current has left behind most of its moisture before reaching it.

There are three fairly distinct zones of rainfall in the district. The three driest taluks are Anantapur, Dharmavaram and Kalyandurg, where (as in the adjoining Rayadurg and Bellary taluks) the total rainfall received is less than 21 inches; Gooty and Tadipatri receive about 23 inches; and in the three southern taluks, where the rainfall is less scanty than elsewhere, between 23 and 24 inches. For the district as a whole, the heaviest rainfall on record was in 1874, the year before the beginning of the great famine of 1876-8, when 38.6 inches was received. The lightest was that in 1876, during that famine, when the district average was only 6.9 inches. Since 1870 the rainfall has exceeded 25 inches in thirteen years and been over 30 inches in four years 1874 (38.6), 1878 (38), 1889 (33) and 1903 (32) inches.

The times at which the showers usually arrive are much the same as in Bellary. December and the first three months of the year are practically rainless, the whole quantity then received averaging less than half an inch; in April and May a few showers arrive; in June and July the south-west monsoon begins to blow and falls continue until the end of the north-east monsoon in November. The wettest months are September and October, and in them nearly half the total annual supply is received. The rain is not only scanty, but it usually falls in light showers (the average works out to under half an inch) which on a stony soil under a tropical sun soon dry up and are insufficient to fill the tanks and wells. Further, it is most capricious and uncertain. The methods of dry land cultivation in vogue in the district require to secure good crops and the showers shall arrive at certain definite periods and intervals and any marked irregularity in the rainfall hampers cultivation in a manner for which showers in subsequent months cannot atone. The absence of rain in June and July, for example, will render it impossible to sow the redsoil in those months and copious falls in September and October will not compensate for the earlier deficiency. The prosperity of a year cannot, therefore, be judged merely by examining the total fall it received. To give good crops, the rain must be timely as well as sufficient.[1]

Liability to famine:

Anantapur district possessing an exceedingly light and uncertain rainfall, as has been explained in previous chapters, a district in which three-fourths of the people are dependent upon pastoral and agricultural pursuits, where most of its soil is poor, and almost all the irrigation works are dependent upon local rainfall is as a necessary corollary, more than usually liable to disastrous seasons. The official records of the bad years which occurred in it before it was severed from Bellary in 1882 usually, however, deal with the old Bellary district as a whole, and it is not now always possible to give separate detailed particulars for the taluks which now make up Anantapur.

Early Scarcities :

Of the famines and scarcities which overtook it before its cession to the Company there is no exact record. Native historians in those days concerned themselves more with courts and kings than with calamities among the common people. Ferishta mentions two famines in the fifteenth century which are said to have spread throughout the Deccan, but gives no exact particulars. The second of them must, however, have been excessively severe, for he says that for two years no grain could be sown "and in the third, when the Almighty showered his mercy upon the earth, scarce any farmers were left to cultivate the lands."[2]

One of Munro's reports makes a passing mention of a scarcity in 1756, and shows that the famine of 1791-92 which was so severe in the Northern Circars (and which is memorable as being the first occasion on which an Indian Government opened relief-works) also seriously affected the Deccan districts. Its intensity was enhanced by the rapacity of the native administration. "Had the officers of Government," says Munro, lowered the assessment or even let it remain as before, the effects of the famine would probably only have been felt while it lasted, but as they raised it near 50 percent, wherever there was a crop, this addition to the high price necessarily occasioned by the scarcity rendered grain so dear that very little could be purchased by the lower classes of the inhabitants, and great numbers of them perished in consequence.[3]

Scarcity of 1802-04:

The first scarcity after the session began in 1802, lasted till 1804. Writing to the Board in May 1803, Munro said that "in no one village perhaps of any district (taluks were called districts in those days) except Adoni (in the Bellary district), was there what is called an average produce." A year later Munroe wrote again that "the tanks nowhere received any water for first crop. In only two out of 37 districts did they receive a full supply for the second. Great numbers of the cattle employed in agriculture and in the transport of grain have perished. All kinds of provisions are from two to three hundred percent, above the average rate."[4] The scarcity (Munro declined throughout to describe it as a famine) ended with the great storm of October 1804.

Scarcity of 1805-07:

In the next year the famine which affected the districts adjoining Madras City spread to Anantapur. The distress continued until 1807. Munro's report upon the situation deprecated interference with the grain trade and suggested the remission of revenue as one of the best means of alleviating distress, both of which principles were adhered to in all subsequent famines. In the Ceded districts the season was in Munro's opinion "beyond all comparison worse than any that has ever been known," for though prices were not so high as they had been in 1804, there was much less crop than in that year. "Not a tank in the country had its due complement of water and many of them remained quite empty."[5] Things were worst in the cotton-soil country, especially in Gooty taluk. Apparently, however, only Rs 20,000 was spent in relief-works. A bad season was began in

1824 and relief-works were again made necessary in the district, but it was less severely affected than several others.

Famine of 1833:

In 1833 occurred the Guntur famine, so called because of its severity in the old Guntur district, where out of a population of 500,000 as many as 150,000 persons were estimated to have perished from want. Mr. F. W. Robertson, the then Collector of the old Bellary district, described the season within his charge in the precise words applied by Munro to the state of affairs 26 years before, declaring it to be " beyond all comparison worse than any that has ever been known."[6] The September and October rains failed, and consequently most of the black cotton-soil was left untilled. Prices went up in places with appalling rapidity, cholam, which in September had sold at from 70 to 75 seers the rupee, rising in a few days to 23 seers. The Collector was authorised to afford gratuitous relief to those in absolute want, to open relief-works and to try and encourage the importation of grain, but what steps were actually taken in Anantapur nowhere now appears. Records show, however, that in six months 12,000 people died of cholera in the old Bellary district and that the loss of revenue was Rs 3.25 lakh.

Famine of 1854:

The next famine in the Presidency was in 1854 and it was almost entirely confined to Anantapur and Bellary. The district had hardly recovered from the damage to its irrigation works caused by the great storm of May 1851 referred to later in this chapter, and in 1852 and the early part of 1853 the standing crops-especially the cholam, the staple food of the people-had been extensively injured by unseasonable rain. The rainfall in June and July 1853, on the other hand, was scanty, and the north-east monsoon completely failed. Hindupur received more rain than any other taluk, but even there the total registered was only 16 inches and in the district as a whole the average fall during the year was only 9.5 inches and in certain of the taluks (Gooty among them) it averaged only 6.5 inches, and was in some cases as low as 3.5 inches. The harvest was consequently a miserable failure and prices began to rise.[7]

By January 1854 cholam was selling at 27 seers the rupee against an average in the ten years 1841-51 of about 58 seers, and by June it had risen to 21 seers per rupee. It continued at this figure until September, and in the northern taluks, which were the worst affected, it was even as high as 14 seers. The highest price touched in 1833 had been Rs 200 per garce and even this had only lasted a short period, the average for the whole year being Rs 140.

But on this occasion, the price in the northern taluks averaged Rs 218 per grace steadily from January to September, and from June to September was even as high as from Rs 240 to Rs 252. In October ten inches of rain fell, prices eased and the famine was over.[8] Figure 6.1 gives the details of relief extended to the victims of 1854 famine.

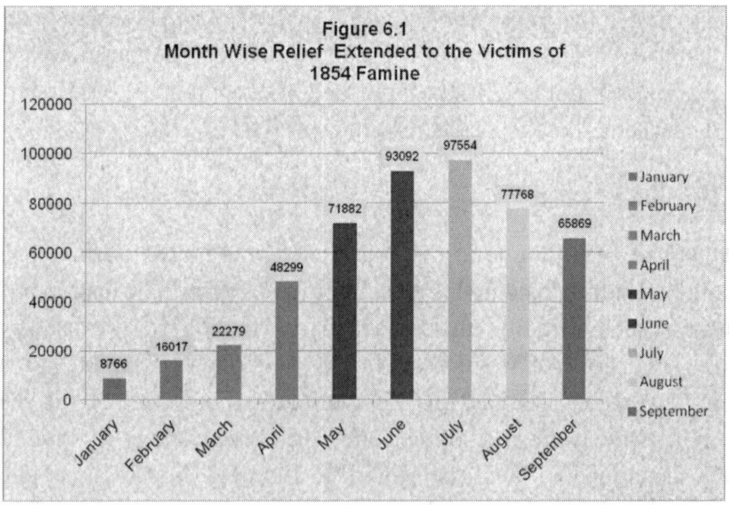

Table 6.1: Month-wise Number of People Received Relief during 1854 Famine

Month	Number of people
January	8,766
February	16,017
March	22,279
April	48,299
May	71,882
June	93,092
July	97,554
August	77,768
September	65,869

Source: Report of Indian Famine Commission 1854.

The number of people on relief-works in the Bellary and Anantapur districts together rose from 9,000 in January 1854 to 97,000 in July and was at one time as high as 100,600, or eight percent. Figures for the first week in each month from January to September are given in the margin. In Gooty taluk as many as 8 percent, of the inhabitants were on relief. Mortality among the people is not referred to in the reports and was apparently slight, but the then Collector, Mr. Pelly, estimated that in the cotton-soil taluks four-fifths of the cattle had perished and the villages were said to be strewn with their bones.

Relief Works undertaken: The relief-works consisted almost entirely of earth-work on new roads and they were chiefly controlled by seven military officers working under the Civil Engineer. The chief of them was the Secunderabad-Bangalore road, which runs from Kurnool through Gooty, Anantapur and Penukonda into Mysore territory. Piece-work rates were nowhere tried. The wages given were at first Rs 2 for men and Rs 1-6 for women and children, but in July they were reduced to Rs 1-3 for men, one anna for women and eight pies for children. The majority of the people on the works were farm-labourers, ordinary coolies and weavers. In the two districts 284 miles of earth-work for roads were completed and another 88 miles partly finished and the expenditure upon works to the end of September was Rs 12 lakhs. It was, however, calculated that the work done was only worth about a third of this sum.

Expenditure to the state: Altogether Rs 16 lakh was spent on the famine and if to this sum is added the actual loss of revenue in 1854, Rs.5 lakh, and a further prospective loss of Rs 4 lakh, the calamity cost the State Rs 251 lakh in the two districts. The cost to the people themselves was, of course, far heavier. Writing to the Secretary of State after the famine, the Madras Government put the losses due to withered crops, land left unsown and diminished cultivation at about Rs 33 lakhs, and those caused by the death of cattle at Rs 13 lakhs, and concluded its calculations with the remark that "the result is a loss in this one Province (i.e. the Ceded districts) of nearly Rs 70 lakhs of rupees in this single disastrous season."[9]

Famine of 1866: In 1866, famine again visited the Presidency and afflicted Bellary and Anantapur, and especially the Gooty and Madakasira taluks of the latter, more severely than any other district except perhaps Ganjam. Events in the district in the years immediately preceding 1866 had in part prepared the way for disaster. The outbreak of the American War in April 1861 had caused a cotton famine in Lancashire and the consequent run upon Indian cotton had been so great that the price rose from about Rs 1-4 per maund of 25 lbs. in 1861 to Rs.3 in 1862, Rs.5 in 1863 and even higher figures at the end of 1864. The ryots, speculating on a continuation of these extravagant rates, raised cotton wherever it would grow until the area under that crop in Bellary and Anantapur was more than double the normal. The crop was wonderfully profitable (it has been calculated that the people made 1.5 million sterling out of it in the three years), but its cultivation at the expense of food-grains in a district cut off from railway communication with outside areas proved a dangerous undertaking. Even while the seasons continued well, this procedure raised prices. In 1863-64 the season was bad and they went up still further.[10] In 1865, the American War ended and cotton went down with a run to Rs 3-12 a maund. Also the season was again unfavourable. No good rain fell and prices went up to 11 seers of rice and 14 seers of cholam per rupee, which was as high as they had ever been in the 1854 famine.

Beginnings of distress : In March 1866 the then Collector of Bellary district asked that relief-works might be started, but received no definite orders. Matters were becoming very serious. According to one of the official reports "the poorer ryots and hired labourers, and especially the Bedar and other low castes, were in a pitiful condition, supporting life upon edible leaves and nuts, pounded tamarind stones and the pulp of the aloe." The people began to wander to Kurnool and Mysore. "Numbers perished by the way during these migrations and it was not unusual to find lying on the roads and streets the dead bodies of these famished way-farers."[11] The one bright spot in the picture was the readiness with which private charity advanced to alleviate the wretchedness of the poorer classes. Some of the richer ryots fed considerable numbers daily.

Works at length opened: In July the District Collector at length made arrangements with the Superintending Engineer to open relief-works from the usual Public Works grant and obtained sanction for an additional Rs 30,000 for improvements to roads and the cleaning of wells. In the Anantapur portion of the district it was arranged to go on with the extension towards Guntakal of the north-western line of the Madras Railway, the rail-head of which was then at Muddantiru in Cuddapah district.

A dearth of food: By August things were at their worst. In places there was an absolute dearth of food. During the latter half of the month second sort rice was four seers the rupee and cholam five seers. The Collector telegraphed to Government asking that Rs 10,000 worth of the cheapest grain in Madras might be sent him instantly. Government made immediate arrangements with the Commissary-General to dispatch the grain, but the difficulty was to get it to Bellary. The railway had just been opened as far as Muddaniiru, but the only means of getting the grain from thence to Bellary was by country cart, which "involved 100 miles of transit of a fodder less region, certain deterioration, if not death, of the bullocks and in many cases of the drivers by cholera." The rate of cart-hire prevailing was Rs.4 per bandy per mile, but even for this extravagant figure it was quite impossible to get sufficient carriage at Muddaniiru and the grain had eventually to be sent to Bellary from Bangalore, 180 miles by road, and took altogether nearly two months to reach its destination.[12] Meanwhile a few more works had been opened, a sum of Rs 12,000 was collected locally for gratuitous relief and the Famine Committee in Madras (the first instance of a private relief fund in the history of Indian famines) sent Rs 14,000 more for the same purpose.

Rain in August: Towards the end of August rain fell, and prospects brightened. Prices, however, remained high, the necessity for relief continued, and the Collector obtained another Rs 1.25 lakhs for works. The rain continued through September and October, but the numbers on relief, instead of declining, increased and continued to increase until January 1867, after which they began to fall. It was not, however, until June in that year that the works were finally closed.

The relief-works carried out: Piece-rates were again left untried on these works. The wages were at first 3, 2, and 1.5 annas for men, women and children, respectively, but in December they were lowered to 2, 1.5 and 1 anna, respectively. Altogether 261 miles of roads were newly constructed in Bellary and Anantapur and another 216 miles of existing roads were improved.[13]

Cost of the famine: The figures in the margin show the average daily number of persons relieved throughout the famine in the two districts. The superfluous relief cost about Rs 1 lakh, but of this sum the Madras Famine Committee contributed Rs.55,000 and nearly all the remainder was locally subscribed. Table 6.2 gives the details of year wise and month wise relief extended during famine of 1866.

Table 6.2: Year-wise and Month-wise Relief Extended during Famine of 1866

Year and Months	On gratuitous relief	On relief works
July-1866	3,613	...
August-1866	15,955	3,090
September -1866	28,693	8,263
October-1866	32,310	9,500
November -1866	19,938	11,616
December-1866	15,590	17,492
January-1867	10,158	19,421
February-1867	6,743	18,109
March-1867	5,019	15,310
April-1867	3,301	7,467
May-1867	3,113	4,378

Source: Indian Famine Commission-1866.

The relief-works cost the State Rs 4.5 lakh and in the two years ending with 1866- 67 remissions amounting to Rs 2.5 lakh more than the normal were granted, so that the expenditure by the Government in the two districts was some seven lakhs of rupees. The loss to the people will never be known. The death-rate was 4 percent, against 1.5 percent, after the famine, but registration of deaths had only begun in the Presidency in June 1865 and the figures were probably worth little. There was, moreover, considerable mortality from cholera (in many villages the panic was so great that the corpses remained unburied) and it is not safe to assume that any increase in the deaths was due to starvation. The loss in cattle and crops was, however, undoubtedly enormous and the mortality among the former was estimated at 35,000 head worth of Rs 9.5 lakhs.

It was the opinion of Mr. Ellis, who, under the orders of Government, visited the district in October 1866, and of others also, that the gravity of affairs was not realised early enough, and that if the action which was at length taken in August and September had been begun in May and June, the people would have been saved a great deal of avoidable distress.

The Great Famine of 1876-78:

Ten years later came the worst affliction that the district or the Presidency has ever known, the Great Famine of 1876-78, the visitation which lasted 22 months, affected fourteen of the 21 districts of the Presidency (eight of them severely), is calculated to have caused the death of 3.5 million people, and to have cost the State Rs.630 lakhs in direct expenditure, besides another 191 lakhs in loss of revenue.

Its severity in the district : Except Kurnool, the old Bellary district suffered more terribly in this visitation than any other region in the Presidency. It has been calculated that in those two years more than one-fifth of its inhabitants (330,000 souls) died of starvation or disease and that, if the effects of the check upon reproduction which resulted are also included, the population at the census of 1881 was no less than one-fourth smaller than under normal circumstances it would have been. In the Madakasira taluk the results were even more disastrous. At the census of 1881 its population was 31 percent, less than it had been at the census of 1871, ten years before. At the census of 1891, fourteen years after the famine, the population of the Anantapur district as a whole continued to be smaller than it had been in 1871, and even by 1901 the total increase in the thirty years since 1871 had amounted to only six percent. But the distress in it was at no time as deep as in the taluks which now form Bellary.[14]

The beginnings of trouble:

The beginnings of this disaster date from 1874, in which year heavy rains destroyed part of the crops. In 1875, the south-west monsoon was scanty and late, prices began to rise and remissions of revenue were necessary. The north-east monsoon of that year was not sufficiently favourable to drive prices down, but, though preparations for the worst were made, it was confidently hoped that the south-west monsoon of 1876 would be a success and remove all anxiety. But the monsoon months passed by one after the other without bringing any sufficient rain and in places the price of cholam rose until it was 16 seers the rupee, or nearly double the normal rate. August and September similarly passed without bringing any good rain and affairs became serious in Penukonda and Anantapur taluks.

September 1876; sudden expansion of distress:

The distress then began to spread suddenly and with great rapidity to the rest of the district. On the 22nd September the Collector (Mr. J. H. Master) reported that it was universal throughout his charge and on the 28th that it was increasing daily in nearly every taluk. Government raised to Rs 75,000 the grants for works in Bellary and Anantapur which already had been made to him, and deputed Mr. G. Thornhill, Senior Member of the Board, to travel through the Ceded districts to see how matters lay. He corroborated the Collector's accounts of the season, but hoped that if only the coming north-east monsoon was a success the shadow would be removed.

October: sudden rise in prices:

Due to the calamity the prices of commodities in the district, however, suddenly went up with a bound. On the 12th October, Mr. Master telegraphed that cholam had suddenly raised to nine seers the rupee and rice to seven, and that the people were everywhere crowding to the works. By the 19th prices had gone up still further and by the end of the month large numbers of people were on relief. Tahsildars were relieved of their magisterial work by the appointment of Sub-magistrates; the allotments for works were increased to Rs 2,19,000 and the rates of wages on them were enhanced to meet the rise in prices.[15] All through November rain held off and the numbers on works and gratuitous relief continued to rise, and eventually the allotments for the two districts were raised by another three lakhs.

December: famine inevitable:

By the end of November all hopes of a favourable monsoon were dead and the district staff seeded down to fight the famine which was now inevitable. Two additional Deputy Collectors and two other officers were sent to help. An extraordinary scarcity of food set in. Grain depots were established in the different taluks, grain being procured (where local supplies failed) from Madras through Messrs. Arbuthnot & Co., and Major F. J. Hicks was appointed as Griain Transport Agent for Anantapur and other districts to arrange for the prompt carting of this food to the places where it was most urgently wanted. The numbers on relief went up by leaps and bounds and by the end of December they reached 148,000.

Steps taken and proposed:

Government ordered (for the first time in the history of Madras famines) that a proper system of task-work should be put in force and suggested moving some of the labourers across to Nelloreto work on the Buckingham Canal. This plan, it may be stated at once, subsequently came hopelessly to grief, only 12,000 persons in the two Steps taken districts of Bellary and Anantapur being induced to travel so far. The Government of India ordered that no work which was to cost more than Rs 30,000 should be put in hand without their sanction, and one result of this was that all the enormous expenditure which was eventually incurred in the district was distributed among improvements to small tanks and the making and repair of roads and it is not now possible to point to any notable work as the outcome of the Great Famine. Mr. Thornhiirs proposal to pay advances to blanket-weavers to keep them engaged at their proper occupation and off the works was also negatived at this time, though, subsequently sanctioned, but endeavours were made to stimulate the local demand for labour by encouraging applications for advances under the Land Improvement Act.[16]

Role of Sir Richard Temple:

At the end of 1876 the Governor of Madras (the Duke of Buckingham and Chandos) attended the Imperial Assemblage at Delhi at which the assumption by Queen Victoria of the title of Empress of India was formally proclaimed, and while there he was consulted by the Viceroy regarding the policy to be followed in Madras in regard to the famine. One result of the deliberations was the discontinuance of the purchase of grain through Messrs. Arbuthnot and the abolition of grain wages except where no grain was purchasable on the spot. Another was the deputation of Sir Richard Temple, who had had famine experience in Bengal in 1874, to the Madras Presidency.

Some of his Suggestions:

Of the hundred and odd minutes and memoranda which Sir Richard wrote in the three and a half months during which he stayed, in this Presidency, those which most directly affected the policy in Anantapur suggested that further stringency should be used in admitting persons to works, admissions being allowed only on the certificate of an officer not below the rank of Deputy Tahsildar, and workers not in danger of starvation being turned away; that the existing wages should be reduced by one-fourth all round; that the works should be limited to certain lines of road already in hand and some 150 large irrigation works each capable of employing 500 persons; that officers of the army should be engaged to assist the civil staff in organising relief; that advances should be made to weavers to enable them to work at their trade; and that special steps should be taken to care for children and the aged and infirm.[17]

Increasing intensity of the famine: The gradually increasing intensity of the famine from this time forth is graphically shown in the attached statement[1] giving the numbers on works and gratuitous relief and the prices of the staple food grains in each month from December 1876 to September 1878.

Table 6.3: Year Wise and Month Wise Relief Extended during Famine of 1876-78

Month and Year	Average number of people relieved during each month of the famine of 1876-78			Total percent, of population in 1871	Average price in seers per rupee	
	On works	Gratui-tously	Total		Cholam	Rice (2nd sort).
December 1876	129,222	18,824	148,046	19.97	7.5	6.7
January 1877	140,110	28,274	168,384	19.97	7.8	6.7
February	79,168	10,346	89,514	22.70	8.7	6.9
March	48, 598	12135	12135	8.19	9.5	7.1
April	54,502	31, 237	54,502	11.57	9.0	7.7
May	74,544	48, 567	74,544	16.61	7.9	7.2
June	70,466	41,095	70,466	15.05	7.2	6.7
July	76,601	43, 811	76,601	16.24	6.2	5.8
August	71,947	65, 400	71,947	18.53	6.1	5.4
September	28,957	92, 578	121, 535	16.40	6.6	5.4
October	17, 244	54, 367	71,611	9.66	9.4	7.0
November	10, 326	15, 673	25,999	3.51	10.6	7.5
December	6,396	9, 781	16,177	2.18	10.3	8.0
January 1878	611	4, 291	4,902	0.66	11.1	8.4
February	0	754	754	0.10	10.9	8.3
March	0	649	649	0.09	11.4	8.3
April	0	809	809	0.19	11.8	9.3
May	51	1,611	1,662	0.22	11.6	9.9
June	455	2181	2, 636	0.36	10.3	9.5
July	1051	1, 657	2,708	0.39	9.9	9.2
August	1788	1,674	3,6,42	0.47	10.3	9.1
September	1969	1, 813	3,781	0.51	11.4	9.7
Average over 22 Months	17,000	22, 160	59,160	7.98	9.6	7.8

Source: Famine Commission-1876-78.

As the months passed by, new difficulties continually arose. Cattle for grain transport became scarcer and scarcer and, in the absence of fodder, endeavours were made to keep them alive by feeding them partly on prickly-pear from which the thorns had been picked out; the works in the district were flooded with immigrants from Mysore; cholera raged at several of them; house to house visitations were found necessary to prevent people starving in their villages; caste prejudices with regard to cooking had to be considered in the relief-camps or the food was refused; cloths had to be provided for the large numbers who came nearly naked to the works; and the desertion of wives by their husbands, and children by their parents, had to be checked. Sir Richard's rule requiring the dismissal of relief-workers who were not in danger of starvation was found to result in their rapid deterioration in health and speedy qualification, for re-admission, and a keen controversy began between him and as the time approached when the south-west monsoon of 1877 monsoon might be expected, hope began to revive. In the first two weeks of fails. June good rain (the first for seven months) fell in most of the taluks and though prices were higher than ever (probably owing to the demand for seed-grain) it was thought that the beginning of the end had come at last. But once more disappointment followed. In the last part of the month the rains held off again.

July: difficulties further increase:

July went by without sufficient rain and the intensity of the distress still further deepened. Parents were reported to have sold their children for food; in some of the camps (Penukonda, for example) the Superintendents had the greatest difficulty in procuring grain of any kind; prices went up in places to 4.5 seers the rupee for both rice and cholam; and owing to the impossibility of getting any green food or any good water sickness spread through many of the relief-works.[18]

August: The Climax reached:

In August the Viceroy came to the Madras Presidency and with the Governor visited Bellary. A result of his tour was that from thenceforth the Duke controlled all famine matters himself, without the intervention of the usual channels of communication.

A definite policy was also laid down regarding the manner in which the different classes of the needy should be treated and the system under which works should be organised and controlled. August was the worst of all the terrible months of the famine. The numbers of those on gratuitous relief and on works in the district ran up to 137,000, or 18 percent, of the whole population according to the census of 1871.

September: Rain Fall:

It was the darkest hour before the dawn, for in the next month; heavy rain was at last and at length received. In the district as a whole 6.5 inches fell in September and in October another eight inches. The streams were in flood, the works were damaged by the rain, and at the famine-camp at Vajrakaruru a violent hurricane blew down the sheds and killed some of their inmates. The crisis was past, but though the numbers on works at once declined prices continued to be high and the totals of those on gratuitous relief in September were larger than they had ever been before. It was not until November that prices eased to any considerable extent and from thenceforth the numbers on relief rapidly declined and at the end of January 1878 works in the district were closed.

Cost of the Famine:

The cost of the famine in the district is not easy to ascertain as the official figures give details only for the old Bellary district as a whole. In 1885, however, Mr. Galton, then Collector of Bellary, worked out the total cost for that district as it now stands, and if this is deducted from the expenditure in the old Bellary district the cost in Anantapur (excluding all establishment charges) comes to Rs 10,32,000 for relief-works and Rs 9,85,000 for gratuitous relief. The loss of revenue is not now ascertainable.[19]

Scarcity of 1884-85:

The famine of 1876-78 has put all subsequent, as it did all previous, afflictions in the shade, but in the quarter of a century which has since elapsed two more scarcities and two more famines have visited this distressful district. The scarcity of 1884-85 was the first of these. Three out of the four preceding seasons had been unfavourable and in 1884, owing to deficient rain, the '*mungari*' harvest on the red soils had been small and the '*hangari*' crops in the black-soil taluks had failed almost everywhere. From March 1885 to June of the same year a considerable number of people were employed on the earth-work of the Guntakal-Hindupur Railway. The total amount spent on this up to September 1885, when heavy rain removed all further anxiety, was Rs 2.80 lakhs, and remissions amounting to 3.5 lakhs had been granted.[20]

Famine of 1891-92:

In 1891-92, famine again visited the district, but it suffered less severely than any of its neighbours in the Deccan. The three southern taluks escaped altogether and matters were never really serious in the others. The north-east monsoon of 1890 had failed in most of the southern and central districts of the Presidency, but in Anantapur the rainfall was sufficient and, thinking that they were safe, the ryots exported large quantities of grain to their afflicted neighbours. But in 1891, they themselves suffered from want of rain, both monsoons failing and the fall to the end of October being only ten inches against an average of twenty-one. In Dharmavaram and Kalyandurg the rain was particularly scanty. The extent cultivated in 1891-92 with all crops was nearly one-fifth less than the average and on one-fifth of this reduced area die crops either withered totally or gave an outturn of less than four annas. Prices consequently rose almost as suddenly as they had done in 1876 and by December 1891 cholam was selling in the north and centre of the district at between 11 and 13 seers the rupee, or more than double (in Dharmavaram nearly treble) the average rates. Part of this rapid rise is thought to have been due to the superstitious terror caused in the minds of the people by the remembrance that the coming Hindu cyclic year bore the ominous name of Nandana, which ever since the famine of 1832-33 had been a household word throughout the Ceded districts. Relief-works were started in December 1891.[21] The course of events thereafter is shown in Table 6.4.

Table 6.4: Relief Extended during Famine of 1891-92

Month and Year	Average number of people relieved during each month of the famine of 1891-92			Total per cent, of population in 1891	Average price in seers per rupee of	
	On works	Gratuit-ously	Total		Cholam	Rice (2nd sort).
December 1891	394	-	394	0.08	12.4	7.9
January 1892	515	278	793	0.17	13.6	8.5
February	487	571	1,058	0.22	14.2	8.7
March	910	240	1150	0.24	14.8	8.8
April	1,159	146	1,305	0.27	15.2	8.7
May	1, 211	131	1,342	0.28	16.1	18.9
June	1, 234	60	1,294	027	15.7	9.1
July	141	20	161	0.03	18.5	10.6
Average over 8 Months	756	181	937	0.09	15.0	8.9

Source: Famine Commission-1891-92.

Cattle mortality heavy:

Apparently no human mortality occurred, except from cholera, but the loss of cattle was very great. In some talukas one-fourth and even one-third of the breeding and young stock died. Grass was allowed to be cut free of charge in all distressed localities but no alterations were made in the rates for grazing in the reserved forests. Efforts were made to induce the ryots to try prickly-pear as fodder, but they usually declared that it gave the cattle liver-complaint.

Cost to State:

The total cost of the relief-works was some Rs 26,000 and gratuitous relief came to some Rs 2,700. Remissions, however, amounted to Rs 2, 85,000. The total cost to the State was thus about Rs 3,14,000.

Table 6.5: Type of Relief Works Undertaken during Famine of 1891-92

Type of Relief Works	Amount in Rs.
Roads	3,648
Irrigation works	6,800
Forest fencing etc	5,249
Establishment	10,445
Total	**26,142**

Source: Famine Commission-1891-92.

Between October 1891 and September 1892, Rs 94,000 were disbursed as advances under the Land Improvement Loans Act and Rs 4,000 for the purchase of fodder, cattle and seed-grain.

In 1896 and 1897 yet another famine visited Anantapur, Distress was general throughout a great part of India, but in Madras the only districts attacked were those in the Northern Circars and the Deccan. Among these latter the area affected in Anantapur was proportionately larger than in any of the others and amounted to over four-fifths of its total extent, including all parts of it except some portions of the three southern taluks. It was the same old story of deficient rains. The south-west monsoon of 1896 failed, and so did the north-east monsoon of the same year and the south-west monsoon of the next.[22]

Famine of 1896-97:

The dry land sowings in 1896-97 were almost up to the average, but of the area of the crops harvested up to the end of November 1896 more than a half gave no outturn at all and more than another one-third a quarter crop. The harvest in the next four months was even worse, over four-fifths of the area reaped giving either no crop at all or less than a quarter of the normal.

Numbers relieved and prices:

The prices of both cholam and ragi rose sharply in October 1896 and were above the scarcity rates in November. They varied greatly, however, in different parts of the district and in Hindupur and Madakasira were as much below the district average as in Gooty and Dharmavaram they were above it. At Hindupur ragi was at one time 34 measures to the rupee while at Dharmavaram, only 40 miles distant by rail, it was 19. Grain was imported in large quantities from Mysore and throughout the hot weather two special trains full were run daily from Hindupur to Gooty. Relief became necessary in November and the numbers on the works grew steadily larger until September 1897, when good rain at last arrived.[23] The average numbers on relief in the district in each month up to October 1897 are shown in Figure 6.2.

Figure 6.2
Per Cent of the Population Relieved during 1896-97 Famine in Anantapur District

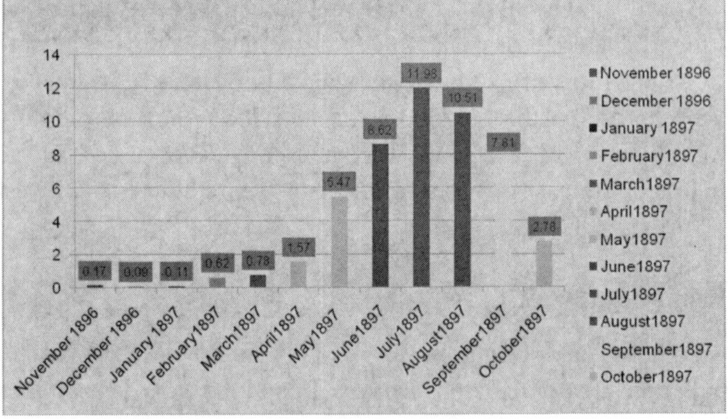

The value of works and average price of cholam in each month up to October 1897 are shown in table 6.6.

Table 6.6: Year-wise and Month-wise Average number of people relieved during each month of the famine of 1896-97

Month and Year.	Average number of people relieved during each month of the famine of 1896-97.				Average price in seers per rupee of cholam
	On relief works.	Weav-ers	On gratuitous relief	Total	
November 1896	1040	...	155	1,195	13.6
December 1896	506	...	111	617	14.2
January 1897	662	...	83	745	14.4
February1897	3957	...	438	4,395	13.8
March 1897	4889	...	661	5,550	14.1
April 1897	10021	45	1,059	11,125	13.9
May 1897	31459	104	7,205 |	1,38,768	13.5
June 1897	48010	154	12,943	61,107	12.8
July 1897	69780	308	14,805	84,893	11.1
August 1897	60500	‘429	13,522	74,451	10.2
September 1897	40948	489	13,932	55,369	11.5
October 1897	13222	869	5,589	19,680	15.1
Average over 12 months	23750	200	5,875	29,825	13.2

Source: Famine Commission-1896-1897.

The previous normal price of cholam had been 30 seers the rupee and it will be seen that in some months it was nearly treble this figure. Weavers were relieved by making them advances of material and taking over the fabrics woven there from at rates which left the workers sufficient for their maintenance for the time spent in weaving. The highest number so relieved in the district was 3,436. A Deputy Tahsildar was appointed to superintend operations and a special Deputy Collector was in charge of this form of relief in the four Deccan districts.

Mortality among cattle:

Human mortality from starvation was apparently unknown, but the cattle as usual suffered severely. Though in May 1897 all the forests of the district were thrown open to free grazing, a measure which was calculated to have benefited 42,000 head, the cattle census of 1897 showed no less than 132,000 head of cattle and 72,000 sheep and goats fewer than that of 1895. In no other district was the mortality so high.

Private charity and loans by Government :

From the Indian Famine Charitable Relief Fund, Rs 1,91,000 was received for expenditure in the district and nearly this entire sum was devoted to setting up afresh those who had suffered most severely by the distress. Fodder depots were also opened with the support of the Fund at seven places in the district and in those at Guntakal and Tadipatri 700 tons of paddy straw was sold.

The amounts advanced by Government under the Loans Acts were as shown below:—

	Rupees
Land Improvement Loans Act—	
For construction or repair of wells	1,54, 781
For other land improvements ...	86,253
Agriculturists Loans Act— ----	
For purchase of fodder	1, 36,281
For purchase of cattle and seed-grain	25,962
Total	**4,03,277**

Cost to the State:

The loss to the State from remissions of land revenue was five lakhs and from the decline in the Forest receipts, due to permitting grazing free, another Rs 6,000; or altogether Rs 5,06,000. The direct expenditure amounted altogether to Rs 9.7 lakhs, of which 1.97 went in gratuitous relief and 7.4 in wages on the works. Nearly all these works consisted of making or repairing roads. The total cost to the State was thus some Rs 14.75 lakhs.[24]

The famine was undoubtedly the severest which had visited the district since 1878, but warning had been taken from the results of the unpreparedness of 1876, the methods of fighting scarcity had been enormously improved, and owing to the great (some folk said excessive) liberality with which the people were treated the distress left few permanent traces behind it. The last bad season on record is that of 1900, but Anantapur was but slightly affected, only one small work (the restoration of the Pinnapalli tank near Yadiki) is opened in it, and the expenditure being only Rs 19,000.

Distress of 1900:

There was a recurrence of acute distress in some parts of the district during 1900 and, although of a short duration, it was caused by the scanty south-west monsoon of 1899, followed by an almost total failure of the north-east monsoon. The failure of the second monsoon was most marked in Anantapur, Kalyandurg, Gooty and Tadipatri taluks. Dry crops over large stretches either failed entirely or yielded far below the average. Parts of North India which were also in the grip of famine made enormous demand for grain from this district as well and this led to an inflation of their prices. The restoration of the ruined Pinnapalle tank near Yadiki in Tadipatri taluk was taken up as a test work but it never went beyond the 'test' stage and had to be closed early in August. Kadiri taluk suffered no less; at the end of July, 1899 less than half of the normal area under dry crops had been sown in the taluk. Collection of material on the Kurli Ghat road was taken up in February 1900 as a test work. Relief measures by way of postponement of collections and grant of advances were undertaken in Rayadurg taluk.[25] In parts of Kalyandurg and Dharmavaram taluks nonworking cattle suffered due to want of fodder and free cutting of grass had consequently to be permitted in the forest reserves.

Scarcity of 1901:

The 1901 again proved a harsh year particularly for the taluks of Gooty and Tadipatri, with a large volume of labour thrown out of employment. Consequently a number of works were executed by the

Public Works Department and at Jakkalacheruvu and Yadiki some-kitchens were opened. The distress, however, ended in September.

Famine of 1920-21:

With both the monsoons failing in 1920, Gooty taluk was particularly affected. Two test works and seven kitchens were opened in January 1921 in Gooty. The Indian People's Famine Trust made a grant from which clothes were supplied to destitutes. But the north-east monsoon proved timely and copious and put an end to the distress.

Famine of 1924-25:

The scarcity of 1924 engulfed parts of Gooty, Madakasira, Penukonda, Dharmavaram and Hindupur taluks. Even in 1923 the rainfall was very disappointing and while the early crops withered, the late ones did not sprout at all. The 'garden taluk' of Madakasira suffered from serious fodder scarcity. These taluks were declared as famine affected and test works were started in February 1924. Large quantities of fodder were imported and sold to the ryots at reasonable rates.

Famine of 1934-35:

In 1934, conditions became once again critical in Penukonda, parts of Hindupur and Tadipatri taluks. Sixty three relief works, comprising 38 irrigation, 19 road and six drinking water supply works were started. To relieve fodder scarcity, depots were opened in Penukonda, Hindupur, Kadiri, Dharmavaram, Anantapur, Tadipatri, Guntakal, Gooty, Kalyandurg and Madakasira. Among those organising relief, the Rayalaseema Central Famine Relief Committee, the Indian Red Cross Society, the Indian Peoples' Famine Trust, The Madras Corporation and the Zamindar of Ellamarri were the most prominent. A good north-east monsoon in 1935 put an end to this famine, the severest of the kind experienced in the district since 1896-97.

Famine of 1937-38:

The whole of Gooty taluk and parts of Tadipatri, Penukonda, Hindupur and Rayadurg taluks were badly affected by a famine in 1937-38. The seasonal conditions were not favourable enough to enable the agriculturists to recuperate from the distress. In April 1937, there was an unusually heavy rainfall, but later the rains receded. The few showers in September and October were untimely. There was a large scale failure of dry crops and the absence of any stocks with land-holders and the contraction of credit intensified the distress. The conditions in Gooty taluk and the Jutur area of Tadipatri taluk were so bad that even women belonging to some 'respectable' families were obliged to seek relief at the famine relief works. Drinking water supply was a problem in Gooty from May to August 1938. The weavers in Uravakonda were in straits and some of them were reported to have migrated to Bombay in search of livelihood. A relief centre had to be opened in the last week of June for providing work to them. The eastern portion of Rayadurg taluk was also affected necessitating the grant of large scale remission of land revenue and the opening of a test work.[26]

The District Board embarked on an expanded programme of road works and undertook the construction of the Kurnool-Bangalore road, the Gooty-Pattikonda road and the Cuddapah-Bellary road. Sixteen more road works were taken up between January and September 1938—one each in Dharmavaram and Hindupur, 12 in Kalyandurg and two in Kadiri taluks. Six relief works were also started by Government, two each in Gooty, Uravakonda and Tadipatri taluks and all these attracted a fairly large volume of labour from the neighbouring Kurnool and Bellary districts. Instead of being provided with cash doles, destitutes in the headquarter villages of each relief camp were fed in the adjoining kitchens.

Fodder scarcity was keenly felt in Rayadurg, Gooty, Kalyandurg and Kadiri taluks and fodder depots were opened at Rayadurg and Kalyandurg. A depot was set up at Bantanahal in Alur taluk of Kurnool district to provide fodder for the Uravakonda area. Hill grass was sold at concessional rates in these depots and the Panchayat reserves were also thrown open for free grazing.

Two non-official committees were formed, one each in Gooty and Tadipatri taluks and a sub-committee in Uravakonda. This sub-committee and a 'White Shirt Association' seemed to have done some good work, by way of distribution of clothing to children and provision of some monetary relief to pregnant women. The Red Cross Society distributed milk powder and cod liver oil to the infants. The High School Teachers' Association at Tadipatri and the Red Cross Societies at Guntur and Calicut collected some old clothes and gave them for distribution among the poor. The Rayalaseema Central Famine Relief Committee spent about Rs 1,400 on relief work. Cloth produced by the weavers in the relief centre and purchased with the help of a grant of Rs 10,000 from the Indian Peoples' Famine Trust Fund was also distributed. The District Co-operative Bank, Anantapur contributed a sum of over Rs 1,000 for sinking drinking water wells.

Famine of 1941-42:

The complete failure of the north-east monsoon of 1942 retarded agricultural operations and resulted in a failure of crops leading to conditions of scarcity. The entire district excepting the taluks of Kadiri and Hindupur was affected and relief measures covering nearly 28 percent of the district population had to be undertaken by Government for almost a year. Thirty- four road works were taken up for providing employment and a portion of the wages was paid in the shape of grain. Six depots were opened to relieve fodder scarcity.[27]

The Divisional Famine Relief Committee at Bukkapatnam organised the distribution of clothes, while substantial donations came from the Maharaja of Mysore and the Indian Peoples' Famine Trust. The Rayalaseema Famine Relief Committee also ran a few cheap grain depots. Towards the end of 1943 conditions slowly returned to normalcy on account of the good rainfall in September-November of the year.

Famine of 1945-46:

Hardly two years passed before Gooty, Tadipatri, Kalyandurg, Madakasira and Penukonda taluks were affected by a severe drought although it did not lead to a grave crisis. The last three taluks suffered from acute scarcity. The Bhogasamudram tank in Penukonda town-the main source of drinking water supply-was completely dried up and water had to be taken from small scoopings made in its bed. Water was also supplied by a Government lorry from Venkatareddipalle, two miles away. Desilting operations were undertaken in the wells and the 'kuntas' in Rayadurg town to relieve drinking water scarcity. In all [1861] relief works were taken up for execution at a cost of Rs 13.42 lakhs. Cash and grain doles were provided and special kitchens for children, two each in Madakasira and Kalyandurg and one in Dharmavaram were set up.[28]

About 31,000 children were fed at these kitchens while 2.84 lakhs of people were given gratuitous relief. To relieve scarcity of fodder, 26 fodder depots were opened and a fleet of 25 lorries maintained to transport both fodder and grain. Over 6,300 lorries of hill-grass were imported to tide over the crisis which lasted till August 1946. Clothes including sarees were distributed in Anantapur, Hindupur, Dharmavaram and Penukonda taluks from out of the donations made by the Indian Association, Jinga and similarly about 600 sets of dress were given to Sugali women out of the donation of the Indian Peoples' Famine Trust. The rains that commenced in July 1946 slowly mitigated the distress.

Floods:

While the worst sufferings of Anantapur have been those caused by deficiencies in the monsoons, there have been several occasions when on the other hand excessive rainfall has brought about disaster.

The disaster of 1804:

The first serious floods after the district was ceded to the Company were those of October 1804. Writing to the Board on the

4th November, Munro said:

> "In consequence of a torrent of rain between the 12th and 15th of last month, during which all the rivers and nullas rose to a height never before remembered, the greater part of the tanks have been destroyed over every part of the country from Harpanahalli to Chitvel. The nullas cut from rivers have been buried in sand and in many places so deep that it is difficult to discover their former channels, and many villages have been swept away with all the property they contained and in several instances with a considerable number of their inhabitants."[29]

In May of the next year he sent some details of the damage done. In the four Ceded districts four dams, 752 tanks, 260 "nullahs" and 855 wells had been either destroyed or greatly injured, and, although only such of them had been restored as possessed sufficient ayacut to repay the outlay in four years, as much as 6.5 lakh of rupees had been spent in repairing the damage they had sustained.

Storm of 1817:

Thirteen years later, on the 19th October 1817, the monsoon again set in with great violence. Writing in the following June, the Collector reported that 117 tanks, 58 channels and 312 wells in Bellary and Anantapur had been either breached or seriously injured. In the latter district the Gooty and Yddiki taluks suffered most. Nearly a lakh of rupees was spent in repairing the damage, and two lakhs more were granted in remissions. Moreover the rain continued to fall for weeks without intermission, and consequently hardly any cholam could be sown; and what little was put down was drowned by a return of very wet weather in November, so that the whole of the country usually grown with this crop presented "one uniform picture of desolation."[30]

Great Storm of 1851:

In May 1851 there occurred perhaps the most disastrous storm that the district has ever known. On the afternoon of the 5th May heavy rain began to fall and it continued without intermission all that day and the next and the day after that as well. The storm swept from north-west to south-east across a tract of country about 50 miles in breadth. The Collector wrote that "the damage done was excessive. Houses have been washed down everywhere. Cattle in hundreds and even thousands have perished in the rain." The roads which lay in the track of the storm were rendered impassable and 253 tanks within its influence in Bellary and Anantapur, having an ayacut assessed at £2 lakhs of rupees, were more or less seriously injured. Channels were swept away or obliterated, much land was ruined by the sand which was deposited on it the great tanks at Singanamala, Anantapur and Dharmavaram were breached, three fourths of the town of Tadipatri were washed away and the great gopuram of the temple on the river bank was brought to the ground. The Singanamala tank was terribly damaged, 840 yards of its embankment being swept away.

The estimates for the necessary repairs in Bellary and Anantapur amounted to three lakhs, and, as before, it was ordered that only those works should be put in order which would cost less than four years' revenue to restore. An exception to this rule was, however, made in the case of the Singanamala tank, the cost of repairing which was over Rs.60,000.

Public Health:

Anantapur is one of quite the healthiest districts in the Presidency. Its extreme dryness is in its favour, it has a short hot season and an unusually pleasant cold weather and Hindupur and Madakasira taluks form part of the Mysore plateau and share the exceptional climate of that tract.

Malaria: Anantapur is almost free from malaria which infests so much of the other three Deccan districts. In no part of it is fever endemic. The hills are as healthy as any other part of it and wet cultivation does not, as is often the case in Bellary, carry with it the penalty of an increase in disease. Dengue fever has recently visited Penukonda and many cases of it have occurred. The people say that it also appeared in 1874.[31]

Cholera: Cholera has yielded to some extent to the spread of sanitary ideas, but every now and again it breaks out again with something of its old energy. It is worst when the season is bad. The mortality from the disease was highest in the unfavourable years 1896 and 1901. When once cholera has begun operations it is the less easy to check owing to the crowded fashion in which so many of the villages are constructed. In days gone by no village was safe from marauders which was not walled and fortified, and often the dwellings were huddled together within the fort walls. The custom so originated still influences the people and dwellings outside the village- site are much rarer than in the south. The extension of well-cultivation, which requires the ryot to live near his land, will probably in time do much to break down this habit.[32]

Small-pox: Small-pox is undoubtedly rarer than of old, owing to the extension of vaccination in recent times. In no year of the past decade did the deaths caused by it reach one per million of the population. It however fluctuates in its effects in a manner which is not always susceptible of obvious explanation, causing extremely few deaths one year and a very considerable number the next.[33]

In 1898, plague was imported from Hubli in the Bombay Presidency to Timmancherla and Guntakal, whence it spread to Gooty, some villages near Uravakonda, and Hindupur. The Tahsildar of Hindupur, was murdered in October by a crowd of excited people who objected to the erection of plague sheds near their villages. The plague died away in the hot weather of 1899 and for the next two years the district was practically free from the disease. In October 1901 it was again imported, this time from Bellary, but it did little damage, the number of fatal indigenous cases being only 24. In 1902, it again appeared, chiefly in Kalyandurg taluk. But again the deaths were few, the total mortality being less than one hundred.

Guinea-worm: Guinea-worm prevails in a number of places in the northern and central taluks, but no accurate statistics are available. One of the worst villages in the district for the disease is Kalyandurg, where the water-supply is particularly defective. As elsewhere, fever, and other causes are claimed to cause a high percentage of the mortality, the reason being that in the unavoidable absence of a proper diagnosis of the cause of the majority of deaths, there is no other head under which the village officers, who compile the returns, can enter anything which is not clearly cholera or small-pox. The registration of these events is, however, compulsory only in Anantapur municipality, the eight taluk headquarters and Yadiki, and elsewhere the accuracy of the figures is not of a high standard.

Vaccination: Vaccination is compulsory only in Anantapur municipality and Vaccination the casba villages of the eleven unions of the district. Operations in Anantapur are controlled by the municipal council and elsewhere by the local boards.

Sanitation: Outside the municipality of Anantapur and the few unions of the Sanitation, district sanitation is, as usual, little understood and less practised. No comprehensive schemes of any kind have been undertaken anywhere in the district.

Anantapur possesses six hospitals and six dispensaries. Apparently the first of these to be established was the Munro Memorial Hospital at Gooty. This began as a dispensary which was located in the verandah of the Munro chattram. In 1869, it was moved to its present quarters, which were erected with the funds belonging to the chattram endowment, and a part of this endowment which had been formerly utilised for feeding travellers at the chattram was set aside for its upkeep. In 1884 the institution was handed over to the care of the taluk board, which now contributes to its maintenance.

The Anantapur hospital is financed by the municipality. Part of it has been recently rebuilt from funds raised for a Victoria Memorial and the foundation stone of a maternity ward has been laid.

The other four hospitals are those kept up by the Local Boards at Tadipatri, Dharmavaram, Hindupur and Penukonda. It is not dear when the last of these was established, but that at Tadipatri was founded in 1873 and the other two in 1884.

Dispensaries: The six dispensaries are all maintained from Local Funds. The villages in which they are located and the dates of their establishment are as under:—Bukkapatnam, 1891; Kalyandurg, 1879; Madakasira, 1890; Pamidi, 1893; Uravakonda, 1883; and Yadiki, 1901.[34] The history of famines in a district where scarcity is almost the rule is bound to be rather tedious but some of them which were either prolonged or intense merit description. Some of the earlier famines wrought upon the district before its formation in 1882. Recorded evidence testifies to large scale relinquishments of land, mass migration of people from Gooty and Rayadurg to Mysore, decrease of population and sale of stocks by the peasants 'to pay their last kists, the following review written in 1886 by Nicholson, the Acting Collector of Bellary, serves to show how frequent and unfortunate the distresses were between 1803 and 1885. The measures taken by the government to deal with such situations related at best to the disbursement of cash doles to the poor to "enable the dealers to introduce supplies of grain", prohibition of export of grain, grant of 'takkavi' loans and remission of assessment of land revenue "according to the ability of the farmer". These remissions were in fact restricted as it was felt that any large scale remission would be regarded rather a proof of the weakness than of the indulgence rendering the "future collection of revenue extremely difficult." Some of the famines during this period shook the district badly.

REFERENCES

1. Digby, The Famine Campaign in South India 1876-78, Vol. I, p. 25.
2. Krishna-Swami, S. Y., "Rural Problems in Madras" Monograph, p. 21.
3. *Ibid.*, p. 23.
4. Krishna, Y.S., A short Report on the Fodder, Milk Supply and Utilisation problems of the State of Madras, p. 25.
5. Report of Indian Famine Commission 1805-07.

6. Sathyanathan, W.R.S., Report of the Agricultural indebtedness, 1935, p. 54.
7. Report of the Indian famine Commission-1854, p. 27.
8. *Ibid.*, p. 29.
9. *Ibid.*, p. 33.
10. Report of the Indian famine Commission-1866, p. 5.
11. *Ibid.*, p. 7
12. *Ibid.*, p. 8.
13. *Ibid.*, p. 10.
14. Report of the Indian famine Commission-1878, p. 21.
15. *Ibid.*, p. 5.
16. *Ibid.*, p. 67.
17. *Ibid.*, p. 82.
18. *Ibid.*, p. 86.
19. *Ibid.*, p. 89.
20. Report of Indian Famine Commission 1882-85, p. 27.
21. Report of Indian Famine Commission, 1891-92, p. 49.
22. *Ibid.*, p. 80.
23. Report of Indian Famine Commission 1897, p. 42.
24. *Ibid.*, p. 48.
25. Report of Indian Famine Commission, 1901-03, p. 63.
26. Report of the Madras Famine Code Revision Committee, 1938, p. 55.
27. Narayanaswami Naidu, B .V., Report of the Economist for enquiry into rural indebtedness 1946, p. 28.
28. *Ibid.*, p. 35.
29. Anantapur District Gazetteer 1970, p. 542.
30. *Ibid.*, p. 548.
31. Report of the Health Survey and Development Committee, 1945, Vol. I., p. 34.
32. Lt. Col. A.T.H. Russel, Geographical Survey of Cholera in the Madras Presidency from 1818-1927, Madras, p. 35.
33. Lt. Col. A.T.H. Russel, Geographical Survey of Plague in the Madras Presidency, Madras, p. 11.
34. *Ibid.*, p. 13.

7

Historical Perspectives of Developments in Andhra Pradesh Under the Colonial Period

The crucial importance of the period of 18th century in the economic history of Andhradesa in general and that of its trade and commerce in particular is too well-known. This period witnessed many fluctuations in the trading and commercial life of the region due to rapid contemporary political changes and also the emergence of certain external forces. The seventeeth and the eighteenth centuries mark a transitional period in the history of India. During these centuries, India, because of the cumulative influnce and total effect of a number of political, social and economic factors, commenced on its course of moving from the medieval age towards the modern age and from the feudal age towards the colonial age. From the limited perspective of trade and commerce these two centuries may also be called as the age of European East India Companies.

In Andhradesa, as elsewhere in some other regions of India, so far as the aspect of trade and commerce is concerned, the seventeenth and the eighteenth centuries have acquired a special significance. This significance lies in the fact that a foreign and extraneous element in the form of European East India Companies, the Portuguese, the Dutch, the English and the French entered the economic scene through channels of trade and commerce; the 'factors' of these Companies founded 'Factories' at several port-towns, along the eastern and the western coasts of the southern peninsula and also at a few places in the interior of the country. Though the Portuguese presence was there in the early part of the seventeenth century on the eastern coast, its effect on the trade and Commerce in Andhradesa, if not next to nothing, was minimal and marginal. It was largely confined to San Thome and Madras and to places and ports south of Madras; to the north of Madras it never extended beyond Pulicat; the trade relations and activities of the Portuguese were mainly with the Vijayanagar empire, which was on the wane of its power. The ruling powers in Andhradesa during the seventeenth and the eighteenth centuries in the chronological order were the Qutbshahis, the Moghuls, the Asafjahis and the Arcot or Carnatic Nawabs who were vassals of the Asafjahis.

Kadiripati's *Sukasaptati, Narayanamatya's Hamsavimsati and Athavana Vyavaharatantramu* a local record in Telugu collected by Kavali Venkata Borraiah an assistant of Col. Colin Mackenzie describe the social and economic conditions of the Dekkan and the South in general and Andhradesa in particular, during the seventeenth and the eighteenth centuries. In this paper, the conditions of trade and commerce, internal and external, with special reference to commodity-structure, as can be gleaned from these three works, have been discussed.

The Maritime Merchant his Establishment and Activities; the Sukasaptati and the Hamsavimsati call a maritime merchant as Odakadu Oda in Telugu means a ship and Kadu. a genitive suffix, indicates ownership; similarly maritime trade is called Oda-beramu, beramu meaning trade.Sukasaptati describes the wealth and commercial activities of a maritime merchant (Odakadu) by name Vasumanta, a 'Gaura' (one of the merchant castes called 'Gaura'. Vasumanta was commissioned by the king of the land to supply to his palace and treasury commodities and articles of luxury. Sukasaptati says that this merchant-magnate, Vasumanta, owner of a number of merchant men, had established a shop (angadi) in every town, thus establishing, as is done in our own times by big business houses, a chain of wholesale and retail shops all over the country, controlled by a central establishment to sell his wares. He helps other lesser traders and merchants with advances of capital to start their trade and business. His wealth, by profits and trade earnings, is indicated by a pennant ('Padaga') raised on his house of business for each crore of accumulated wealth. His house of business was always agog and busy with traders who had assembled there to know the quotation of the commodities for the day, with stockbrokers, wholesale merchants and the assessors of precious stones and lapidaries. In addition to these, the poet Kadiripati says very interestingly, reflecting the contemporary scene, that Ingilishu Mukhamulu or the agents of the English factors waited and goods from Ceylon, Vilanga and Bangala (Bingal) reach him on his mere letter of indent, as he was known for his trustworthy and honest dealings. The descriptions indicates that Vasumanta carried on both inland trade and external trade.Continuing his narration of the activities of the merchant-magnate Vasumanta, Kadiripati says, that commissioned as he was by the ruler of the land to procure multifarious articles of luxury from the islands overseas, he, first reached the Bhagirathi or the Ganga. From there he made a voyage of the sea and reached the island, inhabited by the Parangis or Europeans of strange language and wondrous habits. It may be surmised that the island reached by Vasumanta was one of the islands of the Indian archipelago (probably Java), where the existence of the anthropoid ape, called Orang Utan has been known; for, later, among the ship loads of articles and wares that Vasumanta brought back with him, we find mention of Manisi-Krotulu or ape-men. We also know that in the Indian archipelago, in Sumatra and Java, and in Ceylon as well, the Dutch established their hegemony of trade in the seventeenth and the eighteenth centuries. Now to continue with the narration of Vasumantha's activites, it is said that he lived in the island for several years and established rapport and friendly relations with the Parangis. i.e., the Europeans. Then reminding himself of the royal mission, he loaded his ships with multifarious articles of luxury and voyaged back on the sea to his native place.

Kadiripati, in his Sukasaptati, speaking of another rich merchant called Somadatta says that, as in the case of Vasumata mentioned above, he obtained commodities on his mere letter of indent from all (Ceylon), Mummengi Bangalamu [Bengal and Gova (Goa)]. He also procured a number of high luxury goods from these different centres of trade. Kadiripati does not mention whether Somadatta procured these high luxury commodities to carry on trade on his own or on being commissioned by some rich and high potentate for the supply of these commodities. Narayanamatya, in his Hamsavimsati, speaks of a maritime merchant called Vishnudasa, who was eagerly sought after by the llamu Valavda, that is the Dutch (Valanda) in llamu or Ceylon and the Bandara Inglishu Kalamu that is the English ship merchants to negotiate the purchase of their wares and articles of trade, especially the spices and the scents (Saurabhadravyamulu). We get the impression from Narayanamatya's narration, that Vishnudasa procured numerous articles of luxury from Ceylon and from the marts that were situated on the shores of the Indian sea. It is not mentioned that he had visited any island beyond the sea, except Ceylon. It is also said that Vishnudasa, besides buying multifarious articles of luxury for his own business, helped the numerous traders who reached these marts on the shores of the Indian sea from the different trade centres of South India and of North India, as well, by negotiating for them the prices of the commodities. As already mentioned, these marts on the sea-shore were the factories of the English (Ingilishu) and the other European factors on the shores of India. Narayanamatya names about 250 places, obviously centres of trade, from all over India, and of which nearly three-fourths are in Andhra, from where merchants flocked to the sea-shore marts of the European trading companies. By the time of Narayanamatya, that is the eighteenth century, the presence of the Europeans was felt so much, as to make the poet say that 'Parangulu' (actually Portuguese, but here the word refers to all Europeans), Ingilisulu (the English), 'Barasulu' (the French) and 'Valandulu' (the Dutch) attended the annual festival (tiranallu) of god Sri Ramachandra Perumal.

Merchant magnates like Vasumanta, Somadatta and Vishnudasa, whose extensive activities of trade and commerce were described by the poets Kadiripati and Narayanamatya remind us of the merchants of the stature of VirjiVora of Surat, Malay Chetti, Kasi Viranna and Sunca Rama Chetti of the Coramandel who were masters of commercial empires and of whose extensive trade activities the writings of foreigners bear eloquent testimony. There are many parallels between the activities of the merchants described by Kadiripati and Narayanamatya and the activities of the merchants like Virji Vora, Kasi Viranna, Sunca Rama Chetti etc. known from the descriptions of foreign writers. These parallels are to be found on the items, (i) their trade covered a wide range of commodities and many branches of the inter-regional trade; (ii) their operations extended to most of India's traditional markets; and (iii) they owned fleets of ships to carry on maritime trade. We may not be exaggerating when we say that the poets had, in their minds, some living model of a merchant-magnate of their times, when they delineated in their Kavyas the characteristics and activities of their merchant heroes, Vasumanta, Somadatta and Vishnudasa.

Prof. Das Gupta who wrote on "Indian Merchants and the trade in Indian Ocean, c.1500-1750" in the Cambridge Economic History of India observes that the Indian merchants during these centuries fell into three categories. The first category were the "substantial merchants" "who travelled in style with their valuable cargoes and establishment of domestics, claiming and often obtaining special treatment on board as well as in the Indian Ocean ports". The second category were the merchants who travelled as agents of their principals and also managed their business at home. The third category were the small merchants who travelled with a bale or two of textiles every year on the ocean routes. The merchant-magnates Vasumanta, Somadatta and Vishnudasa, furnished above, it becomes clear that good rapport and trade relations had been established by the Indian merchants with the English and other European factors in India, settled on its shores and in the East Indian Islands. This rapport between the Indian merchants and the European factors did not miss the notice of even poets with a creative sense of curiosity like Kadiripati and Narayanamatya. It is also clear that the Indian merchants, who were commissioned by the kings, zamindars and rich landlords for a variety of large number of luxury articles, procured them from the European factors, who monopolised the trade in these aricles. The European factors acted as middlemen, and as such should have garnered huge profits, at least in some specified items of these luxury goods.

The descriptions of the trade activities of merchants, described by Kadiripati and Narayanamatya, leave us with the impression that the Indian merchant had not yet lost his initiative in trade and commerce. Economic historians are of the opinion that during the seventeenth and the eighteenth centuries, the Indian merchant investing in the trade of the Indian Ocean was "the most important figure in the country's overseas trade". This observation is especially true of South India, one of the cis-vindhyan macro-region of trade, and of Andhradesa, one of the 'perennial nuclear regions' of this narrow region. Burton Stein observes: "It is nevertheless arguable that for the first two centuries or more of the European presence, European sea power and sea-trade remained marginal to South Indian developments, commercial or otherwise, in contrast to Bengal. For most of the seventeenth and eighteenth centuries European traders were content with a small volume of trade from these stations along the coast and content also to remain at the fringes of the increasingly chaotic polity which threatened even their small-scale commercial operations".

Both Kadiripati and Narayanamatya furnish us with a long and interesting list of commodities which their merchant heroes,Vasumanta, Somadatta and Vishnudasa, had brought back after having purchased them from the marts of the English and other European factors, situated either on the shores of the Indian Ocean or in the islands of the sea, i.e. the Indian archipelago. Some of these commodities might also have been procured from trade centres in the interior of the country and Narayanamatya gives the names of more than 150 such trade marts within Andhradesa. The commodities, named in the lists furnished in the works of the poets are identical to a great extent and consist of mostly fancy and high value luxury goods. A good number of these commodities do not find mention in the writings of foreign traders and travellers.

Andhra Ports and the Maritime activity in Textile trade:

Ports play an important role in the economy of a country. Andhra enjoyed special privileges that accrue to a coastal country as it has a long coast-line of nearly a thousand kilometers. When ships were the only means of bulk transport, Andhra coasts had many centres of brisk trade. Western coast of India was brought under the Portuguese who claimed maritime supremacy over the Indian Ocean with a view to having monopolistic hold on the entire produce of spices. The Dutch, English, French companies who appeared late had to get spices mainly from other parts of Asia and in their quest for these commodities they entered the trade in textiles and a number of other items whereby they hoped to collect more spices and other valuable items which were in great demand in their motherland. As a result, we find a significant change in commodity composition of the export from India in the early part of seventeenth century and it was in this context that the East coast became the target of the contending European powers. Of all the important ports of coromandel Machilipatnam was the leading port before Madras was even thought of. The other ports of Andhra too had their own share in maritime trade of the seventeenth century.

Machilipatnam was known as Bandari Mubarak in the Indo-Persian chronicles of late Qutb Shahi period. The actual rise of this port town is attributed to the rise and stabilisation of the kingdom of Golkonda in the sixteenth century. The British East India Company and the Dutch East India Company formed in 1600 and 1602 A.D, respectively, established their factories at various ports on the Indian coast. The word factory does not convey any meaning in the modern sense of the term. These factories were the trade centres, where the Europeans unloaded goods from their own countries and where the Indian goods were collected, processed and shipped off.There were nearly 40 ports big or small on the Andhra coast visited by the western ships in the early seventeenth century but they had ceased to be ports any more as the sea has receded considerably. Treaties were signed with the local rulers and it was a sea-saw of favours for the European traders depending on the peshcush they could afford. The first European factory to be established in Machilipatnam was that of Dutch which was established on the strength of the Firman issued by the Sultan of Golconda, Mohmad Quli in August 1606. It was in the early seventeenth century that the English landed at Surat with a strong economic motive. Their interest in India rose mainly when they discovered that there was a great demand for Indian Textiles in south-east Asia. The company, therefore, decided to force its way into the textile trade of India inspite of fierce Portuguese opposition. The English opened negotiations with rulers of Golconda for trading facilities on the coast of Andhra.

The earliest English factory on the eastern coast was established at Machilipatnam in 1611. The company was willing to wage battles against the other Europeans powers as they knew that the calicoes, chintzes and palampores of Andhra were in large demand in markets of south east Asia. With a view to exporting locally woven piece goods to Persia and Bantam the English started the factory in Machilipatnam. The port became heaven to the Muslim, Hindu and European merchants the participation of merchants from various nations speeded up the production in various sectors. The growing export market for textiles enhanced their production which is evident in the proliferation of weaving settlements in its immediate and in the far interior areas. The varieties of cloth produced were of high specialisation, some of the most important varieties being batellies, Salemporis Morris, guinea cloth and long cloth most of which found their way to south east Asia, Persian gulf and also to Europe. Diamonds were exported to Achin, Ormuz, Persia and Europe. Indigo produced in the hinter land was mostly used for domestic market which had an export potential. One major advantage the port had was its capacity to correspond its exports with imports. This exceptional potential of the port was due to its link with the kingdom of Golconda which was indispensable.

This port town of Andhra grew at a tremendous speed in the seventeenth century because of the factor that it had access to the hinterland. The hinterland of Machilipatnam included the fertile lands of Krishna-Godavari deltas where cotton and dye-yielding crops were raised on large areas. In fact the hinterlands of this port was so vast that textiles and other export items were brought here from places as far as 350 miles interior. Thus, the port became the greatest one in these parts and came nearest to an enterpot.

Apart from Dutch and the English, the other European powers worth noting is the French who opened their commercial establishments at Machilipatnam in 1669 by obtaining a firman from the Sultan of the Golconda. In fact the contact established by French at Machilipatnam later paved way for closer relations between the French and the Nizam. Nizampatnam mentioned by Ferishta as Arjunpatnam was a known centre for ship building industry. The English and Dutch vied with each other for trade in salt-petre.

Textile Exports:

The Andhra coast was traditionally a region of variegated weaving. The best textiles along the entire cost were produced in the Nizampatnam area. Apart from coloured woven of material, 'Ikat', was also manufactured. The Tamil Nadu coastal area was better known for its fine kalamkari ware. The products of both regions, the woven material of Andhra coast and the kalamkari fabrics of the Tamilnadu coast played an important role in the spice trade. Nutmeg mace and cloves in which Indonesia possessed a monopoly were bartered in exchange for these textiles.

Under the aegis of Vijayanagar, the southern unit also received considerable fillup, although there are references to the kalamkari technic being practised in the second century of the Christian era very little is known about the patterns in vogue or the identity of the artisans. The establishment of Vijayanagar suzerainty was also accompanied by a degree of demographic change with the settlement of Telugu speaking immigrants in Tamil country. Members of Telugu Naidu community now came to exercise an exclusive hold on the painting of Kalamkari ware.

The Qutub Shahi rule saw the reopening of earlier areas of trade. Apart from the spice Islands, a demand was established in the markets of the Red Sea and more particularly in Iran. This led to the fashioning of a new range of textiles. Kalamkari ware began to be made on a commercial scale. The Persian market was a potent one and patterns tended to fall in line with consumer preferences. As in the Tamil Nadu region the painters of Kalamkari were drawn from among members of the Naidu community.

Although the tradition of kalamkari was much more firmly entrenched in the Tamil Nadu region, the painted ware of the Golconda coast soon established a name, perhaps as a result of court patronage, for superior quality. Although the Motupalli charter and the grandiose activities of Raja Chola and Rajendra Chola are suggestive of an indigenous tradition of maritime activity carried on a considerable scale, the actualities of local maritime skills remain shrouded in mystery. When the Europeans entered the field, the Chettiars played a role in the south while the existence of an Arab settlement had been associated with the early history of Masulipatnam. It was because of their participation in the spice trade that Europeans were drawn to the east coast. The Dutch enjoyed a particularly favourable position in Golconda. Not only did they possess distinct advantages in the spice trade, but they were the only Europeans tolerated on Japanese soil. This enabled them to bring Japanese gold and copper into Golconda. The same advantage provided the Dutch with an edge over other European competitors in the Persian market. Although the Dutch themselves were primarily interested in Persian silk they were fully cognisant of the additional fact of Persian demand for Golconda painted cottons. Dutch counters in Golconda comprised those established at Masulipatnam (1605), Petapoly (1605), Palakollu (1606) the capital city, Golconda (1661), as also Datcheron, Nagalwanse and Bimlipatnam

The other items of exports from the Andhra coast were diamonds, iron, steel, silks. The diamonds were exported to countries like Persia, Holland, Portugal and Turkey. About 23 diamond mines were found in the Kingdom of Golconda towards the second half of the seventeenth century. Those who were rendered helpless on account of famine and other natural or man-made calamities were purchased and sold for the European colonies, and Masulipatnam was one of the chief exporting centres of slaves. As seen above an ever-increasing demand was made for the slaves who could be sent to the estates of cloves nutmegs etc., in the South East Asian countries. Both Indian and foreign merchants traded in slaves. Thus merchant's capital established a strong on various sectors of economy through Masulipatnam in the seventeenth century.

The imports of the period were Nutmeg, Sandal wood, Gold from Siam, Pepper and ivory, Japanese and Chinese camphor were also imported.The fort towns of Andhra had a life different from that of the hinter land and the middle men kept contacts with the foreign traders. Local people not only prepared goods for sale but also were employed as porters, cooks, washermen, gardeners, house keepers, soldiers, peons and clerks. No wonder the agriculture labour slowly began moving to the coastal areas in quest for money and livelihood of a different nature.

Textile Trade and Commerce in Andhradesa:

We hardly ever listen to the ticking of the clock as long as the clock continues to tick. Once the clock stops ticking for some reason or other, then only do we realise that the clock had been ticking smoothly since a long time and had proper care been taken it may not have stopped ticking. That the phenomenon has relevance to trade and commerce as well, can be understood very well, if we were to take cognizance of the spate of suicides of cash crop farmers in contemporary Andhra Pradesh or Telangana to be specific. All sorts of reasons are being attributed for the sad state of affairs which has resulted in so many suicides. One marvels at the ingenuinity of man in the context of search for the reasons of the spate of suicides of the farmers. The latest reason offered has a physchological explanation given by a team of psychiatrists. It says that the suicides of farmers are the result of a phenomenon of mass hysteria in which a person initiates others in a state of depression. People in distress have a tendency to copy the behaviour of others who have solved similar problems and copying the behaviour of role models is natural. If a role model solved his problem by committing suicide hundreds of others in similar plight would follow suit.

Viewed in this light, it would appear that the sudden decline and finally the total disappearance of the textile trade of Andhra Pradesh deserves serious investigation. It may be mentioned, however, that this paper is not the result of any such investigation but only deals with the desirability of such a project for a doctoral thesis and offers some suggestions regarding the approach to be adopted,

The craze for cotton goods especially muslins and betilles produed in the Golconda region had commenced in Europe a century earlier than the period focussed in this seminar but reached its peak around 1680. The escalating export of textiles from the Andhra region can be deduced from the growing orders for muslins and Warangal bettilles in the Despatches from Holland. In 1642, the Dutch had shipped between eight thousand to ten thousand pieces of Guinea cloth from Coromandel to Holland. In 1682, forty years later, two lakhs thirty five thousand pieces of Guinea cloth that is calico were shipped from the port of Masulipatnam alone, besides forty thousand pieces from various other factories in Coromandel. It is obvious that the textiles of this region were valued more than the textiles of other regions and thus it has been estimated that the export from the Andra region was six fold more than the Tamil Nadu region. Similarly it far exceeded the export from the Western coast.

It is no wounder that the entire North Deccan was dotted with villages engaged in the production of textiles for meeting the export demand. These centres of North Deccan have been listed in some detail by the well known Dutch Chronicler, Daniel Havert. Similarly, the Golconda region also had many traditional weaving villages going back to the pre-Qutbshahi and even Kakatiya period. The earliest European Merchant Company's trading stations, the factories, were established in the towns which sprung up at the centre of these rural weaving villages. Havert informs us that near about Warangal, 72 miles North West from Masulipatnam, there were twelve prosperous weaving centres, which produced bettiles, araals, serongs and fine cloth. At Ellur and eight villages there abouts, about twelve miles from Maulipatnam, were woren blue Salamporees, Madapollams named after the place where it was made, and every kind of blue cloth. The other textile centre mentioned by Havert in the vicinity of Masulipatnam are Linga with ten villages, Mangalagiri with fourteen weaving villages, Malipora with twenty-two weaving villages and Doorapindy with fourteen weaving villages. All these textile weaving centres also witnessed a thriving trade and commerce.

It is not surprising, therefore, that the weavers living at these places were fairly, satisfied lot. Medieval inscriptions and Telugu literary accounts give the picture of a happy continuity, satisfied with its place in the community in which they lived. It must be realised, however, that those connected with the export trade were slightly better off than those engaged in meeting the demands of the local requirement. Artisans like weavers and smiths seem to have come within the lower-middle strata of society as distinct from the rural poor or the low caste artisans like the potters and the leather workers. On the other side of the scale were the merchants and bureaucracy who were quite well off. Yet, the Ramadhanya Charitra of Kanakdasa, the sixteenth century saint and poet would suggest that most of the weavers could subsist on only Ragi and could not afford even coarse rice. Perhaps the general standard of living of all the people was rather low for in the fifteenth century Srinatha commented that in Palnad even the king had to plough and the queen had to spin. As far as millet is concerned according to Srinatha even Manmath had to subsist on millet. May be Srinatha's account has more of poetic fancy and yet it would appear that rice was not available easily. The truth is that a clear idea of a weaver's income can be had only from the seventeenth century western accounts and the earlier indigenous sources do not provide specific information. If we take note of Methwold's account, a weaver earned about Rs 3 per month, which was also the standard wage of smiths and other artisans. In contrast a domestic servant was paid only around Rs 2 per month. Another Dutch record of 1652 confirms that the monthly wage of an ordinary weaver was Rs.3. It appears that this wage remained the same throughout the period with which we are dealing i.e. the seventeenth and eighteenth centuries. In 1737-38, the monthly wage of Rs 5 demanded by the Bombay weavers was considered a high figure. In 1790, a weaver at Vishakapatnam earned Rs 4 a month. Hamilton Buchanan describing the state of affairs around 1800 gives daily earnings which workout to be Rs 2 and a half per month for the weaver of fine cloth. It must be remembered that prices in seventeenth and eighteenth century Andhra were such that it was possible to survive on such low wages, even if one lived from hand to mouth. Travellers like Palsaert and Bernier, however paint a miserable picture of the weaver who had to reckon not only with low wages but also with feudal oppression.

The flourishing textile export on the one hand and the pathetic picture of the weaver on the other hand offers a strange contradiction. The reasons for this contradiction are many but one reason surpasses all the other reasons. The capabilities of the weaver as a weaver were inversely proportional to his capabilities as a trader. In fact he hardly ever dealt directly with the European purchaser. For one thing there was the difficulty of communication, and the foreign merchant hardly ever dealt directly with the craftsman. They employed brokers who in Golconda were generally termed as "Committees" on account of their belonging to the Komati class. For painted Kalamkaris, the Komatis received 'musters' from the foreign merchants i.e. master drawings and also advance. The majority of the workers were so poor that no work could be undertaken without advance. Conversely, it was through the advance that the foreign merchant exercised any control over the artisan. If the producers were scattered, the brokers would sub-contract to others of the same caste (described as inferior committees). It were not only the European merchants who made use of Komatis to give orders. The Persians also adopted the same procedure and thus it were the middle men who were the real beneficiaries of the export trade in cotton.

While the middle men gained the most of the advantages they did not participate in the disadvantages. It has been mentioned that the Europeans supplied 'musters' to the weavers in order to conform to the length, breadth and thickness. For Kalamkaris, the musters supplied the specimen for design and colour. If the ultimate product was not to their satisfaction the companies would not make full payment to the merchants and the money promised to the weavers would be reduced proportionately.

The royalty apart from purchases in open market, was also involved with the production of textile items for their own use as article of clothing the Jamas (coats) and the Patkas (girdles) and as wall hanging in their tents. Bernier has given a detailed description of one of Emperor Aurangzeb's encampments in 1665. He mentions that the principal tent was lined inside "with beautiful hand jointed chintz manufactured for the purpose at Masulipatnam" and "the Emperor's private enclosure was also hung with Masulipatnam chintz, painted over with flowers of a hundred defferent kinds." The Qutbshahi royal tents should have been no different.There was so much competition in procuring painted textile for the Mughal and Qutbshahi tents that "Wakya Nigars" i.e. the writers of news letters stationed in Qutbshahi territory reported the acquisition of these items by Qutbshahi kings to the emperor Aurangzeb. Thus, among the hazards of the trade one may also include the hazard of royal wrath in the event of failure to supply the wanted items of textile. Various justifications for the Mughal attacks on the Deccani Sultanates have been given. The greed for Deccani textiles could have been yet another reason. The English factors had planned to shift their trading stations from Masulipatam on account of the monopolistic procurement of the textiles at that centre by the Qutbshahi rulers. The written testimony is available in the communication of the English factors stationed at Bantam (Java) dated 31st January 1636, addressed to their bosses in London in which the factors laments the increased shortages of goods due to the acquisition by the Golconda king for his own use.

It is not necessary that the Qutbshahi royalty should have acquired local textiles only for their personal use. Trading and barter could have also been the real reason. The Qutbshahi kingdom had close relations with Persia. Mohd. Quli Qutb Shah (1580-1611) had given one of his daughters in marriage to Shah Abbas the ruler of Persia. There were diplomatic exchanges and the safavid Court of Persia too valued Golconda Kalamkaris quite a lot and made use of Golconda textiles for the clothing of Irani soldiers. On the other hand Persian horses were in great demand in the Golconda kingdom and were exchanged for textile items. Thus, it would appear that undesirable royal interest in textile production was a serious hazard.

If the changes in fashion were responsible for the popularity of Indian textiles in France and England among the privileged classes and among the peasant class in Holland and other European nations, the changes in culinary taste of the Europeans proved to be a hazard for the textile trade with Far East. Originally the European Companies used to acquire Kalamkaris and other textile items for barter in spice trade from the Far East. Bullion was exchanged for textile in India and textile was exchanged for spice in the Far East. However, the spice trade declined in later seventeenth century and first half of the eighteenth century as a result of changes in European culinary tastes. This was marked by decreasing reliance on salted meats as an item of diet during winter months. There was a resultant fall in demand for spices which had earlier been used to make salted meat palatable by masking its unsavoury smell. This hazard of changing tastes was however oft set with the growing popularity of the Indian textiles in the European market on account of changing fashions.

The thugs and brigands who infested the highways were yet another hazard for trade and commerce in the seventeenth and eighteenth century Andhra region. At times they were very well organised. While some account of their methods and tactics is available in the English language the vernacular literature has not been explored exhaustively for their activities.

Recently some serious investigation, has been done regarding famines of late medieval period. Yet few people realise the severity of famines of medieval times. Poor means of communication and transport hampered any sort of help and areas of plenty and areas of famine could not be far apart.The Golconda region experienced a severe famine around 1687 immediately after its annexation by the Mughals. The internal political chaos coincided with the growing agitation in England against the import of Indian calico. Danial Havert has left behind a very touching picture of this tragedy. In a letter to his friend he describes in great detail the plight of thousands who lay dead on the streets and how women and children sold themselves into slavery. Of Masulipatnam he says, "it has become so bad from morality and death from this year 1687 as most of the merchants and weavers are dead, that Masulipatnam is at present a sketch of what it was before. He also discusses the rejection of goods in Europe and the failure of Company in making payments. The unsettled conditions of the region are further described as, "The trade are quite dead, added here to the bankruptcy of the weavers as well from their dead as from flight and the plunder of the robbers who keep themselves so near the village." Havert further informs "where there were eighteen merchants earlier 1682, now there are but nine. The rest are dead or poor and at present every thing is transacted by five merchants who are very scarce with money." Havert indicated that the Dutch were thinking in terms of closing their establishment at Golconda.

The Industrial revolution in Europe, the discovery of aniline dyes and the growing political power of the British in India put the final nails in the coffin of textile trade in India. Lord Bentick summed up the situation when he observed, "the bones of the cotton weavers are bleaching the plains of India". It is up to us to ponder over why have we always been so careless about research and development and why do we fail to study and analyse the hazards of trade and commerce.

The East India Company consolidated its position in Andhra during the first half of the nineteenth century. It reorganised the administration by dividing the entire region into many districts and appointed collectors over them. The collector was entrusted with the responsibilities of revenue administration and general adminstration of the district. The entire area of coastal Andhra was divided into five collectorates of Ganjam, Visakhapatnam, Godavari, Krishna and Nellore. The Rayalaseema area ceded by the Nizam to the East India Company in 1800 was constituted into a single collectorate with Anantapur as its headquarters. Four sub-collectors namely Thackeray, Cochrane, Graeme and Stoward were appointed at Harpanahalli, Adoni, Cuddapah and Cumbum to assist the collector in his work. In 1808, the area was placed under two collectorates of Bellary and Cuddapah.

The next benefit is concerned with the economic field. At the beginning itself, the British observed that there were three radical evils in South India. They were the insubordination of the Zamindars, and palegars, the lack of recognised laws and law courts and the uncertainties of the land revenue system. By subjugating palegars, Zamindars they not only established peace but also evolved their own land revenue policy which caused benefits to both the government and the ryots to a certain extent.

Anantapur District is one of the twenty-three(13 districts) districts of the state of Andhra Pradesh and also one among the four districts of Rayalaseema namely Chittoor, Cuddapah, Kurnool and Anantapur. The district consists of three revenue divisions and further divided into 63 revenue mandals. The area of the Anantapur District is about 19,130 Square Kilometers.[1] The district is situated between 13°-10'. and 15°-15' Northern latitude and 76° and 78°-30' Eastern longitudes. Geographically the district is located at the Northernmost point of the Mysore plateau. Its elevation towards the south is about 2,200 ft., and its declination is about 1000 ft. at Gutty in the north and 9009 ft., at Tadipatri in the north east.[2]

Anantapur district is the place where dry and hot climate prevails most of the time in a year. Evasion of monsoons is the main cause for precarious agricultural conditions in the district. As the district is far away from the seam, the north-east monsoons do not visit this region. The Western Ghats prevent the south-western monsoons from entering into this district. The rainy season is mainly experienced during the months of May-November. The average rainfall in the district is 440.4 mm. The month of November is recorded for the highest rainfall of 88.4 mm in the year 1992-93.[3]

Agriculture is the main stay of the people of the district. The main crops that are produced in the district are paddy, jowar, bajra and maize. The important commercial crops in the district are grams and peanuts. Though the district relies much on rains for agriculture, cultivation in certain area, is under major and minor irrigation projects.

The systems of land revenue administration in Ananthapur district:

Anantapur region was under the rule of various divisions dynasties during the ancient period. Different systems of land revenue policies came into vogue in this region. In the early times 'Samudayam' or group tenure was in existence. The main features of this group tenure are (1) the periodical and (2) using the special number of ploughs and labourers of tilling the land and sharing the gross produce among the cultivators themselves, only after paying the fixed state share. The responsibility of the administration of land revenue was entrusted to a village corporate body, which consisted of the staff of village servants. The lands were divided into three kinds. They were 1. Nirunela (Wet Land), 2.Velichenu (Dry Land), 3.Tonta Bhumi (Horticulture). The rates of assessment fixed were varied on these different kinds of land. No land revenue was charged on waste lands 'Poramboke' and 'tarasu'[4]. The same system was continued with little modifications until the region was came under the Vijayanagar empire.

The method of assessment of the land tax:

The method of assessment has undergone change under the Rayas of Vijayanagar. To assess the land tax certain factors were taken into account. They are, (1) The nature of village, (2) The tenure of the land, (3) The nature of the soil and (4) The kind of the crop cultivated in the soil. At first it was to be traced out whether a piece of land was a devadana or brhmadeya or dalvayagrahara or in kraragrama. The nature of the crop was also considered for fixing the land tax. Tax was charged on the lands producing dry crops and horticulture. According to a record of 1311 from Tirvennaimallu, a tax called 'tottapumvu' i.e., tax on garden lands was collected.[5] Moreover several factors were taken into consideration by the rulers for fixing the rate of assessment. However, in the post Vijayanagara Period, the Sultans of Bijapur and those of Golconda who held sway over the region adopted the system of equal sharing of crop by the state and on the basis of actual survey of the land, which was that in use. But under the rule of the Nizam of Hyderabad i.e., between 1792 A.D. and 1800 A.D. there was a decrease in revenue collection. This was because of severe famines which affected the district during the years 1792 and 1793.

After the third Mysore war in 1799 A.D. the Nizam of Hyderabad entered into an alliance with British East India Company which is known as Subsidiary Alliance in A.D. 1800. According to which the districts of Bellary (inclusive of Anantapur district) Cuddapah and Kurnool passed into the hands of British East India Company. Anantapur was made headquarters in 1807 A.D. and the region was called ceded districts. This region was divided into two Collectorates of Bellary and Cuddapah and so remained until 1858 when Kurnool was constituted into separate district.

As soon as the district came under the control of the British, Thomas Munro was appointed by the Madras Government, as the principal Collector of the region in 1800. Thomas Munro was to face the powerful Poligars who were wielding enormous power in the region and were not ready to accept the authority of the British. Thomas Munro issued proclamations to these Poligars to lay down their arms and also pay peshkush to the East India Company. It took 18 months for him to bring them to terms. In Anantapur region, there were some prominent Poligars who at first offered stiff resistance against the British and surrendered later on.[6]

Thomas Munro as principal Collector, for better supervision and administrative convenience, divided the region into four Sub-Collectorates. These were Harpanahalli, Adoni, Cuddapah and Cumbum and they were further divided into 37 revenue tolohs.[7] Thus, systematic administrative units based on geographical conditions, headed by officials to look into revenue administration in the region, came into existence for the first time under the regime of British East India Company.

The Village-wise settlement :

Thomas Munro soon after assuming charge as Principal Collector introduced 'Mauzawar' or village-wise revenue settlement. The main principle of this system of land revenue was the fixation of land revenue for every village and the ryots of that village were to make collective payment, according to their shares of land. But at the end of the same year, this village-wise settlement was replaced by the Ryotwari system of land revenue. The year 1788-89 was taken as the standard year for the assessment of land revenue in the region. That year approximately 11 lakhs of pagodas of land revenue was collected.[8]

On the introduction of ryotwari system, Thomas Munro opined that the system would bring mom revalue to the government with the rise in yielding capacity of soils. The fundamental principles on which the settlement of ryotwari depended were the settlements should be ryotwari. The prime motive of ryotwari system was to determine the taxable capacity and general prosperity of the inhabitants of a village. A radical change in the nature and extent of the land tax under ryotwari also caused troubles to the ryots.

The Ryotwary system that was implemented by Thomas Munro Numb Miami affected the peasant community economically who were not in a position to take up cultivation unless the government came to their help. Thomas Munro realising the condition of the peasants decided to advance loans to purchase bullocks, grains and carts. The steps taken by Munro to ameliorate the ryots had no effect because of prevailing famine conditions. Land had no salable and ryots started migrating to far off places in search of livelihood.

Under Ryotwari system Thomas Munro, the Principal Collector of Anantapur ordered for systematic survey of the land and settlement of the land revenue to be collected. The survey of land was started in June 1802 and was finished by 180 a survey parties were formed in this purpose. Surveyors surveyed the areas of all rinds, sites, towns, villages, agricultural fields, tanks, rivers, waste land and identified the area under forests. While surveying the agricultural lands the names of the ryots were registered and numbers were given to their fields. The surveyors used the standard measure, i.e. a chain of thirty-three feet, forty of which made an acre. The head surveyors supervised the surveying process by surveyors. A revenue survey is one of the stages and it is directly related to the land revenue.[9] The main aim of conducting systematic land survey was to determine the wealth of the various Provinces and their power to hear taxation.[10] For conducting a regular and systematic land survey the Madras Survey Department was constituted in the year 1854. The aims of this act were the establishment and maintenance of boundary marks and facilitating the settlement by avoiding boundary disputes in the presidency of Fort St. George.

For assessment purpose, the assessors followed the surveyors. The assessors went round of the surveyed lands with the assistance of village officers namely munsif and karanam along with ryot of the field. While assessing the field the land in question was classified under the heads of wet and dry. Both wet and dry land was further into 1st, 2nd and 3rd sorts agreeable to their supposed respective produce. The classes of wet land in a village were often increased to five or six and those of dry to eight or ten. However, allowance was made for distance from the village and even other incident by which the expense of cultivation was augmented. While surveying and accessing the dry land, black and red lands were classified separately. If 1/4th of the land was cultivated by a peasant the entire field was registered for assessment as waste land. If only 1/2 of the land was cultivated, the cultivated part was registered fertile and the other half as waste. If three quarters were cultivated and only one quarter was left waste, the entire field was recorded as cultivated land. Uncultivated lands were classified into fallow lands. The surveyors registered the names of the royts and the numbers of their field. They marked out the division of fields all surveyed and recorded.[11]

Provision for maintaining land records :

To avoid land disputes the Madras Survey Act made a provision for maintaining land records after survey. The system of maintaining land records with the purpose of providing the relevant and current information about land holdings in the district was introduced.

Maintained survey records in Anantapur District of Madras Presidency:

The survey records that were maintained in Anantapur District of Madras Presidency are as follows:

(a) A village map of an 8 inch or 16-inch scale. (b) A field measurement book. (c) A demarcation sketch. (d) A stone register. (e) Village Accounts (Revenue assessment). (f) Field register. (g) Register of Inam lands. (h) Register of irrigation fields. (i) Register of migrated area occupied and charge under each source and (j) Land Revenue Settlement for a series of years.

The Government framed certain policies on which the Ryotwari system was implemented; 1. Assessment was to be fixed on the land. 2. Soils were to be classified for the purpose of assessment. 3. The fixed assessment amount was not being more than half the value of the net produce after deducting the expenses of cultivation. 4. It was not to be levied any tax on the second crop of dry land but in the case of wet lands, the tax collected on second crop to be one-half of the first crop assessment. 5. Remissions to be allowed wherever and whenever there was failure of monsoons. 6. In the circumstances of incessant supply of water, the special settlement officers was empowered with the task of making the charge on second crop. 7. Lands were divided into two categories namely wet and dry. 8. Lands, cultivated under the ayacut or Doruvu well must be considered as dry lands. The water-cess levied on them should be atone fourth or one-eighth of the difference between the wet and dry rates of assessment because water was provided by single or double lift. 9. The ryot was the complete owner of his land and was given the power of selling, 10. Relinquishing, mortgaging and obtaining more land.11. A reduction of 25 percent on all land should be made in the survey rates of assessment.12. An additional reduction of 8 percent or 33 percent in the assessment should be allowed on lands watered by wells or by water raised by machinery from rivers and mullahs. A similar reduction should be allowed on the lands watered by small tanks wherever the cultivators agreed to bear the expense of repairs. 13. Thy ryot should not be harassed by the revenue officers in any way so long as he paid the fixed assessment. But in the cases of non-payment, the ryots should be evicted from his land by the government. 14. Taccavi advances were sanctioned to the ryots to purchase bullocks, seeds, agricultural implements, forage etc., to repair old irrigation wells, to construct new ones etc., which were repayable by ryots in easy instalments to the government and 15. All unoccupied land should be in the lands of government.

After the completion of the classification of soils, the work of fixing the assessment on land was to be started by the government. The share of the government was fixed to be one half of the net produce of land. The net produce was only the remaining produce alter making all necessary deductions, from the total produce. The fixation of assessment was made by taking the value of gains into consideration. The grain value determined was convened into money at the commutation price. The soils of equal gain value were classified under various groups called taram (classes) each with its own rate of assessment.

Policy of Land Revenue administration :

The settlement made for a 'Fausali' the harvest year was called 'Jamabandi' was introduced as a policy of Land Revenue administration. The Government issued an order No. 521 on 27a May 1887 in which the procedure for conducting a detailed jamabandi and the duties of officers. Revenue officers from village to the district level to conduct jamabandi were appointed. The aim of conducting jamabandi was to verify the estimated data of all items of land revenue including the demand for permanently settled Estates, Inam villages and minor Inams. According to the terms laid down in the Government order, the officer appointed to conduct jamabandi, should verify the compilation of statistics prescribed for economic and administrative purposes. A detailed statement of village and taluk registers and accounts was to be prepared by the officers for ascertaining the above referred particulars. In terms of the Government order referred above the process of jamabandi of every revenue taluk was to be completed before the end of the fusali year and after the completion of jamabandi, the taluk-wise demand statements were to be closed within fifteen days.

Machinery and revenue administration:

The Board of Revenue of Madras Presidency in its Regulation I of 1803 created a well defined machinery to head the general and revenue administration. According to the regulation, four categories of officers in each district and their powers and functions were defined. They are 1. District Officers, 2. Taluk Officers, 3. Village Officers in Ryotwari villages and 4. Village Officers in proprietary estates.

The District Collector, the Head Assistant Collector, the Divisional Officers like Deputy Collectors, belonged to the first category of 'District Officers', Tahsildar Deputy Tahsildars and Revenue Inspectors were grouped together under the category II and the village officers were placed under the category III. They are (1) Village headman (Munsif); (2) Karanam (Accountant); (3) Talaayary and 4) Vetti (Village servants) in Ryotwari villages.

The District collector was the Principal revenue collecting authority in the district on both the cultivable and uncultivable lands in the district. The Head Assistant Collector assists the Principal Collector in day to day administration.

The Deputy Collectors who were ranked second in the administrative hierarchy were over all in-charge of the Revenue Divisions. The officers supervised the administration. They had to supervise the annual settlements of the villages within their jurisdiction. They had to attend to the complains from the ryots on the question of the encroachment of lands and distribution of water, issuing pattahs, investigating the claims of remission under till conditions of failure of crops, drought, famines, storms etc., and ordering for the repair of tame sand water sources. These officers were to conduct the annual jamabandi every year at the Divisional level.

The Tahsildars were overall in-charge of taluks and they were assisted by Deputy Tahsildars in day to day general and revenue administration. Revenue Inspectors were appointed to look after the revenue and land administration in a group of villages within his jurisdiction. They had to report every affair to the tahsildars.

The village officers belonged to the lowest cadre of Revenue Officials. The British Government respected the age old custom of inheritance of the post of village officer and allowed to continue the persons of the family in the post of village administration. They did not disturb the administrative fabric at village level. The facilitated for smooth conduct of revenue and general administration at the grass root level which is hub of all activities. The village level officers played a key role in the revenue administration.

Historical Perspective of Irrigational facilities in India Under the British Supremacy:

An important period in the agrarian history of India, it witnessed an enormously varied and complex situation as far as its agrarian conditions were concerned. The land tenure system, land revenue assessment, rates, nature of collection during this period. In the life of ordinary peasant and the agriculture labour became miserable. There was no major development as far as the system of irrigation, extension of cultivation and the process of agriculture were concerned. A significant development of this time was that India known for certain crops like tobacco, potato, chillis etc. another phenomenon of this period was that while the cultivation of crops like that of cotton, indigo, ginjalie etc. got a tremendous impetus became of European trade. There were also sub-regional variations in the crop pattern.After their foothold in India, the British government continued the policy of its immediate preceding rulers who sought to glorify their reign by undertaking the irrigation works but their policy in the first half of the nineteenth century was not satisfactory and they only revived the old ones. Their policy was changed only in the second half of the nineteenth century. The question arises why they were interested in the second half of the nineteenth century. The answer is, the fundamental trait of the British Indian Government irrigation policy during the period was an expansion in the irrigation services, and they experienced famines, floods and unfavourable seasons, in the first half of the nineteenth century. To avoid this, they had to pay more attention irrigation works are a good safeguard against famines and droughts. Moreover, they could be constructed as a measure to relieve distress caused by them. A general increase in the wealth of a country as brought about through irrigation works raises the taxpaying capacity of its inhabitants. An extension in the irrigated area increases agricultural production and improves the material well being of the peasantry. They also expected political advantages from the construction of irrigation works.

It was believed that the native population would lead a Peaceful life and the Raj would be free from dangerous agitations etc. the most important consideration appears to be their usefulness in years of famines and droughts. On the whole the Government undertook the execution of irrigation works because they were impressed by similar works completed by proceeding rulers. They thought that the irrigation works proved to be a solution to the problems of the day and they had their own self interests. With the above views in their minds they undertake the great works like Godavari, Krishna, Pennar etc., by the close of the first half of the nineteenth century. Mr. White at the beginning of the period asserted that not a single scheme has been projected "Since the establishment of the company's administration on the coast".[12] The Government of Fort St. George declared in 1799 "It is the wish of the Government to leave the construction and care of tanks and Water sources entirely to proprietors who will however encourage improvement and be assisted with loans from the treasury".[13]

The Existing of Irrigation Works:

Thousands were left in drought every year, as both the project of the old Governments and those of the public spirited donors were left uncared for the Company. Occassional loans for repairing old irrigation works were given by the company, only when they could help the payment of revenue without arrears. More than half the existing irrigation works were constructed by the ryots themselves. Otherwise vast tracts could not be protected against drought every year.[14] If repairs were ever carried out, they were always at the expense of the renters, who had to keep a deposit with the company.[15] Local authorities used to take up the smaller works, while the bigger ones were entrusted to supervisors. The problem of irrigation received more attention from the then British rulers. Generally the collectors were responsible for the collection of revenue with the assistance of the civil engineering department.[16] There was a superintendent of Tank Repairs and water sources in 1809. His duties were divided between two Civil Engineers in 1809 and they were raised to four in a decade[17] to suggest and construct canals wherever necessary Taccavi loans were given to ryots to carry out repairs."repayable with interest at 12 percent on the security of their estates and under prescribed regulations."[18]

Later on, the Collectors were authorised to lend on security at 10 percent the amount to be paid in a moderate period.[19] These taccavi loans in Chicacole proved very profitable on the whole the expenditure on irrigation works was inadequate. The Company was more particular about the revenue and neglected to improve the sources of irrigation. The public works commission noted that the charge incurred for repairs was less than half percent on the probable original cost of the works, under two percent of their total commercial yield and little more than four percent on the revenue derived from them"[20] The Maramut (repair) department was organised by civil engineers in 1838 which worked with great zeal and proved most beneficial, both the Government and the ryotzamindari areas also, Maramut continued in full vigour.

As the collectors of revenue and their subordinates could not bestow their entire attention of this, the Government appointed committees to enquire about the situation of the irrigation works in 1832 Arthur cotton was asked to report on the condition of these minor works. In the words of Arthus Cotton. The revenue actually derived from them was by no means a full measure of their value and advised the authorities to bestow more attention on their upkeep and maintenance as he felt that the aim of Government was not the creation of revenue but the good of the people.[21]

Prior to 1854 the Construction and management of all the public works except railways was entrusted to the military engineers of the three engineer corps of the East India Company Armies, working under the control of the Military Board and Subsequently to the corps of the Royal Engineers.[22] Some of these engineers became famous for their pioneering works on the great irrigation projects which they executed with remarkable courage and skill. Amongst them the most famous names are John Calvin, Proby T. Cautley Arthur Cotton, and S.L. Jacob. In the year 1854 Lord Dalhousie abolished the military boards[23] and in order to improve the irrigation facilities, a separate public works department was organised in 1854 with a Chief Engineer assisted by a number of engineers to supervise and control the works of irrigation.[24] After the establishment of the public works department which came directly under the control of Government of India Public Works Department was divided into two branches in 1866 viz, the civil works branch including irrigation, roads etc., and a Military works branch. The kudimaramat also gradually ceased. Such was the public of the Company with regard to minor irrigations works shall now study their policy regarding the major irrigation works.

The Construction of Irrigation Works:

The great irrigation projects were constructed during the end of the first half of the nineteenth century. Arthur cotton was at the summit of his fame in the fifties, with the successful execution of large irrigation projects like the Cauvery delta system, the Godavari and the Krishna delta system of canal under his supervision and guidance. All these proved to be financially quite sound and every new project, therefore, came to be looked upon as a potential Gold mine.[25] In order to further the exploitation of irrigation potential of the country the private enterprises under what was known as the guarantee system was also undertaken. Under this system, the Government of India guaranteed a return of five percent on the capital outlay.[26] Shortly after the mutiny, great pressure was put upon the Secretary of State to construct irrigation works by means of private companies. The Madras Irrigation and Canal Company was the first company in India in 1858[27] and the East India Irrigation and Canal Company in 1863 was the second one. It was an unsuccessful experiment and the progress was very slow. These two companies were a financial failure. Warned by this example and the experience elsewhere of the unsuitability of the agency of private companies in the construction of irrigation works. Government constructed all other irrigation works in the Madras presidency by the direct agency of their own Officers. This decision was arrived at in 1867, when the policy of guaranteed companies for the construction of irrigation works was finally abandoned in favour of what was then called the "extraordinary" public.

Works policy, whereby large works of irrigation expected to prove remunerative were to be constructed by Government from money borrowed annually by the state, when the ordinary revenues were insufficient for the purpose. This capital expenditure incurred on the large irrigation works of the Godavari, Krishna rivers continued upto the year 1879 partly to be met from Loan Funds and partly from ordinary revenue.[28] In 1876, the term 'Extraordinary' was abolished in favour of productive and very strict rules were laid down. Under this policy some of the greatest irrigation works of the country were constructed like Krishna, Cauvery, Sirhind etc. Productive canals i.e. those expected to yield within ten years of their construction, net revenue sufficient to cover the annual interests charges on the capital investment were undertaken. These productive public works proved remunerative.

Protective Public Works:

By the year1881 new class of works, called protective public works, as instituted. They may be defined as works, which although not directly remunerative to the extent which would justify their inclusion in the class of productive public works were calculated to afford a protection against famine and to guard against probable future expenditure in relief of the population. The only work yet classed under this head is that known as the Rushikulya project in the Ganjam District. The work was sanctioned by the Secretary of State.

In 1883 and the preliminary operations for commencing work were undertaken towards the close of the official year 1883-84.[29] The progress up to 1880 had not been so rapid. The value of irrigation in times of famine had always been recognised and the extension of irrigation facilities was always one of the main recommendations of all Famine Commissions.[30] The Famine Commission of 1880 recommended a programme of construction of irrigation work and by the end of the century most of these were completed. The commission of 1896 also drew up a definite programme, but the lines on which works was afterwards carried out were laid down by the Irrigation commission. So the beginning of the present century was marked by an important event in the history of irrigation in India. Lord Curzon's Government appointed in 1901 an Irrigation Commission, which was presided over by Sir Colin Scott Moncrieff.[31] This Commission toured throughout the country and a very comprehensive review of the whole problem was taken by this commission in its report and detailed recommendations regarding particular works under consideration as well as the general line of policy were made. The company attention was specially directed towards the desirability of the extension of irrigation as protection against famines. In Madras province, the irrigation commission had recommended that the systems of the three great deltas of Godavari, Krishna and Cauvery should be completed[32] and the Rushkulya project in Ganjam should be executed.[33]

The history of irrigation in India under the British rule is story of plan less and uncoordinated efforts by a government which has failed to realise the potentialities of offering irrigation facilitates to a country where water has been said to be more valuable than land.[34] Truly speaking their policy was to develop productive irrigation works and to neglect protectiveness. The irrigation Commission emphasised the protective value of irrigation works and appointed out that the indirect savings they might bring about by reducing the cost of famine relief and by obviating the need for remissions of the land revenue, would often make up for the expenditure on such works.

The drive for improvement did not entirely die out, but by mid-century the Agricultural Society of India, one of its principal champions, had lost much of its improving zeal in favour of a more decorative and recreational role. The perceived need for improvement in Indian agriculture remained: indeed, it was enhanced by the massive famines of the late nineteenth century and the rise of a more technically advanced agricultural science. But, despite the widely perceived failure of the zamindari system, the practical implementation of improvement was left either to once-despised Indian initiative or the reluctant intervention of the colonial state. Moreover, the quest for improvement remained largely as it had begun, a European movement, and failed to generate among Indians the necessary enthusiasm and resources for substantial agrarian change. Despite its continuing evocation into the 1840s and 50s, the British model of improving landlords and tenants had all but failed on Indian soil.[35]

The Establishment of Property Land Relations in Colonial Andhra (1800-1850):

Agrarian conditions in Andhradesa cropping pattern, growth of commercial agriculture and its impact on the economy. The agrarian system of Andhradesa during this period of two centuries is essential for an understanding of the nature of colonial exploitation in the succeeding period in its proper perspectives. The agrarian exploitation and the crisis of the colonial period is more truly the vestige of the agrarian system prevalent in the area during the pre-colonial period. To understanding of the economic history of this region in particular and that of India in general.[36] By the end of the eighteenth century, the whole of Andhra came under the control of East India Company. After the establishment of British political and administrative control. The Andhra region was progressively brought into the orbit of world capitalist economy in a "subordinate."or colonial position[37]. In the beginning the main concern of the company was to get more revenues from the land in order to finance their trade and expansionist needs[38]. Therefore, they created new land revenue systems which in turn transformed the agrarian social structure in Andhra. The colonial system of land tenures legitimised a new pattern of peasant relationship to and it was that framework within which agricultural production was carried out. The nature of land tenurial systems conditioned not only by production methods. but also the distribution of produce. Hence, in this paper, an attempt has been made to analyze the pattern of changes that were introduced in the land revenue settlements in Andhra during the first half of the nineteenth century.

In the pre-British period, the land revenue was collected from peasants by zamindars, poligars and other local petty chiefs[39]. The state conferred on these intermediaries the right to collect land revenue from the peasants.The peasants in turn held their lands on sharing system. Generally, the States share was half of the total produce. This system was called Asamhsystem. Though most of the lands were either under the direct control of zamindars or the government. The actual cultivation was organised not directly by them, but through an hierarchy of intermediary. It with these intermediaries who took the villages on rent and in turn made agree and with the individual peasants for the cultivation of lands in those villages. In some cases, the zamindars directly made arrangements with the village heads taking them responsible for the revenues[40]. Whatever, might have been the arrangements from peasants, in general, were collected in kind. In fact, there were only a few instant of fixing of money rents.

It was into this type of pre-colonial economy that the East India Company sought to introduce new tenurial system. To legitimize the new system, several ideologically loaded reports were produced, denouncing pre-colonial system as oppressive and unjust and the cultivators were reduced to object poverty under the weight of arbitrary demands and exactions, which always were beyond the stipulated rents.[41] This inhuman condition was supposed to have continued only until the advent of Britishers in Andhra. The disturbed political situation under the Golconda rulers was identified and highlighted as a cause for the oppressive demands on peasants from local Zamindars.[42] Though the East India Company had fixed the land revenue demand at a very new level. Those exactions were justified by contrasting them with the deliberately exaggerated 'oppressive and unjust' taxation system in the pre-colonial period .It is in the context of this ideological framework, we propose to analyze the introduction of various tenurial systems in Andhra in the early nineteenth centaury.

Ryotwary Experiments:

In the Ceded districts, Sir Thomas Munro, abolishing all the earlier revenue settlements based on sharing system, had introduced a new tenurial system with individual peasant proprietorship. In the Ceded districts, Munro preferred individual settlement with peasants to the permanent zamindari, settlement that was in operation in Bengal. Through these individual settlements called ryotwary. Munro undertook an elaborate survey and settlement of the land revenue demands.

To systematize the revenue appropriation from peasants, Thomas Munro had introduced a system of systematic survey of the entire land cultivated lands were surveyed by fields which were registered by name and with a number. This survey was completed by 1806. The assessment was taxed uniformly for an entire district, after comparing it with the collections under the earlier governments, the estimates of the ordinary and head assessors and the opinion of the most intelligent native people. The assessment was made on the basis of half of the gross produce Alta fixing the net assessment for the whole district, the share of cacti village was finalised. If the villagers objected to their share of assessment, the issue was examined by the peasants of others wages. In fact, each claim was examined and if found necessary modified seceding to the terms aimed upon between both the parties. This system, which was introduced in the beginning, had run into difficulties. There upon Thomas Munro initiated what is known as the ryotwari settlement. Under this system the individual peasants were given pattas, with particulars on land revenue assessment, area under the occupation of each pattadar. The ryotwary system was maintained throughout Munro's period of service, as Collector up to 1807. Munro advocated adopting this ryotwary system permanently.

The assumption was that the zamindary settlement would be comfortable, and assure more revenues. Despite all these uncertainties. Munro, was able to convince the government to fix moderate assessment in the first three years and a gradual increase in fourth year. Munro also pleaded that the initial assessment was too high in view of the impoverished condition of the people.[43] When the British government asked to submit a report on the feasibility of introducing permanent settlement, instead. Thomas Munro recommended the ryotwary system which he thought was suitable for the socio-economic conditions of the Ceded districts.

In 1808, the Madras Government considered the introduction of permanent ryotwary settlement, as advocated by Munro not only improper but impracticable and directed to introduce a village lease system for three years. In this system, the villages were rented out to the highest bidder - generally the Reddys and Karnams - and the revenue demand being fixed on the average assessment of former years.[44] Even in this system, the lands were over assessed and therefore, it failed. Heavy arrears remained outstanding at their close, and the peasants had to suffer much from the hardness and rapacity of the renters.

At this point, the Madras Government thought that better results might follow if leases were for a longer term period. In 1811, the triennial leases were exchanged for decennial village leases. The Madras government decided to settle this system permanently. In future, if it was approved by the British government and Court of Directors. The majority of villages were rented out under this system, though some of the villages, which remained without renters, were settled on ryotwary tenures. The competition among the renters was so great to get villages for rent, that the outsiders were in many instances found to outbid the local Reddys and Karnams, who actually can judge the real value of lands and how to utilise them. As a natural consequence, the demands thus fixed were almost in all such cases turned out to be too high. The villagers were either zufted (auctioned) for arrears or thrown out by the ryots as a losing concern. In both eases the renters not only exhausted all the resources of peasant's before they gave up but in the process got impoverished themselves. This system, therefore, proved to be disastrous both to the renters and ryots. In 1820, for instance, there was an outstanding balance of Rs 3,21,248, while many renters were bemoaningtheir temerity in prisons. As the assessment was high both the renters and ryots got ruined. In the Rayadurg taluk alone, remarked Thomas Munro that[45] nearly half the ryots, had emigrated, most of the headmen were reduced to poverty and many of them had been sense to had the substantial ryots whose stock supported the agriculture of the villages, were gone.

The ryotwary system as it was reintroduced after 1820 was a modified form of the old ryotwary. The Board of Revenue tried to introduce it in two different forms, viz., pulcutryotwary and field ryotwary. After consultation with the ryots all the lands, both cultivated and waste, were made over to the villagers on the condition that they pay a certain sum as government share. This system was called apputticut, ryotwary settlement[46] which resembled the joint village rents in Rajahmundry and Masulipatam Districts. (Later called as Godavary and Krishna districts).

The other type of settlement was 'annual field ryotwary' of sharratryotwary system. This was a settlement on fixed terms, prevailed in the irrigated villages. It was a joint arrangement among the ryots in conformity with the visabadikamatams, i.e., maintaining joint interest in the cultivation with fixed shares. As in the earlier ryotwary, the assessment was fixed on the basis of half of the gross produce. Individual pattas showing the particulars of land assessment were given to the individual peasant proprietors. As the rates were found to be injuriously high, the government in 1820 had accepted to lower the assessment to the extent of 25 percent on all dry and wet lands and 33 percent on all garden lands.

However, we cannot argue that the assessment under ryotwary system from 1822-23 was very light, there are indications that the assessment during this period, in the ryotwary areas tended to retard the agricultural development. Between 1822-23 and 1856-57 there were four exceptionally bad harvesting years : among the remaining years, except in 1841-42, 1842-44 and 1993-94 in no year had the land revenue reached that of 1822-23, the first year of the ryotwary settlement, as the revenue demand had been dependent on the acreage under cultivation. There was difference of opinion among the British officials on the cause for this agricultural depression. While some believed, that this was due to heavy assessment, the others argued, that since the over assessment was very low there was decrease in cultivation due to fall in prices of grain.[47]

Broadly speaking, the real cause for the heavy assessment in the initial stages was the insistence by the Court of Directions on large revenue remittances from agriculture. Under the pressure from the Court of directors, the officials had always tried to increase the revenue exactions in every mode of settlement. Except in the ryotwary system, in which the individual peasant was responsible to pay the land revenue, which in turn was revised at fixed intervals, there was no elasticity to increase the revenue demand in other tenurial systems and hence they proved to be a failure. In other words, unlike the other tenurial systems, the ryotwary system had allowed the government to impose increased new revenue assessments after every resettlement. We further illustrate the complex history of ryotwari system with the case study of Nellore district for there are regional variations to this history.

Nellore district by the British, in 1801:

Nellore district was acquired by the British, in 1801, it was under the management of few renters fixed the Carnatic Nawab. These renters, as for the assertion of the colonial administrators did not keep any regular accounts and collected revenue on the basis of sharing system. The first Collector of the district Travers, got all these renters removed and in their place, introduced the ryotwary system. The justification given for this change was to stop confusion and willful mystification of former revenue administration. He, moreover, started to make arrangements with the inhabitants of each village regarding the area to be brought under cultivation, and the probable produce to be derived there from. Lands were measured roughly and affixed an estimate of outturn. The government share was fixed at 55 percent per punt of grain. Further deduction of 3.75 percent was made for village fees. This left 41.25 percent to the peasant. The conversion of money rates for the government share was fixed at Rs 40 per punt for jowar, and Rs 26 and Rs 30 for paddy.[48]

Cultivators completely under the subjection:

After sometime this system was modified, under the assumption that a few of the principal inhabitants, who monopolised all advantages at the expense of the mass of cultivators, secured to themselves the best lands and usurped the greater proportion of the pasturage. These rich and powerful ryots said to have held the poorer cultivators completely under their control by advancing the money or grain for their revenue payments on the security of the produce at low prices, and reselling to them the grain they had need of at a considerable advancement or profit. As C. Rundall Deputy Director of Revenue Settlement. Nellore commented on these principal inhabitants. "they were wealthy as well as powerful and held the poorer cultivators completely in subjection; advancing their lists on the security of the produce at low prices. Therefore, a system of fixed money assessment was introduced in 1802-03, after conducting inquiry and classification of soils. The government share (land revenue) was fixed at 55 percent after deducting 6.5 percent for villages. The commutation rate was lowered to Rs 20 per punt for wet and Rs 28 for dry grains. This resulted in 15 types of dry rates from Rs 9.21 to Rs 0.25 per acre. and 38 types of wet rates from Rs 27.19 to Rs 2.25 per acre. The waste lands were given to the cultivators, which were regarded till then as common property of the community. This settlement was known as the Ryotwary Muria Settlement. As in the ceded districts, the mucta system was abandoned in favour of village rents. In 1807-08, first Triennial and afterward Decennial settlements. This system of village rentals was introduced by the Collector of Nellore Fraser, Even under this system most of the renters, as in it. Case of Ceded districts, could not pay the arrears and half of the rented villages in the Nellore district had been resumed by 1820-21. The Collector of Nellore, Smalley, who came after Fraser, commented on the evils under these leases.

Again. in 1826-27, Smalley, the Collector of Nellore introduced a new land revenue settlement in eighty ha villages, based on his own experimental survey. This however had not satisfied the Board of Revenue and consequently the survey started by Smalley was stopped. There upon the villages under thematic; system were brought back into Travers's mucks ryotwary settlement. The situation in 1830 was guist confusing with simultaneous existence of different land revenue systems not work. In some villages, the Travers nutria ryotwari settlement its modified My Smalley form, while in other villages. Smalley's own experimental settlement. These varied revenue systems continued until 1859-60.

In 1839-40, while 67 villages of the Udayagiri Jagir were resumed, in 1841, the Sydapuramtainindary was sold for arrears of peish rush which was purchased by the government. The Collector of Nellore, Stonehouse settled these villages by fixing government share at 55 percent of the grass outturn, after deducting six and half percent for village fees, and commuting the rates at Rs 22 per putti for dry, and for wet crops. By 1859-60, several modes of settlements were in existence in Nellore district. They were:

S.No.	Mode of Settlement	Number of Villages
1	Traver'smucta villages	127
2	Smalley's mucta villages	381
3	Smalley's surveyed villages	86
4	Settled by Stonehouse	67
5	Under rent	57
6	Under amani system	1
	Total Villages	**719**

Thus, out of 719 villages only one village was continued under the traditional sharing system.

In the ryotwary areas, the basic change that was introduced by the British mu fixing of the government land revenue in money, completely abolishing the sharing system. The major and the immediate consequence of this change was the increase in land revenue burden. In the sharing system, which was very common in the pre-British period peasants paid their share to the state depending on the season and the harvest. Though they paid a large quantity of produce (according to their share) in favourable seasons, the peasants paid less during unfavourable seasons this turned out to be a blessing in disguise for peasants. But under the new system the peasants were compelled to pay their revenue share (in fixed money rates) which was same in favourable and unfavourable seasons. Therefore, under the new system while the peasants benefited from high commodity prices at the time of favorable seasons, which existed for a short period, they had suffered in the long run to a long spell of had years and low prices. Added to this was the compelling need of the peasants to sell their produce immediately after the harvest to pay their fixed government revenue demand in money. Here, the commodity prices played a very important role; they were always low during the harvest season. So the ordinary peasants hardly benefited from the commodity market. They suffered due to the land revenue demand in money as it forced the peasants to alienate their produce at an unfavourable time and commodity rates. A.K. Bagchi rightly remarked.[49]

Under the British, not only was the payment fixed in money, it was also realised in money, exactly at harvest times. So the riskiness of prices was added to the riskiness of the harvests and aggravated the peasant burden.

Zamindary Permanent Settlement:

In the Northern Circars, at the time of its acquisition by the British, the lands were under the control of reminders, besides some hay lands which were maintained directly by the Government, to meet the needs of garrisons and civil establishments.[50] As early as in 1769, the Madras government formed Provincial Councils to supervise zamindaries. Initially the Company followed a policy of annual settlements with zamindaries but only low paid their rents punctually taking advantage of the prevailing political anarchy.[51] Traditionally the zamindars employed sub renters to collect the revenues from the ryot and said to have exploited the peasants with unauthorised exactions. Like in the zamindaries, the Provincial

Councils also employed the renters in heavily lands, which were under the government control to collect revenues sometime; whole 'sirkar' was let out to a renter. Unfortunately, mostly eking strangers, the renters inhavely areas abused their powers even more grossly than those under the zamindars. However by 1796, Government of India, encouraged by their success in Bengal, insisted on introducing permanent zamindary settlement in the Madras Presidency. Though the Madras Government and its Collectors were unwilling to introduce the permanent zamindary system, the Regulation XXV of 1802 made the tenure zamindary permanent one.[52] It gave them a right to hold their zamindaries forever on fixed revenue to the government, call peishcush, with heritability and transferability of property however, the ancient Zamindars were given only title namely the sanad-milkyyat-istimrar, under which their Zamindars were neither divisible nor alienable the other zamindaris on the other hand were brought into existence by an agreement called Cubliat and their estates were freely transferable, and could be sold, gifted or mortgaged peishcush was fixed 2/3 of the half of the gross produce.[53]

Several causes were attributed for the decline of the zamindari estates. Firstly, the demand of peishcush on many estates was arbitrary and too heavy. For instance, entire Charmahal estate in Krishna district was bought in by the government by 1843, for the estate could not pay the high peishcash.[54] In some cases, course, the demand was fixed very low and they obviously continued to survive. Second many of the zamindaries had become extinct from the bad management of their estates. Thirdly, frequently visit of famines and bad seasons effected the agricultural production adversely and prevented them from collecting enough to pay the peishcush. For instance, when the famine of 1833 badly effected all the zamindaries in the Krishna district, the Government did not give remissions on the peishcush and struck to their rule: pay the peishcush and keep the land. This expropriated several of them. Lastly the actual cultivators did not get any chance to improve their lands as there was no help forthcoming from the zamindars, rather they were oppressed by the burden of heavy rentals.

Zamindars received rents in money:

The lands under the zamindary system were never surveyed, not even roughly. Therefore, the fixation of rents was done based on certain traditional practices. The Rent was fixed on the division of produce, i.e., asarah system, (it was called, kailing system in the Krishna district), often effected by the intervention of the zamindars. In Ganjam district, the ryot's share was generally from seven to eight nowties out of nowties, in paddy and half a share in dry grains.

Under the zamindary system, the proprietary rights on the lands were not given the peasants, but were given, in practice, to the zamindar as long as he paid the peishcush to the government. In this system, even the waste lands were under the control of the zamindar. He could assign the waste land to any person and the occupation of it was protected by the custom. We do not see any instance, in which a single peasant was ejected from his land. However, in practice to recover the arrears of rent, often the peasants immovable property was auctioned.

Before the introduction of permanent settlement in Madras, the Governor General issued instructions, which the Board of Revenue also accepted, not to acknowledge the proprietary rights of zamindars (existing or those to be created) in any respect of affect the rights of the ryots who were under the authority of the zamindars. They also felt that the proposed regulation should not prevent the government, in future, from passing any law for the protection of the rights of the ryots. Surprisingly, not withstanding all such declarations and instructions, no provision was made to safeguard the rights of the cultivators in Regulation XXV of 1802. After 20 years, at the instance of Thomas Munro, another regulation (IV of 1822) was passed. It declared that the Regulation XXV of 1802 was not intended to define, limit, Infringe or destroy the actual rights of any description of tenants. No major dispute arose on the issue of the rights of the ryots under the zamindaries, atleast not until 1863, when the peasants of the Mungapakazamindary in Vizagapatam opposed the enhanced rents.

Inamdary system:

Another important tenurial system that existed in pre-British period and remained untouched by the British government, was the inamdary system. Inam were rent free or favorably assessed lands grants generally given to the religious institutions or to individuals and families in lieu of performing certain specified functions in the society. These grants were made by native governments before the advent of the British. The existence of inams was more pronounced and extensive in South India, than in North. This was perhaps, argued Eric Strokes, due to the disturbed political conditions and unstable central authority which paved the way to grant villages by zamindars and poligars to their kinsmen.[55] Inams were given to the Brahmins temples and artisans for services due to village communities, village employees and lastly and most importantly to the persons who look after particular irrigational works. The last one was also called dasabandaminam. If an inam was comprised of a whole village or a group of villages they were categorised as major inams, of it was only certain land holdings, generally they were called, minor inams.

The British Government in the beginning did not interfere in the management of inams, though they existed in the entire Andhra region along with ryotwary and zamindary areas, with a view to continue the existing whims and traditions of the society. They even granted some mama on favorable tenures. However, the government did not encourage the granting of rooms, particularly after receiving the dispatches from the Court of Directors, dated 2nd January 1822 and 27th May, 1829.

Thus, the government had resumed several moms, particularly kattubadi mains in the Ceded districts. But, after the insurrection of Narsimha Reddy of Koilkuntla, in1846, the government had realised the need for caution in proceeding against the inams. They have given instructions to report the cases.

To sum up, from the foregoing discussion it is very clear that no settlement was up to the satisfaction of the government. The government wanted a revenue system which would give them more land revenue without any mounting arrears. B.V. Narayanaswamy Naidu, rightly remarked that the land tenures in South India are the result, in the main, of a policy of government which aimed at first at ease and readiness of collection and later as high a revenue as the company could manage to get several modes of settlements, therefore were initiated by the various officers, which added further confusion. It was only the Ceded districts which continued under one type of settlement from 1821-22 to 1858-59. Baden-Powell rightly remarked that: “a record of a series of experiments in assessments, reductions and enhancements, changes in one direction and another following each other in somewhat bewildering order. To remove the confusion and various anomalies and errors. The Government had created a new department under the Director of Revenue Settlement in 1858. This department had started the survey and settlement, which was completed only by the end of the nineteenth century, for the entire Presidency.

The most important result of these settlements was the establishment of a new type of property relations in the land, especially in the ryotwary areas. All the settlements in the Ceded districts, Northern Circars and Nellore, were made with individual peasants and past as were issued. The peasants can hold the land in perpetuity as long as they paid the land revenue to the government. They could not be ejected by any law or person; they can sell, mortgage and gift the land on which they were paying land revenue to the government. However, the individual peasant ownership of the land could not be established real sense of the term, especially due to the non commodification of the land. One the other hand the less valuation of these lands was due to the productiveness of the land, the lack of irrigational and the frequent visit of unfavourable seasons. As a result, peasants relinquished their lands very frequently. Added to these problems was the heavy burden of land revenue demand in the initial periods of settlements. It was only after the 1860s and 1870s, with the development of new irrigational facilities and communications that the real ownership in the land was realised by the peasants, it was the zamindaries who acted as the owner of lands. In all these systems, the peasants suffer very much due to heavy assessment, low prices, and frequent occurrence of bad seasons.

The land revenue policy evolved at the time of the British came out successful in satisfying both the government and the ryots as it could secure a sizeable revenue to the state and at the same time provided relief to ryots to a reasonable extent. The ryots of Rayalaseema faced the problems because of faulty implementation of the policies touching upon certain aspects of agrarian life such as teervajasthi (water rate) and forest regulations of local officials. The policy of Ryotwari system that was introduced by Thomas Munro in the Anantapur and other ceded districts with the sole aim of increasing taxation and establishing direct contact with ryots was successful as it started paying dividends. As a result of Ryotwari system more waste land was brought under plough in the district. Actually 32 lakhs of acres of land was brought under cultivation in the ceded districts.The land revenue policy evolved at the time of the British came out successful in satisfying both the government and the ryots as it could secure sizeable revenue to the state and at the same time provided relief to ryots to reasonable extent. The well defined administrative machinery from village to district brought the ryot to direct contact with the government avoiding the middlemen. This administrative machinery is being still continued in the Republic of India for governance. For instance, even though the Government passed in 1854 exempting water rate on lands irrigated by private channels and tanks, natural pools, jungle streams and other improvised water sources on which Government incurred no expenditure, the rate continued to be collected by the local officials, and the ryots did not know about the provision of relief. The region being in a disadvantageous position with regard to rainfall and irrigation facilities, this issue became a sensitive one. When the ryots came to know about the exemption of the water rate in 1880's they began to question the proprietorship of the Government in collecting water rate on the lands which formed ayacut under private sources authorities were not disposed to grant them the exemption on various, often conflicting grounds.

Till 1919 i.e. before the introduction of Montagu. Chemsford reforms irrigation works were virtually under the control of the Central Government and were sanctioned with the approval of the State. No major irrigation works could be undertaken without the sanction of the Secretary of State for India. Under the reforms of 1919 irrigation was classed as a provincial subject. Since then there has been greater activity in regard to irrigation. So from 1919 onwards the irrigation has been the concern of state Governments. As per the Reforms, an irrigation department was created in each state with responsibility of maintaining and developing irrigation works.Although there was no clear consensus among British commentators as to the cause of its deficiencies, the identification of the Indian countryside and agriculture with poverty in the late eighteenth and early nineteenth centuries gave authority to a widely deployed strategy of improvement. India was seen to be ripe for improvement–whether for an anglicisation of its agriculture after the British model. While the late nineteenth century debates about India's poverty concentrated upon economic arguments, these earlier debates presented a wider environmental and moral critique of India and proposed a correspondingly wide variety of solutions, including a greater role for European settlement and enterprise. By the late 1840s many of these improving ambitions and experimental schemes had already failed, whether from want of state support or from their innate impracticality and ignorance of Indian conditions.

REFERENCES

1. Hand Book of Statistics of Ananthapur District 1991-92 & 1992-93 compiled by Chief Planning Officer, Anantapur, p. IV.
2. *Ibid.*, P. V.
3. *Ibid.*, P. V. 43-44
4. Sampath, M.D., *Chittor Through the Ages*, (Delhi, 1982), pp. 143-158.
5. Rao, P. R., History of Modern Andhra (New Delhi, 1983) p. 45 see also Jaya Rao, S.S. Census of India,1981 Series-2 Andhra Pradesh District Census Hand Book Anantapur District. (Hyderabad, 1985), p. 5.
6. John Kelsall, Manual of Bellary District, (Madras 1872), pp. 52-59.

7. Nilamani Mukherji, *The Ryotwari System in Madras*, 1772-1872, (Calcutta) pp 1-16.
8. Siva Sankara Narayana, Bh, (Ed), Andhra Pradesh District Gazetteers Anantapur District – (Hyderabad, 1970) pp. 85-86.
9. Munro's Instructions to Surveyors: Board's Consultations. 24 August, 1807.
10. Clements, R Markham, A Memoir of the Indian Surveys, p. 180.
11. Munro's Instructions, *Op. cit.*
12. W.K. Firminger, The Fifth Report from the Select Committee of the House of Commons on the Affairs of the East India Company in three Volumes. (London, 1812) Vol.II, F.133 (Hereafter cited as the Fifth Report).
13. *Ibid.* p. 184
14. Report of the Indian Irrigation Commission (1900-1901) Vol. 1, Part-1 (Calcutta, 1901). p. 44.
15. General Report of the Board of Revenue, Vol. II, p. 97.
16. First Report of the Madras Public Works Commissioners appointed to enquire into and Report upon the system of Superintending and executing Public works in the Madras Presidency (Madras, 1856) (Hereafter cited as First Report of the Public Works Commissioners). p. 7.
17. *Ibid.*, p. 3
18. The Fifth Report, Vol. III. p. 184.
19. Revenue Consultations, dated September 16, 1813.
20. First Report of the Public Works Commissioners, p. 139.
21. *Ibid.,* p. 3.
22. N.D. Gulhati, Administration and Financing of Irrigation Works in India (New, 1965), p. 15.
23. N. Benjamin, "Irrigation Policy of the British (1850-1900)", The Quarterly Review of Historical Studies. Vol. XVI, (Calcutta, 1976), p. 20.
24. Report of the Commissioners appointed to enquire into and report upon certain matters connected with the working and organisation of the Public Works Department in the Madras Presidency. 5th April (Madras, 1870), p. 11.
25. K.L. Bhatia, Development of Irrigation in India (New Delhi, 1985), p. 46.

26. C.D. Maclean, Manual of the Administration of the Madras Presidency. Vol.1, Part II (Madras, 1885), p. 387.
27. N. Benjamin, *Op. cit.*, p. 30.
28. C.D. Maclean, *Op. cit.,* p. 388
29. *Ibid.*, p. 407.
30. V. Sundara Rajan, An Economic History of India 1757-1947 (Baroda, 1955), p. 64
31. K.L. Bhatia, *Op. cit.*, p. 51.
32. Report of the Famine Commission 1878-80, part II, p. 99
33. *Ibid.*
34. V. Sundara Rajan, An Economic History of India 1757-1947 (Baroda, 1955), p. 67
35. Voelcker, John Augustus, 1893. Report on the Improvement of Indian Agriculture. London: Eyre and Spottiswoode.
36. P. Jyothi, Agrarian system in Andhradesa during the pre-colonial period, pp. 1-4, Basanta Kumar Mallik (ed), 2021, *Utkal historical research journal*, Vol. XXXIV, Bhubaneswar, Odisha, India.
37. Bipan Chandra, Colonialism and Modernisation'. in his Nationalism and Colonialism in Modem India (Delhi, 1981).
38. For details, see Irfan Habib. "Colonialisation of the Indian Economy, 1757-1900" in Social Scientists, No. 32. Match 1975, pp 23-53, and studying a Colonial Economy Without Perceiving Colonialism, in Social Scientists, No. 139, Dec. 1984, pp. 3-27.
39. M.P. R. Reddy, Peasant and State in Modern Andhra (Kavali 1986), p. 49, and Nilamani Mukherji, The Ryotwary System in Madras, 1792-1827, (Calcutta, 1962). p. 4.
40. "Stuart's Report on the settlement of Palkonda Taluk in the Proceedings of the Board of Revenue (Revenue Settlement, Land Records and Agriculture) No. 109, 9th March 1889, p. 19 (Hereafter PBR (RS.LR & A).
41. Dharma Kumar (ed.), The Cambridge Economic History of India, Vol. II (Hyderabad, 1984), p. 214; B.V. Narayana Swami, "Rural Economic Conditions in South India (1800-1890)" in Indian Journal of Economics, Vol. XIII, part 3, January 1933, p. 420:
42. W.K. Firminger, The Fifth Report from the Select Committee House of Commons on the Affairs of the East India Company, (Calcutta, 1917). p. 151.

43. Nilamani Mukherji, *Op. cit.*, p. 24: S.C. Ray, Land Revenue Administration in India, Calcutta, 1915.
44. "Cox's Report on the Settlement of the Pattikonda Taluk in PBR, No. 2352 dt. 10th June, p. 4228.
45. Quoted in S. Srinivasa Raghava Iyangar, Memorandum of the Progress of the Madras Presidency during the last forty years of British Administration. (First pub. in 1893, Reprinted in 1988, Madras), p. 26.
46. "C. Rundals Report on the Settlement of the Principal Division of Nellore District", in PBR., No. 1399, dt. 24th July. p. 3861
47. General Report of Board of Revenue, dt. 5th Oct 1804, p. 27
48. "C. Rundall's, "Report on the Settlement of Nellore", *op. cit.*, pp. 3860-63.
49. Amiya Kumar Bagchi. "Land Tax, Property Rights and Peasant Insecurity in Colonial India". In Journal of Peasant Studies. Vol. 20, No.1, Oct. 1999, p. 9.
50. R.C. Dutt, *Op. cit.*, Vol. I. Under Early British Rule (New Delhi, 1989 reprint). p. 79.
51. B.H. Baden Powell, Land Systems of British India, Vol. III, (Oxford. 1892), (Madras, 1941). p. 41.
52. S. Sundararaja Iyengar, *op. cit.*, p. 76, P. K. Gnanasundara Mudaliar, Note on the Permanent Settlement, Madras, 1940, pp. 37-41.
53. B.H. Baden Powell, A Short Account of Land Revenue and its Administration in British India : with a sketch of Land Tenures, (Oxford, 1913), pp. 199-206.
54. "Morriess Report on the settlement of Masulipatam Portion of Krishna District, in PBR, No. 6927, dt. 17th Oct. 1862, pp. 2762-3.
55. Eric Stokes, The Peasant and the Raj: Studies in Agrarian Society and Peasant Rebellion in Colonial India (Cambridge, 1980), p. 60.

8

Summary and Conclusions

Local history tends to be less documented than other types, with fewer books and artifacts than that of a country or continent. Many local histories are recorded as oral tales or stories and so are more vulnerable than more well known issues. Artifacts of local history are often collected in local history museums, which may be housed in a historic house or other building. Individual historic sites are inherently local, although they may have national or world history importance as well. Many, however have little overall historical impact but add depth to the local area. Local history can be defined as the study of the past of some significant local unit, developing as a community, in its context and compared with such other units. Local history is the study of the past of smaller communities such as a town, rural, or suburban area, or a city neighbourhood. Local history has been used and supported in many countries as a way of active learning.

The interest in local history has grown over the years and especially in recent decades, debates about the potential threat of globalisation to the local culture and identity have prompted a growth of local and regional studies in social science and history. Although local history is frequently used to illustrate broader historical developments, it has also been recommended for technical and methodological reasons. It is argued that the general objectives of local history should include 'not only understanding of the national and local history of a certain period or a certain theme and their interrelationship but also, skills and interests which they intended to dcvelop'.

With this background the present study attempted to study the general socio-economic conditions of the people in Anantapur District during colonial rule from 1800-1947. The study is mainly confined to then eight Taluks of Anantapur District in Andhra Pradesh. It deals with the various issues like social, industrial, banking, local self government, means of communication and the response of British Indian Government to the frequent famines and epidemics in Anantapur district, and examines, whether the district has made any progress under colonial rule.

The present thesis has adopted a combination of historical and descriptive methods and keenly observed various developments while going through the primary sources. In addition, the scholar has also collected the secondary data from the Government records at the State and District level archives. The present chapter deals with the summary and conclusion of the study presented in the thesis.

The chapter is an introductory in nature and it deals with general description of the problem, review of literature, statement of the problem, objectives of the study and the methodology applied for the study are presented in this chapter. The objectives of the present study are to portrayed the historical background of Anantapur district with special reference to political developments; to evaluate the role of British Indian Government in mitigating the miseries of the people of the district during famines and epidemics; to study the demographic features and socio-religious life of people under colonial rule in Anantapur district; to analyze the contribution of British Indian Government for industrial and banking development in the study area and, to evaluate the developments taken place in rural and urban local self governments during British rule.

The study is both analytical and descriptive and is based on primary and secondary data. The method employed is a combination of historical and descriptive. The source available for the present study includes both literary and archaeological material. The present study is chiefly based on the information contained in the numerous lithic and other inscriptions found in various parts of the district to trace the history of the district during ancient and medieval times. The secondary source material includes the district gazetteers, reports various commissions and committees, administration reports of various municipalities before and after independence. The other sources include books, magazines, journals and others.

The history of Anantapur district before the commencement of British rule was presented for the continuity of the thesis. As part of the thesis, it presents a brief historical sketch of the district and describes the early history of Anantapur region and the historical conditions of people in the district under the rule of different dynasties like, Mauryas, Satavahans, Pallavas, Kadambas, Chalukyas of Badami, Banas, Rashtrakutas, Nolambas, Chalukyas of Kalyani,Yadavas of Devagiri, Hoysalas of Dvarasamudram,Nidugal Cholas,Vaidumbas etc., in this part of the country. A special mention is also made the extent of Vijayanagara rule over the district, their socio-cultural contribution to the region and seizure of the district by muslim rulers.

Further the demographic features of the district along with myths and realities of the society are presented in the thesis. After careful study it is very clear that there is deficiency of female population in the district as it is today covering the emigration and immigration of people into and outside the district. The linguistic development with special reference to mother tongue is also analysed. The development of education and educational institutions in the district under colonial rule are discussed in this chapter. The conditions of several occupational classes like agriculturists, gunny weavers, cotton-weavers, cotton dyers, silk-weavers, silk-dyers, cotton-printers, blanket weavers, cotton cleaning and pressing people, jaggery- makers etc., are discussed in detail. The status of religions like Hinduism, Jainism, Christianity, Islam and the celebration of festivals in the district are elaborated in this chapter. Special mention is made about the tree and serpent worship, ancestor worship and vows of Hindus. The conditions of villages, their houses, their dress and ornaments, food habits, amusements etc., and the conditions of various castes, beggars,women and dancing girls in the district are presented.

The development of agriculture under colonial rule was briefly discussed in chapter. The development of old time industries like earth salt, bangle making, handmade paper, dyeing and printing, handloom weaving, indigo dyeing etc., are analysed. The developments taken place in mining and heavy industries like diamonds, gold, silver, ruby mica are also covered. The history of indigenous banking in the district, like nidhis registered under the Indian Companies Act, the role of private money lenders and financiers are elaborated. The development of joint stock banks, co-operative credit societies and banks, primary agricultural credit societies and land mortgage banks are discussed. The contribution of colonial government to the development of banks in the district is negligible. The currency and coinage, trade and commerce, weights and measures in the district under colonial rule are discussed. The efforts for the development of roads and communications and railways are made by the Colonial rulers are well presented.

The chapter devoted to discuss and present the developments in running rural and urban local self governments in the district during colonial rule. The establishment, composition and financial position of the district and Taluk Boards are elaborated in this chapter.The working of Gram Panchayats, their composition and classification were part of the study. The financial position of class-I Panchayats during the colonial rule in Anantapur district is presented in a tabular form. The developments taken place with regard to urban local bodies and the status of Anantapur, Gooty, Hindupur and Tadipatri Municipalities are discussed at length and the efforts made for the development of towns through town planning are examined in this chapter.

The conditions, which often results in the scanty rainfall in the district leading to famines vividly delineated in chapter six. The early scarcities like the scarcity of 1802-04, scarcity of 1805-07 and bad season in 1824 and their impact on the life of people are presented in this chapter. It makes an elaborate study of relief works undertaken, cattle mortality and the expenditure incurred by the government during the Famine of 1833, the devastating effects of the Famine of 1854, the Famine of 1866, the Great Famine of 1876-78, Scarcity of 1884-85, Famine of 1891-92, Famine of 1896-97, Distress of 1900, Scarcity of 1901, Famine of 1920-21, Famine of 1924-25, Famine of 1934-35, Famine of 1937-38, Famine of 1941-42 and theFamine of 1945-46. It also includes the impact of floods in 1804, the Storm of 1817 and the Great Storm of 1851. The state's response to epidemics like Malaria, Cholera, Small-pox and Guinea-worm etc. and the number of medical and health institutions and dispensaries in the district established during British rule.

Indian society underwent many changes after the British came to India. In the nineteenth century, certain social practices like female infanticide, child marriage, sati, polygamy and a rigid caste system became more prevalent. These practices were against human dignity and values. Women were discriminated against at all stages of life and were the disadvantaged section of the society. They did not have access to any development opportunities to improve their status. Education was limited to a handful of men belonging to the upper castes. Brahmins had access to the Vedas which were written in Sanskrit. Expensive rituals, sacrifices and the practices after birth or death were outlined by the priestly class.

It can be concluded that the agricultural population was numerically unimportant and their welfare was also indirectly bound up with that of the cultivator, inasmuch as they subsist by supplying him with the little luxuries and conveniences in bad seasons, when money was scarce. Few of the ryots of the district are great landholders. On only three percent, of the pattas is the assessment over Rs 50 per annum, and in the case of 69 percent, of them it is less than Rs 10. It is therefore only the smaller farmer that need be considered. The economic condition of this class depends upon two of factors, namely the natural characteristics of the country in which they live and their energy and ability in combating the unfavourable characteristics.

The natural conditions of Anantapur could scarcely be more inimical to agricultural prosperity than most of the soil is wretchedly infertile, the rainfall is light and uncertain, fuel and fodder are scarce, irrigation facilities are few, the indigenous cattle are bad, manure is difficult to get and the people are few in number. The qualifications of the ryot for meeting these adverse characteristics and his resultant condition are very bad.

This port town of Andhra grew at a tremendous speed in the seventeenth century because of the factor that it had access to the hinterland. The hinterland of Machilipatnam included the fertile lands of Krishna-Godavari deltas where cotton and dye-yielding crops were raised on large areas. In fact the hinterlands of this port was so vast that textiles and other export items were brought here from places as far as 350 miles interior. Thus, the port became the greatest one in these parts and came nearest to an enterpot.

Apart from Dutch and the English, the other European powers worth noting is the French who opened their commercial establishments at Machilipatnam in 1669 by obtaining a firman from the Sultan of the Golconda. In fact the contact established by French at Machilipatnam later paved way for closer relations between the French and the Nizam. Nizampatnam mentioned by Ferishta as Arjunpatnam was a known centre for ship building industry. The English and Dutch vied with each other for trade in salt-petre.

The Industrial revolution in Europe, the discovery of aniline dyes and the growing political power of the British in India put the final nails in the coffin of textile trade in India. Lord Bentick summed up the situation when he observed, “the bones of the cotton weavers are bleaching the plains of India”. It is up to us to ponder over why have we always been so careless about research and development and why do we fail to study and analyse the hazards of trade and commerce.

In the matter of education and intellectual status, the district is probably the most backward in the Presidency. Real education is too important a factor in the problem to be ignored, and so long as ignorance holds entire sway, there seems little hope of such a general advance, at all events along the agricultural line, to push back the famine.

The history of the district, as of similar ones, shows that the pressure of food failures is absolutely insufficient per se to induce decided advances; whether the apathy arise from frequent failure, or from fatalism, or from improvidence, or from ignorance, or from hereditary conservatism, or from want of example and emulation, it is certain that there is at present a total absence of effort and determined struggle except on the old lines; no marriage in this district has ever yet been delayed for fear of not being able to provide for a family, or because the family property would have to be sub-divided, or because capital was wanting to stock and work a new farm; no new agricultural departure, save only in the matter of a few ploughs in the richer part of the district, has been taken; no determined effort has been made to force an unwilling soil to yield more than it has hitherto yielded; not even patent advantages, such as those of wells in wet land, of fencing and tree-planting, of due manurial conservation, or of cattle treatment, have been even moderately adopted; only in the matter of water supply do they follow the ancestral custom of laboriously bringing rills of water to their distant fields. The ryots are only fairly industrious, and that only in the ancestral grooves.

It cannot be doubted that real education must be looked to for the mental development of the ryot; self-interest such as acts upon Europeans and impels them to the accumulation of wealth, to the hereditary struggle with nature, to new developments whether of agriculture, manufacture, or trade, to the acquisition of knowledge and to prudence in marriage, is wholly insufficient as a motive power in this district. Such education as is given has little or no connection with a lad's after-life; there is nothing in it to help him to farm; it does not teach him to observe, or make him think about, or to think new thoughts about, his processes and products. Probably an adaptation of the educational scheme to the wants of the agriculturist will go far to help us to face the famine problem. As for the wealth of the district, it is simply non-existent. Taking the ryot first, his cultivation is good evidence of his poverty, while there is a terrible absence of jewellery amongst the females; this latter want is very marked to one coming from the south. The ryot has little exchange value in his land; to judge by registration transactions, it is, except in Tadipatri generally and in some parts of the other taluks, hardly a marketable article: at all events the ryot can borrow but little upon it; this stands in his way should he wish to make improvements; though on the other hand it tends to prevent reckless indebtedness. Another evidence of poverty is the small number of money-lenders in the district, and these generally deal with very moderate sums. On the whole, the district is without doubt, the poorest and most backward of all districts, whether as regards agriculture or other industries.

Bibliography

PRIMARY SOURCES

A. REPORTS

A Collection of Papers Relating to the Inam Settlement of Madras Presidency: Selections from the records of the Madras Government, New (Revenue) Series, No. 1, Government Press, Madras, 1948, in A.P. State Archives A.P.S.A., Hyderabad.

A Concise History of the Jagheers in the Northern Division of Arcot, T.N. Slate Archives T.N.S.A., 1922.

A Selection of Papers from the old records of Cuddapah District, "Official Report of a Revolt by Palegar Narasimha Reddy in Koilkuntla Taluk (which found part of Cuddapah District) in 1846, 5 Vols, A.P. Gezetteer Office, Hyderabad.

Administration of Karvetnagar estate, Jagirdar of Avalkonda and Chittoor Palyam and others, 1818-1826, T.N.S.A.

Administration Report of Hindupur Municipality, 1920-21 to 1922-23, 1925-26, 1927-28 to 1941-42.

Administration Reports of Anantapur Municipality, 1884-85 to 1886-87, 1888-89, 1889-90, 1891-92 to 1927-28, 1929-30 to 1944-45, 1946-47 to 1964-65.

Administration Reports of Gooty Municipality, 1869-70, 1871-72 to 1879-80.

Administration Reports of Tadipatri Municipality, 1920-21 to 1935-36, 1937-38 to 1941-42.

Administration Reports of the Director of Town Planning from 1938-39 to 1940-41.

Bayly, W.H., Memorandum on Mirassi Tenure, Madras, 1856.

Dasabandam Inams, Cultivation Hukumnamahs, remission rules.

District Records of Madras Presidency, in T.N.S.A.

Ellis, F.W., Papers Relating to Mirassi Right, Madras, 1814.

Firminger, W.K. ed., The Fifth Report from the Select Committee on the affairs of East India Company, 1812, Delhi, 1983, Vol. 3.

G.O.'s of Revenue Department from 1858-1900.

Hyde's Report on the Introduction of a Ryotwari Settlement into the South Arcot Collectorate and the Correspondence relating thereto, Cuddalore, 1904.

Letters from Board of Revenue to Collector Lushinton, 4 Sep., 1799, T.N.S.A.

Papers regarding the land revenue system of British India, T.N.S.A., 1902.

Papers relating to the Survey and Settlement of the Godavary District, T.N.S.A., 1869.

Papers Relating to the Treaty with the Nawab of Arcot and the Zamindaries of Venkatagiri, Kalahasti, etc., 1802-1872, ASO, D-40, T.N.S.A.

Papers Relating to the Village Panchayats and other Judicial systems of Administration, 1812-1816, Madras, 1916.

Permanent Settlement Records

Proceedings of Board of Revenue from 1859-1870, in A.P.S.A.

Proceedings of the Court of Wards (PCW), T.N.S.A.

Proceedings of the Judicial Department, T.N.S.A.

Replies to Seventeen Questions proposed by the Madras Government of Fort St. George Relative to the Mirassi Right, with two appendices, Madras, 1818.

Report of the Indian Famine Commission 1805-07.

Report of the Indian Famine Commission 1882-85.

Report of the Indian Famine Commission 1897.

Report of the Indian Famine Commission, 1891-92.

Report of the Indian Famine Commission, 1901-03.

Report of the Indian Famine Commission-1854.

Report of the Indian Famine Commission-1866.

Report of the Indian Famine Commission-1878.

B. Manuals and Gazetteers

Boswell, J.A.C., Manual of Nellore District, Madras, 1873.

Brakenbury, C.F., Madras District Gazetteer: Cuddapah, Madras, 1915.

Carmichael, D.F., Manual of the Vizagapatnam District, Madras, 1869.

Chetty, A. Gopalakrishnaira, A Manual of the Kurnool District in the Presidency of Madras, Madras, 1886.

Francis, W., Anantapur District Gazetteer, 1905.

Madras District Gazetteer: Bellary, Madras, 1916.

Cribble, A Manual of the District of Cuddapah in the Presidency of Madras, Madras, 1875.

Kelsall, J.A., A Manual of Bellary District, Madras, 1872.

SECONDARY SOURCES

A. ARTICLES

Anjaneyulu, M.S.R., "Beginning of the English Settlement at Vizagapatnam," in Itihas, Journal of A.P.S.A., 3.2, 1975, pp. 81-89.

Appadurai, Arjun and Carol Breckenridge, "The South Indian Temple; Authority, Honour and Redistribution" In Contribution to Indian Sociology, CIS, 10.2, 1976, pp. 187-211.

Penukonda Jyothi, "The Establishment of property land relations in colonial Andhra in perspective of areas (1800-1850)" pp. 177-184, Shodhsamhita : Journal of Kavikulaguru Kalidas Sanskrit University, Ramtek fundamental & comparative research Vol. VII, No. 9(1): 2021

Appadurai, Arjun, "Kings, Sects and Temples In South India," in Indian Economic and Social History Review, JESHR, 14.1, 1977, Pp. 47-73.

Arasratnam, S., "Weavers, Merchants and Company: The Handloom Industry in South-eastern India, 1750-1790," in Indian Economic & Social History Review, 1980.

Arnold, David, "Looting, Grain Riots and Government policy in South India," in Past and Present, PGP. 84, 1979, pp. 211-145.

Baker, C., "Economic Reorganisation and the Slump in South and South East Asia," in CSSH, 23.2, 1981, pp. 325-349.

Baliga, B.S., "Home Government and the end of the Policy of Permanent Settlement in Madras, 1802-1818," in IHRCP, Vol. XIX, 1942.

Bandopadhyay, Arun, "The nature of Landownership in Tamilnadu from 1820 to 1855," in The Calcutta Historical Journal, CHJ, Vol, III, No. l, July to December, 1978.

Bayly, Susan, "Hindu Kingship and the origin of Community; Religion, State and Society in Kerala, 1750-1850, in MAS, 18.2, pp.. 177-214.

Beck, F. Brenda, "The Right and Left Division of South Indian Society" Journal of Asian Studies, JAS, 29, 1970.

Beck, F. Brenda, "The Right and Left Division of South Indian Society," in Journal of Asian Studies, JAS, 29, 1970, pp. 779-798.

Bhattacharya, Neeladri, "The Logic of TenancyCultivation: Central and South-east Punjab, 1870-1935," in Indian Economic & Social History Review, 20.2, 1983, pp. 121-170.

Champakalakshmi, R., "Peasant State and Society in Medieval South India," in Indian Economic & Social History Review, 18.3-4, 1981, pp. 411-427.

Chandavarkar, Rajnarayan, "Industrialisation in India before 1947: Conventional Approaches and Alternative Perspectives," in MAS, 19.3.1985, pp. 623-668.

Cohn, S. Bernard, "Comments on Papers of Land Tenures," in Indian Economic & Social History Review. 1,2, 1963.

Commander, Simon, "The Jajmani System in North India: An Examination of its Logic and Status across two centuries," In MAS, 17, 1983, pp. 283-312.

Dewey, C.J., "Image of the Village Community: A Study in Anglo-Indian Ideology," in MAS, 6.3, 1972.

Dhanaraju Vulli, "History of 'Colonial Education' in Andhra: Response from Various Castes",Research Journal of Educational Sciences, Vol. 1, No.6, September2013.

Dirks, B. Nicholas, "Political Authority and Structural Change in early South Indian History," in Indian Economic & Social History Review, 13.2, 1976, pp.125-157.

Dua, J.C., "Poligars: Their rise in the Ceded District," in PIHC, 33 Session. Muzaffarpur, 1972, pp.467-474.

Eaton, M. Richard, "The Court and the Dargah in the Seventeenth Century Deccan," in Indian Economic & Social History Review, March, 1973, pp. 50-63.

Galanter, Marc, "The Aborted Restoration of Indigenous Law in India," In Comparative Studies in Society and History, Vol.14, 1972, pp. 53-70.

Ganesh, Kamala., "Jajmani Relations in Tirunelveii District: A Case Study of the Kottai Pillaimar, 1839-1979," in Indian Economic & Social History Review. 22.2, 1985, pp. 175-200.

Guha, Sumit, "Society and Economy in the Deccan, 1818-1850," in Indian Economic & Social History Review, 20.4, 1983, pp. 389-415.

Gupta, S. Anil, "Karl Marx and India," in Society and Change. Vol. VI. No. 1, April-June, 1989, pp. 1-34 and 89-94.

Habib, Irfan, "Classifying Pre-colonial India," in Journal of Peasant Studies, JPS, 1985, pp. 44-53.

Hall, R. Kennath., "Peasant State and Society in Chola Times: A View from the Tiruvidaimurudur Urban Complex," in Indian

Economic & Social History Review, 18.3-4, 1981, pp. 393-410.

Irschick, F. Eugene, " Order and Disorder in Colonial South India," In MAS, 23.3, 1989, pp. 459-492.

Iyengar, P. T. S., 'Misconceptions about the Andhras', Indian Antiquary, 42, 1913.

Jagannadhan, A., "Some Aspects of Socio-economic Conditions in Ceded Districts, 1800-1810," in Itihas, 4.2, 1976, pp.138-147.

Jagatheesan, P., "Inam Settlement in the Madras Presidency during nineteenth century," in P1HC, 45 Session, Annamalainagar, 1985, pp. 552-558.

Kolver, Bernard, "On the origin of the Jajmani System," in Journal of Economic and Social History of the Orient, 31.3, 1988, pp. 265-85.

Kumar, Dharma, "Landownership and Inequality in Madras Presidency: 1853-54 to 1946-47," in Indian Economic & Social History Review, XX. 1975, pp. 229-263.

Kumar, S. Siva, "Transformation of the Agrarian Economy in Tondaimandalam: 1760-1900," in Social Scientist, SS, Vol. 6, No. 10, May, 3978, pp. 18-39.

Lee, "Crisis of Representation," in Contemporary Sociology, 1994, pp. 15-25.

Ludden, David, "Patronage and Irrigation in Tamil Nadu: A Long-term view," in Indian Economic & Social History Review, 1980, pp. 347-365.

Mangamma, J., "Land System and Muttas in the Visakapatnam Agency," in Itihas, 7.2, 1979, pp. 101-117.

Metcalf, Thomas, "Rural Society and British Rule in Nineteenth Century India," in The Journal of Archaeological Science, 39.1, 1979, pp. 111-119.

Morris, D. Morris, "Economic Change and Agriculture in Nineteenth Century India," in Indian Economic & Social History Review, 3.2, 1966, pp. 185-210.

Murton Brian, "Key People In the Countryside: Decision Makers in Interior.

Naidu, B.V.N., "Rural Economic Conditions in South India, 1800-1890," in Indian Journal of Economics, IJE, Vol.xxi, 36, 1935.

Natalie, Davis, "Possibilities of the Past," in The Journal of Inter disciplinary History, JIH, 12.2.1981, pp. 267-276.

Perlin, Frank, "Of White Whale and Countrymen In the Eighteenth Century Maratha Deccan: Extended Class Relations, rights and the problem of rural autonomy under the old regime," in JPS, 5.2.1978, pp. 172-237.

Price, Pamella, "Raja-dharma In Ramnad: Land Litigation and Largess," in CIS, 13.2, 1979, pp. 207-240.

Ramachandran, C., "The Acquisition of Northern Circars by the East India Company," in A.P. History Congress Proceedings, A.P.H.C.P., 4, 1980, pp. 1-9.

Rao, G.N., "Agrarian Relations in Coastal Andhra under early British Rule," In SS, 6.1, 1977, pp. 20-29.

Rao, T.V, Seshadri, "Land Litigation in Andhra Pradesh, 1800-1950," in Artha Vijnana, AJ, 1966, Vol. 3.

Reddeppa S., "The Role of Christian Missionaries in Madras Presidency – A Historical Study", Indian Journal of Applied Research, Vol. 4, No. 2, February 2014.

Reddy, K. Venugopal, "The Role of the lower Peasantry in Narasimha Reddy's Revolt in Koilkuntla Taluk, in PIHC, 44 Session, Burdwan, 1983, pp.441-443.

Reddy, M. Atchi, "Rich Lands and Poor Lords: Temple lands and tenancy in Nellore District, 1860-1986." in Indian Economic & Social History Review, 24,1, 1987, pp. 1-33.

Reddy, M.R.P., "Aspects of Agrarian Revolution in Andhra, 1800-1820: The Munro System-Extermination of Poligars," in A.P., History Congress Proceedings, A.P.H.C.P., R.C. Puram, 1976.

Reddy, R. Pattabhi, "1846, Nati Rayalseema Raltangu Thirugubatu, (Peasant Rebellion of Rayalseema, 1846), in Kadalika (a monthly Journal from Anantapur), September, 1985.

Reddy, Subramanyam, "Changing Agrarian Relations and the State of Peasantry In Andhra during the early Nineteenth Century," in SS, 15.6.1986, pp. 20-41.

Reddy, V. Ratna, "Irrigation in Colonial India: A Study of Madras Presidency during 1860-1900, in EPU, May 5-12.1990, pp. 1047-1057.

Richard M. Swiderski, "Oral Text: A South Indian Instance", Oral Tradition, Vol. 31, No. 2, 1988, pp. 122-37 .

Robb, Peter, "Law and Agrarian Society in India: The Case of Bihar and the Nineteenth Century Tenancy Debate," in WAS, 22.2.1988, pp. 319-354.

Satyanarayana, A., "Peasantry in the Zamindari System," in APHCP, 2, 1976-1977, pp. 27-39.

Semih Aktek N.,"The Place and Importance of Local History in the Secondary History Education", Journal of Theory and Practice in Education, 2009, 6 (1): 86-105.

Shulman, David, "On South Indian Bandits and Kings," in Indian Economic & Social History Review, 17.3. 980, pp. 283-306.

Simmons, Colin, "De-industrialisation, Industrialisation and the Indian Economy, c. 1850-1947," in WAS, 19.3.1985, pp..593-622.

Spencer, G.W., "The Politics of Plunder: The Cholas in Eleventh Century Ceylon, in JAS, 35, 1976, pp. 405-419.

Stein, Burton, "The Economic Functions of a Medieval South Indian Temple," in JAS, 19.2.1960, pp. 163-176.

Subramanyam, Sanjay and Bayly, C.A., "Portfolio Capitalist and the Political Economy of Early Modern India," in Indian Economic & Social History Review,, 25.4, 1988, pp. 401-424.

Talbot, Cynthia, "Temples, Donors and Gifts: Patterns of Patronage in Thirteenth Century South India," in JAS, 50, No. 2, May, 1991, pp. 308-340.

Tamil Nadu in the late Eighteenth Century," in Indian Economic & Social History Review, 10.2.1973, pp. 157-180.

Tomlinson, B.R., "The Historical Roots of Indian Poverty: Issues in the Economic and Social History of Modern South Asia, 1800-1960," In WAS, 22.1.1988, pp. 123-140.

Reddy Venugopal, K., "Revisiting History: A Post-Colonial Representation Of Anti-Colonial Struggle In Andhra", Journal of History & Social Sciences, Volume: III, Issue I, January-June 2012.

Wallerstein, Immanuel, "Incorporation of Indian Sub-continent Into Capitalist World-economy," in Economic and Political Review, 21.4.1986, pp. 28-39.

Washbrook, David, "Law, State and Agrarian Society in Colonial India," in HAS, 15.3.1981, pp. 647-721.

B. BOOKS

Aiyangar, Krishnaswami S., "The Beginnings of South Indian History", The Modern Printing Works, Madras, 1918.

Aiyangar, P.T.S: History of the Tamils to 600 A.D. Madras. 1929.

Appa Rao, G.V., The Annals of Handeh Anantapuram.

Appadurai, Arjun and Carol Breckenridge, "The South Indian Temple; Authority, Honour and Redistribution" In Contribution to Indian Sociology, CIS, 10.2, 1976.

Arnold, David, Police, Power and Colonial Rule, Madras, 1859-1947, New Delhi, 1986.

Ball, "Economic Geology of India", Cosmos book limited, 1987.

Barbara, D. Metcalf and Thomas R. Metcalf, "A Concise History of Modern India, Cambridge University Press, Cambridge, 2006.

Bayley's Memorandum on Weights and Measures (1857), p.23.

Bhattacharya, S., Financial Foundations of the British Raj, Simla, 1971.

Boag, G.T., The Madras Presidency 1881-1931.

Brown C.P.: The wars of Rajas. Asian educational service. New Delhi, 1988.

Bruce Foote, R., "Indian Pre-historic and Proto-historic Antiquities".

Captain, R. V. Littlewood, Livestock of Southern India, N.D.A., D.A.S. A. I. R.C.

Carol Kammen and Norma Prendergast, Encyclopedia of Local History, Lanman, Maryland: Rowman, Alta Mira, 2000.

Chandra, Satish, Medieval India: Society, the Jagirdari Crisis and the Village, Macmillan, Delhi, 1982.

Chandrasekar, A., Fairs and Festivals of Anantapur District, Census Publications, Andhra Pradesh, 1961.

Chatterjee, Partha, Nationalist Thought and the Colonial World: A Derivative Discourse, London: Zed, 1986.

Desai, P.B., Ritti S.H., A History of Karnataka, Karnataka University, Dharwad, 1970.

Dewey, C.J. and Hopkins, A.G. ed., The Imperial Impact: Studies in the Economic History of Africa and India, London, 1978.

Digby, The Famine Campaign in South India 1876-78, Vol. I.

Dutt, N.V.B.S., Mineral Resources in Ceded Districts of Andhra Pradesh.

E. Thurston, Castes and Tribes of Southern-India-Volumes I.

Epstein, Scarlett, "Customary System of Rewards in Rural South India," in Dalton George ed., Economic Development and Social Change, New Delhi, 1971.

Francis, W. Madras District gazetteers, Anantapur District gazetteer 1905, Addison & Company, Madras, 1905.

Gadgil, D.R., The Industrial Evolution of India in recent times, 1860-1939, Delhi, 1988.

Gopal G.R., History of Andhra Pradesh. Part-I. Agam Kala Prakashan, Delhi, 1981.

Gopala Krishnamurthy, P., Khadri Sthalapuranamu (unpublished Manuscript), Khadri, 1983.

Gopalachari, K., Early History of the Andhra Country: University of Madras, Madras 1976.

Gribble, J.D.B., A History of the Deccan, Vol. II.

Guha, Nikhiles, Pre-British State System in South India, Mysore 1761-1799, Calcutta, 1985.

Hanumantha, Rao, B.S.L., Religion in Andhra, Department of Archaeology and Museums, Government of Andhra Pradesh, Hyderabad, 1993.

Havell, E.B., Report on the Arts and Industries of certain districts of Madras Presidency.

Hayavadana, Rao, The History of Mysore, Vol. III.

Henry Heras, S.J., The Aravidu Dynasty of Vijayanagara, B.G. Paul. & Co. Publishers, Madras,1927.

Jawaharlal, G., Antiquities of Budagavi and Kotha Sivaram, Andhra Pradesh History Congress Proceedings XIII Session, Sri Sailam, 1989.

John, History of the rise of the Mahomedan power, Vol. III.

Karashima, Noboru, South Indian History and Society: Studies from Inscriptions, A.D. 850-1800, Delhi, 1984.

Krishna Murthy, M.S., The Nolambas, University of Mysore, 1980.

Krishna Sastri, V.V., The Proto and early Historical Culture of Andhra Pradesh, Government of Andhra Pradesh, Hyderabad, 1983.

Krishna, Y.S., A short Report on the Fodder, Milk Supply and Utilisation problems of the State of Madras.

Krishnamurthy, M.S., The Nolambas, University of Mysore, 1980.

Krishnaswami, S.Y., Rural Problems in Madras, Monograph, Madras, 1947.

Krishnaswamy Ayyar, S., Sources of Vijayanagar History.

Kumar, Prasanna & Murthy, V. Linga & Ravi, K. (ed), Government & Politics in Andhra Pradesh, S. Chand Co., New Delhi, 1982.

Maclean, C.D., Manual of the Administration of the Madras Presidency, Madras, 1885, Vol. I.

Mangalam, S.J., Historical Geography and Toponomy of Andhra Pradesh, Sundeep Prakashan, New Delhi, 1986.

Manual of Administration in Madras Presidency, 1885, II.

Meadows Taylor's paper in Journal of Bombay Branch of R.A.S., IV, 412, 1852.

Mudaliar, Chandra, State and Religious Endowments in Madras, Madras, 1976.

Narayana Charyulu, P., Penukonda Lakshmi, (unpublished Manuscript), Proddutur, 1980.

Narayanaswami Naidu, B .V., Report of the Economist for enquiry into rural indebtedness 1946.

Narayanaswamy, S., Report on the preliminary investigation of Ramagiri Gold Fields 1958.

Nilakanta Sastri, K. A., Early History of the Andhra Country, Madras University Historical Series-No. 16, G. S. Press, Madras, 1941.

Pandit Hisselle Dhammaratana Mahāthera, Buddhism in South India, Buddhist Publication Society, Kandy, Sri Lanka, 1968.

Rama Mohan Rao, K., Directory of Monuments Antiquarian, Subramanyam B. Remains of Andhra Pradesh. Dept. of Archaeology and Museum A.P., Hyderabad, 1993.

Ramakrishna, V., Social Reforms in Andhra (1848-1919), Vikas Publishers, Delhi 1983.

Ramamohan Rao, K. (Ed.), Directory of Monuments, Department of Archeology and Museums. Andhra Pradesh, Hyderabad. 1993.

Ramesh, K.V., Inscriptions of Western Gangas, Vol. XXV.

Ramesh, K.V., Chalukyas of Vatapi, Agamkala Prakashan. Delhi, 1984.

Rami Reddy, G. 1989, "Caste, Class and Dominance in Andhra Pradesh." Francine R. Frankel and M.S.A. Rao, eds. Dominance and State Power in Modern India. Vol. I, Oxford University Press, Delhi.

Rangacharya, V., "Inscriptions of the Madras Presidency", Vol. I.

Ranganatham, G.B., History and Monuments of Penukonda (un Published Ph.D. dissertation), SK University, Anantapur, 1990.

Rao Narayana, D., Survey of Cottage Industries in Anantapur District, H.K. Publishers and Distributors, Delhi.1958,.

Rao, Narasimha, Corporate Life in Medieval Andhradesa, Secunderabad, 1967.

Rao, P. Raghunadha, History of Modern Andhra, Sterling Publishers, New Delhi, 1983.

Rao, P. Raghunadha, Ancient and Medieval History of Andhra Pradesh, Sterling Publishers, New Delhi, 1985.

Rao, Umamaheswara C.,"Land Revenue Administration – A Historical Look", Land Cell, AMR-APARD, Hyderabad.

Reddy, R. Pattabhi, "1846, Nati Rayalseema Raltangu Thlrugubatu, (Peasant Rebellion of Rayalseema, 1846), in Kadalika (a monthly Journal from Anantapur), September, 1985.

Romila Thapar, "The Penguin History of Early India: From the Origins to AD 1300", Penguin Books, London, 2002.

Rubies, J.P., Travel and Ethnology in the Renaissance: South India through European Eyes, 1250-1625, Cambridge University Press, Cambridge, 2000.

Russel, A.T.H., Geographical Survey of Cholera in the Madras Presidency from 1818-1927, Madras.

Russel, A.T.H., Geographical Survey of Plague in the Madras Presidency, Madras.

Sampat Kumar, M.D., Chittoor through the Ages. B.G. Publishing Corporation, Delhi, 1980.

Sardesai, G. S., New History of the Marathas, Vol. III.

Sathyanathan, W.R.S., Report of the Agricultural indebtedness, 1935.

Settar, S., Hampi, A Medieval Metropolis, Kala Yatra, Bangalore, 1990.

Sewell, Robert, A Forgotten Empire (Vijayanagar): A Contribution to the History of India, reprint, Asian Educational Services, New Delhi, 2000.

Shiva Shankar Narayana (E.D), Andhra Pradesh District Gazetters Anantapur District, Govt. of Andhra Pradesh, 1970.

Singh, A.K. 1990, Devadasis System in Ancient India. H.K. Publishers and Distributors, Delhi.

Sinopoli, Carla M. 2003. The Political Economy of Craft Production: Crafting Empire in South India, c. 1350-1650. Cambridge University Press.

Sircar, D.C., Epigraphia Indica, Archaeological Survey of India. 1957-58.

Soma Reddy, R. 1980, History of Religious Institutions in Andhra Desa from A.D. 1300-1600, Hyderabad.

Srinivasa Raghavachariar, Memorandum on the Progress of the Madras Presidency during the last forty years of British Administration, 1893.

Statistical Altas Madras Presidency, 1940-41.

Subba Rao, B., The Geographic Factors in Andhra History and Archaeology', BDCRI, Poona, No. 12, 1948.

Sundaram, K., Studies in Economic and Social Conditions of Medieval Andhra (AD 1000-1600 AD), Triveni Publishers, Machilipatnam, 1969.

Tejaswini, Yarlagadda, Social History of the Deccan, Bharatiya Kala Prakashan, Delhi, 2003.

Terry Barnhart, "Of Whole and Parts: Local History and the American Experience," Research and Review Series, 7, 2000.

Thurston, Monograph of the Silk Fabric Industry in Madras Presidency.

Vaikuntham, Y., Education and Social Change in South India: Andhra, 1880-1920, Madras.

Venkanna, Agricultural Implements, Allied Publishers, New Delhi, 1975.

Venkata Ramana, K., Early Rulers of Anantapur District, Budagavi and Kotha Sivaram, Andhra Pradesh History Congress Proceedings XIV Session, Warangal, 1990.

Venkataramanayya, N., Studies in the Third Dynasty of Vijayanagar History.

Venkatarangaiya, M., "Development of Local Boards in Madras Presidency".

Vijay Tunga, J., "Nagarjunakonda" The Publication Division, Ministry of Information and Broadcasting, Government of India, 1956.

Vipen, A., Scheme of Road Development for the Madras Presidency, 1935.

Wagoner, Phillip B., Tidings of the King: A Translation and Ethnohistorical Analysis of the Rayavacakamu, University of Hawaii Press, Honolulu, 1993.

William, D. Rubenstein, "History and 'amateur' history" in Peter Lambert and Phillipp Schofield ed., Making History: An Introduction to the History and Practices of a Discipline London: Routledge, 2004.

Yazdani, The Early History of the Deccan, Part-6.

Yusuf Hasain Khan, Nizam-ul-Mulk Asaf Jah-I.

Index

B

H